POSITIVE YOUTH DEVELOPMENT THROUGH SPORT

Cutting through the political rhetoric about the power of sport as a tool for social change and personal improvement, this book offers insight into whether, how and why participating in sport can be good for children and young people. As the first text to focus on the role of sport in positive youth development (PYD), it brings together high-profile contributors from diverse disciplines to examine critically the ways in which sport can be used to promote youth development.

Now in a fully updated, revised and expanded new edition, *Positive Youth Development through Sport* covers a wider range of disciplines including sport psychology, development psychology, physical education, sport development and sport sociology. Its three main sections focus on:

- the theoretical and historical contexts of PYD
- quantitative and qualitative methods for assessing PYD in sport
- the potential of PYD in sport across different ages and abilities.

With expanded guidance on how to apply positive youth development in practice, this is essential reading for all students, researchers, educators, practitioners and policy makers with an interest in youth sport.

Nicholas L. Holt is a professor and leader of the Child and Adolescent Sport and Activity lab in the Faculty of Physical Education and Recreation at the University of Alberta, Canada. He conducts research examining psychosocial aspects of participation in sport and physical activity among children, adolescents, and their families.

POSITIVE YOUTH DEVELOPMENT THROUGH SPORT

Second edition

Edited by Nicholas L. Holt

LONDON AND NEW YORK

First published 2016
by Routledge
2 Park Square, Milton Park, Abingdon, Oxon OX14 4RN

and by Routledge
711 Third Avenue, New York, NY 10017

Routledge is an imprint of the Taylor & Francis Group, an informa business

© 2016 Nicholas L. Holt

British Library Cataloguing-in-Publication Data
A catalogue record for this book is available from the British Library

Library of Congress Cataloging in Publication Data
Names: Holt, Nicholas L. Title: Positive youth development through sport / edited by Nicholas L. Holt. Description: 2nd Edition. | New York : Routledge, 2016. | Series: International Studies in Physical Education and Youth Sport | Includes bibliographical references and index. Identifiers: LCCN 2015041200 | ISBN 9781138891791 (Hardback) | ISBN 9781138891814 (Paperback) | ISBN 9781315709499 (Ebook) Subjects: LCSH: Sports for children. | Sports for children--Social aspects. | Physical education for children. | Physical fitness for youth. Classification: LCC GV709.2 .P68 2016 | DDC 796.083--dc23 LC record available at http://lccn.loc.gov/2015041200

ISBN: 978-1-138-89179-1 (hbk)
ISBN: 978-1-138-89181-4 (pbk)
ISBN: 978-1-315-70949-9 (ebk)

Typeset in Bembo
by Saxon Graphics Ltd, Derby
Printed in Great Britain by Ashford Colour Press Ltd

This book is dedicated to the people around the world who work tirelessly to make youth sport a positive and enriching experience for children, adolescents and their families. It is also dedicated to the founding members of Team Holt Canada (Carole, Josie, Juno and Alis), all of whom strive to make sport fun—whether through coaching or playing soccer, or as ultramarathon training partners.

CONTENTS

ILLUSTRATIONS

Figures

Tables

CONTRIBUTORS

Jennifer P. Agans, PhD is a postdoctoral associate at the Bronfenbrenner Center for Translational Research at Cornell University (US). Her research focuses on youth experiences in sport and other movement contexts (dance, circus arts) and the promotion of positive development and health across the life span.

Veronica Allan is currently a second year PhD candidate in the School of Kinesiology and Health Studies at Queen's University (Canada). Her doctoral work will examine the sport experiences of youth-athletes with physical disabilities and the role of coaches in the disability sport environment.

Corliss Bean is a PhD candidate in the School of Human Kinetics at the University of Ottawa (Canada). Her research focuses on examining program quality and psychosocial development within youth sport and physical activity programs, particularly with marginalized youth.

Brian M. Burkhard is a doctoral student in the Institute for Applied Research in Youth Development at Tufts University (US). His research focuses on the character and moral development of youth.

Martin Camiré, PhD is an assistant professor at the University of Ottawa's School of Human Kinetics (Canada). Through his research, he is interested in examining how positive youth development can be facilitated in the context of sport and how coaches learn to implement strategies to promote the development of life skills.

David Carless, PhD is a professor of narrative psychology at Leeds Beckett University (UK). Through a variety of arts-based, narrative, and performative methodologies, David's research explores how identity and mental health are developed, threatened, or recovered in sport and physical activity contexts.

Jay Coakley, PhD is professor emeritus of sociology at the University of Colorado at Colorado Springs (US). He has studied and done research on connections between sports, culture, and society with much attention given to the play, games, and sport participation of young people.

Fred Coalter, PhD is professor of sports policy at Leeds Beckett University (UK). He has broad research interests relating to sport's claimed contributions to various aspects of social policy. He has undertaken extensive research on sport-for-development in Uganda, Tanzania, Malawi, Senegal, South Africa, Brazil and India (Mumbai and Kolkata).

Jean Côté, PhD is professor and director in the School of Kinesiology and Health Studies at Queen's University at Kingston (Canada). His research interests are in the areas of youth sport, coaching, positive youth development, and sport expertise.

Steven Danish, PhD is professor emeritus of Counseling Psychology at Virginia Commonwealth University (US). Steve founded the Life Skills Center at Virginia Commonwealth University. His research focuses on developing and evaluating the effectiveness of sport-based life skills programs (e.g. the GOAL Program and the SUPER Program).

Colin J. Deal is a PhD student in the Faculty of Physical Education and Recreation at the University of Alberta in Edmonton, Alberta (Canada). His research interests include coaches' influences on PYD outcomes and transferring PYD outcomes beyond the context of sport in the form of contributions to the community.

Kitrina Douglas, PhD is director of the Boomerang Project (UK), an ambassador for the National Coordinating Centre for Public Engagement, and a member of the National Anti-doping Panel for sport. Her research explores identity development, physical activity and mental health through narrative and arts-informed methodologies.

Karl Erickson, PhD is an assistant professor in the Institute for the Study of Youth Sports within the Department of Kinesiology at Michigan State University (US). His research examines youth development in sport contexts, with a particular focus on interpersonal processes.

Blair Evans, PhD is an assistant professor within the Department of Kinesiology at the Pennsylvania State University (US). Merging theories and methods from several domains of psychology (i.e. social, organizational, sport, and health psychology), his primary area of focus is on how peer group dynamics and social relationships shape adherence and involvement in sport and physical activity.

Kaitlyn A. Ferris, PhD is a postdoctoral scholar in the Institute for Applied Research in Youth Development at Tufts University (US). Her research focuses on out-of-school time activities, especially organized sports, health-related behaviors, and under-served populations, including rural youth.

Tanya Forneris, PhD is an instructor at the School of Health and Exercise Sciences at the University of British Columbia–Okanagan Campus (Canada). Her field of expertise is the development, implementation and evaluation of community-based programs, including sport and physical activity programs, to enhance positive developmental outcomes in youth.

Jessica Fraser-Thomas, PhD is an associate professor in the School of Kinesiology and Health Science at York University in Toronto (Canada). Her research in PYD includes a focus on social influences, such as coaches, family members, and peers. She recently co-edited *Health and Elite Sport: Is High Performance Sport a Healthy Pursuit?*

Lauren A. Gardner is a PhD candidate in the School of Psychology at the University of Wollongong (Australia). She is conducting research exploring the psychological and social factors associated with participation and dropout in youth sport, including a focus on coach–athlete relationships.

Daniel R. Gould, PhD is a professor and director of the Institute for the Study of Youth Sports in the Department of Kinesiology at Michigan State University (US). His current research focuses on how coaches teach life skills to young athletes and developing youth leaders through the sport captaincy experience.

Tanya Halsall is a PhD candidate in the School of Human Kinetics at the University of Ottawa (Canada). Her primary research areas are in positive youth development, program evaluation, and community-based research in child and youth mental health.

Chris Harwood, PhD is a reader in applied sport psychology in the School of Sport, Exercise and Health Sciences at Loughborough University (UK). He conducts applied research in the psychosocial aspects of youth sport with a particular focus on empowering the roles of coaches and parents in the psychological development of athletes.

Don Hellison, PhD is a professor emeritus at the University of Illinois at Chicago (US). Don has spent over 40 years working with underserved youth. His work has focused on the development, implementation, and evaluation of an alternative physical activity model that focuses on teaching life skills and values through physical activity and sport.

Ken Hodge, PhD is a professor in sport and exercise psychology at the School of Physical Education, Sport and Exercise Sciences, University of Otago (New Zealand). His research focuses on the psychosocial effects of participation in sport. He has investigated issues such as prosocial and antisocial behaviour, moral development, and life skills development through sport.

Nicholas L. Holt, PhD is a professor and leader of the Child and Adolescent Sport and Activity lab in the Faculty of Physical Education and Recreation at the University of Alberta (Canada). He conducts research examining psychosocial aspects of participation in sport and physical activity among children, adolescents, and their families.

Julie Johnston, PhD is a lecturer in Sport and Exercise Psychology in the Department of Sport Science at Nottingham Trent University (UK). Previously she was a research associate in the area of psychosocial development in youth sport at Loughborough University. Her research interests are in the area of youth sport with a particular focus on coach and parent interactions.

Kelsey Kendellen is a PhD candidate at the University of Ottawa's School of Human Kinetics in Ottawa (Canada). Her research focuses on the development of life skills through sport and more particularly how the life skills transfer process can be facilitated.

Richard M. Lerner, PhD is the Bergstrom Chair in Applied Developmental Science, Director of the Institute for Applied Research in Youth Development, and Professor in the Eliot-Pearson Department of Child Study and Human Development at Tufts University (US). His research investigates what goes right in the lives of youth.

Sarah K. Liddle is a PhD candidate in the School of Psychology at the University of Wollongong (Australia). She is conducting research examining mental health and related factors in sport participation, with a particular focus on young people.

Dany J. MacDonald, PhD is an assistant professor in the Department of Applied Human Sciences at the University of Prince Edward Island (Canada). His research focuses on the development of positive contexts in which youth can participate in organized sport and the development of instruments capable of measuring the sport experience.

Tom Martinek, PhD is a professor in the Department of Kinesiology at the University of North Carolina at Greensboro (US). Tom has directed and taught in

Project Effort which is an after-school sport and leadership program for underserved youth. Most recently, he has established an alternative high school for at-risk students on UNCG's campus.

Travis McIsaac is a graduate student in the Department of Applied Human Sciences at the University of Prince Edward Island (Canada). He is interested in how various sport experiences can be used to predict the development of positive outcomes in youth sport participants.

Adam Miles is a doctoral student in sport and exercise psychology at the School of Physical Education, Sport and Exercise Sciences, University of Otago (New Zealand). His research project is focused on evaluating the effectiveness of a needs-based life skills programme to help elite athletes prepare for retirement from sport.

Kacey C. Neely is a PhD candidate in the Faculty of Physical Education and Recreation at the University of Alberta (Canada). Her research examines athletes' experiences of deselection and in youth sport settings and positive growth.

Kendra Nelson-Ferguson completed a Master of Arts degree in the Faculty of Kinesiology and Recreation Management at the University of Manitoba (Canada). Her line of research explored sibling relationships in elite youth sport as well as biofeedback. Currently, Kendra is a doctoral candidate in sport psychology at Western University (Canada).

Christine L. Smyth is a Master's student in the Child and Adolescent Sport and Activity lab in the Faculty of Physical Education and Recreation at the University of Alberta (Canada). She is interested in coaching and youth development.

Leisha Strachan, PhD is an associate professor in the Faculty of Kinesiology and Recreation Management at the University of Manitoba (Canada). Her research is focused on individual and contextual factors related to PYD in sport. She is one of the creators of Project SCORE!—a program focused on helping coaches provide positive experiences (www.projectscore.ca).

Katherine A. Tamminen, PhD is an assistant professor in the Faculty of Kinesiology and Physical Education at the University of Toronto (Canada). She conducts research examining stress, emotions, and coping in sport, as well as sport experiences among young athletes, parents, and coaches.

Jennifer Turnnidge is currently a fourth year PhD student in the School of Kinesiology and Health Studies at Queen's University (Canada). Using both quantitative and qualitative methods, she is interested in exploring how coach–athlete and peer relationships can promote positive development in sport.

Stewart A. Vella, PhD is a research fellow in the Early Start Research Institute at the University of Wollongong (Australia). His research examines the relationship between sports participation and psychosocial development during childhood and adolescence. He has a particular interest in interventions to promote well-being and in working with coaches.

Andrea Vest Ettekal, PhD is a research assistant professor in the Institute for Applied Research in Youth Development at Tufts University (US). Her research examines adolescents' participation in out-of-school time activities, with special interests in organized sports, peer influence, and ethnicity and culture.

Matthew Vierimaa is currently a fourth year PhD candidate in the School of Kinesiology and Health Studies at Queen's University (Canada). Using a wide range of methods, his research broadly focuses on understanding how social and contextual factors influence youth's performance, participation, and personal development in diverse sport contexts.

Maureen R. Weiss, PhD is a professor in Kinesiology, and adjunct professor in the Institute of Child Development, at the University of Minnesota (US). Her research focuses on the psychological, social, and physical development of children and adolescents through participation in physical activity, with interests in self-perceptions, motivation, moral development, and social relationships.

ACKNOWLEDGMENTS

The production of this book was supported, in part, by a Partnership Development Grant from the Social Sciences and Humanities Research Council of Canada (grant # 890-2014-0022) held by Nicholas L. Holt (as principal investigator). I would like to acknowledge the work of Meghan Ingstrup and Shannon Pynn, both from the Child and Adolescent Sport and Activity lab in the Faculty of Physical Education and Recreation at the University of Alberta, who worked tirelessly to check and review chapters for consistency and accuracy.

INTRODUCTION TO THE SECOND EDITION

Nicholas L. Holt

Positive youth development (PYD) is part of the positive psychology movement. Positive psychology itself arose in reaction to the deficit-reduction perspective that dominated the field of psychology in the latter half of the twentieth century (Snyder and Lopez, 2002). During this period psychologists focused their attention on "fixing" individuals' deficiencies. Positive psychology, on the other hand, was about promoting strengths. As Martin Seligman (2002), one of the founding fathers of positive psychology, explained: "psychology is not just about illness or health; it is also about work, education, love, growth, and play" (p. 4). Here we see a natural connection to PYD, whose proponents adopt a strength-based approach and regard youth as having "resources to be developed" rather than "problems to be solved" (Damon, 2004). I think of PYD as an area of research that includes a range of different approaches, models, and constructs sharing some common characteristics. Specifically, these characteristics include taking a strength-based perspective and viewing youth as having resources to be developed rather than problems to be fixed. Since the early 2000s PYD has been used to examine youth development through participation in sport.

Why a second edition?

I had been mulling—or perhaps procrastinating—over the idea of compiling a second edition of *Positive Youth Development through Sport* (Holt, 2008) for some time when Dr. Martin Camiré from the University of Ottawa suggested it may be time for another edition. Dr. Camiré noted that not only was the book widely used, the number of scholars studying PYD had grown significantly since 2008. When the first edition was published PYD was a fledgling movement in the youth sport literature. In fact, part of my motivation in compiling the first edition was to promote and recognize this emerging area of research. Since that time I have been impressed by the number of scholars who have studied PYD. Many of their graduate students have gone on to launch their careers with coherent programs of research dedicated to understanding more about PYD.

Accordingly, my first objective in curating this new edition was to reflect the growth of PYD research in sport. In a sense this was quite easy to achieve because there are so many more scholars studying PYD now compared to the 2000s. The first edition of this book had ten chapters from authors working in four different countries (the United States, Canada, the United Kingdom, and New Zealand). This second edition has eighteen chapters from authors working in five different countries (the United States, Canada, the United Kingdom, New Zealand, and Australia). Clearly, researchers from WEIRD (Western, Educated, Industrialized, Rich, and Democratic) societies still dominate the literature and I hope to see more PYD research emerging from scholars around the world. As someone who grew up and now resides in countries with two official languages (Wales and Canada) I know it can be incredibly difficult to communicate in one's second language. I hope journal editors and reviewers will be flexible in their attitudes toward reviewing such work in the future.

Another motive for this second edition was my desire to stimulate critical scholarly debate about PYD through sport. I have a long-standing belief that unless there are differences of opinion about how to conduct research in a particular area, that area will slowly "die" because new studies will lack novelty, will add little to the literature, and will eventually become difficult to publish. For these reasons I invited some authors who are outside of the "mainstream" psychologically oriented PYD literature in sport to contribute to this book and to provide alternative perspectives that may provoke scholarly debate. I also encouraged all contributors to critically examine the literature and highlight limitations and areas for future research.

Overview of contents

The first part of this book is devoted to theoretical and conceptual issues. I invited Dr. Maureen Weiss to contribute the first chapter because I recalled her Albert V. Carron Distinguished Lecture keynote presentation at the Société Canadienne D'Apprentissage Psychomoteur et de Pyschologie du Sport/Canadian Society for Psychomotor Learning and Sport Psychology conference in Winnipeg, Manitoba (Canada) in 2011. During this keynote address Dr. Weiss argued that PYD researchers have paid insufficient attention to the historical legacy of developmental work in sport psychology. I was pleased she accepted my invitation to contribute to this book and she has provided a challenging but balanced chapter that provides much food for thought.

Further reflecting my desire to promote scholarly debate, Dr. Jay Coakley (Chapter 2) provides a sociological perspective on PYD which highlights several broader issues psychologically oriented researchers may wish to further consider. I realize it may seem a little odd that the first two chapters in this book challenge PYD, given that this book is essentially promoting PYD as an area of research and practice. However, as Dr. Coakley's critique so eloquently demonstrates, it is fundamentally necessary to understand and to question dominant ideologies underpinning youth development so as to improve work in this area in the future. I encourage more critical debate as the field matures.

We then have three chapters (Chapter 3 by Agans and colleagues, Chapter 4 by Hodge and colleagues, and Chapter 5 by Strachan and colleagues) which depict various theoretical approaches to studying PYD. Given that there are many atheoretical studies of PYD through sport (as Hodge and colleagues point out), I view these theoretically oriented chapters as "required reading." I would also like to take this opportunity to direct readers to some sport-specific models of PYD through sport that are not extensively covered in this book (e.g. Gould and Carson, 2008; Petitpas et al., 2005).

Part 2 focuses on measurement. Vest Ettekal and colleagues (Chapter 6) discuss the application of the Richard Lerner's Five Cs model while MacDonald and McIsaac (Chapter 7) consider a range of measures to assess PYD. Coalter (Chapter 8) offers a different perspective based on measures of perceived self-efficacy he has used in his sport-for-development work across the globe. These chapters by no means address all the measurement issues associated with PYD through sport, but they offer vitally important insights because there is a need to improve the measurement and design of studies. In particular, Dany MacDonald and Travis McIsaac (Chapter 7) highlight the need for the precise use of measures to assess PYD *outcomes* versus PYD *experiences*. They also note the need for new measurement approaches to assess the *processes* through which PYD may be acquired through sport.

In Part 3 we dive into the "meat" of PYD research. I wanted to show how PYD has been studied in different types of sporting contexts. Harwood and Johnston (Chapter 9) draw parallels between PYD and talent development. Chapters 10 (Camiré and Kendellen), 11 (Turnnidge and colleagues), and 12 (Gould) focus on coaching. Together, they reflect the critical role of the coach in promoting PYD through sport. The final chapters in this section (Chapter 13 by Forneris and colleagues and Chapter 14 by Martinek and Hellison) look at programs to promote PYD across a range of different contexts, with particular attention given to what might be described as "at risk" or "marginalized" youth.

In Part 4 I wanted to push some other perspectives that may be useful for advancing PYD research in the future. Tamminen and Neely (Chapter 15) discuss theories of positive growth and draw parallels to the PYD literature. Understanding more about positive growth—and in particular, ways in which individuals can "grow" from managing negative or traumatic experiences—is an important issue for PYD researchers to consider. PYD research runs the risk of being "Pollyanna" or overly optimistic, and it could be useful to consider how the "darker" sides of sport may actually contribute to development. Continuing my desire to extend PYD research, in the closing chapters, Stewart Vella and colleagues (Chapter 16) and David Carless and Kitrina Douglas (Chapter 17) discuss how sport participation may play a role in promoting mental health.

As I mentioned, I asked all the authors to highlight limitations of existing work and suggest important areas for future research. Indeed, each chapter includes suggestions for much-needed future research projects and I hope that readers—especially graduate students searching for topics for their thesis and dissertation research—will find many of these suggestions useful. Accordingly, the final chapter in this text (Chapter 18 by Holt and colleagues) represents our own attempt to highlight some of the important issues that require scholarly attention, particularly in terms of theoretical, conceptual, and methodological features for future research.

In closing

This second edition provides the most expansive and complete account of the PYD literature ever produced. I hope it will be a useful resource for scholars, both those new to the field and the seasoned veterans. However, I understand there are many other scholars who work with PYD yet do not have chapters in this book. This by no means diminishes their work and is due to my own errors of omission. Finally, I would like to express my gratitude to Ms. Meghan Ingstrup and Ms. Shannon Pynn who diligently reviewed each chapter. Their support was invaluable and led to the timely publication of this book.

References

Damon, W. (2004). What is positive youth development? *Annals of the American Academy of Political and Social Science, 591,* 13–24.

Gould, D., and Carson, S. (2008). Life skills development through sport: Current status and future directions. *International Review of Sport & Exercise Psychology, 1,* 58–78.

Holt, N. L. (2008). *Positive Youth Development through Sport.* London: Routledge.

Petitpas, A. J., Cornelius, A. E., Van Raalte, J. L., and Jones, T. (2005). A framework for planning youth sport programs that foster psychosocial development. *The Sport Psychologist, 19,* 63–80.

Seligman, M. E. P. (2002). Positive psychology, positive prevention, and positive therapy. In Snyder, C. R., and Lopez, S. J. (Eds.), *Handbook of Positive Psychology* (pp. 3–9). Oxford: Oxford University Press.

Snyder, C. R., and Lopez, S. J. (2002). *Handbook of Positive Psychology.* Oxford: Oxford University Press.

PART 1

Conceptual and theoretical perspectives

1

OLD WINE IN A NEW BOTTLE

Historical reflections on sport as a context for youth development

Maureen R. Weiss

For centuries, sport has been touted as a domain where children learn physical skills, develop moral character, and attain leadership qualities that generalize to life situations (Wiggins, 2013). Belief in the power of sport to enhance personal skills is often communicated through testimonials, such as this quote by Mike Krzyzewski (Duke University): "I don't look at myself as a basketball coach; I look at myself as a leader who happens to coach basketball. I want my players to develop as students, as players, and as human beings." However, scientific studies dating back to the 1930s show that positive outcomes are *not an automatic consequence* of participating in sport—along with favorable outcomes are examples of negative experiences, owing in part to misguided coach and parent behaviors (Fraser-Thomas and Côté, 2009). Therefore, optimizing youth development requires that programs carefully conceive an intentional curriculum to teach life skills, systematically train coaches to deliver lessons, and ensure supportive relationships within a positive learning climate (Weiss et al., 2012).

The purpose of my chapter is to trace the historical roots of research on positive youth development through sport—which precedes the formal naming of this framework. Sport, as a context for youth development, has been studied for nearly a century (Weiss and Gill, 2005), and delves into social and environmental factors associated with youths' psychosocial and behavioral outcomes. Robust findings bolstered many community programs' desire to accentuate a child-centered philosophy—by adopting core values and creating curricula to help youth attain life skills and healthy outcomes (Weiss and Wiese-Bjornstal, 2009). Thus, it is not surprising that sport researchers enthusiastically embraced the positive youth development (PYD) framework.

In studying PYD through sport for many years, I notice a consistent oversight in the literature. Psychologists and many kinesiology professionals do not cite relevant studies from broader youth sport psychology in their literature reviews. They cite papers by psychologists mentioning sport as a developmental context or studies that include sport data as part of a larger study of extracurricular activities. For example, a special issue of *New Directions for Youth Development* (Fall 2007) on "sports-based youth development" included seven papers and seventeen authors, of which only one (second) author is in the sport sciences. The lead article ("An overview of how sports, out-of-school time, and youth well-being can and do intersect") cited 50 references—only one was from the youth sport literature. The editors state, "This volume ... examines youth sport programs as potential contexts that promote positive youth development ... authors explore the potential benefits and possibilities of youth sports to be a context that makes a positive difference in the lives of young people in terms of physical, cognitive, and socioemotional development" (p. 2). This statement, coupled with selective authors and citations, comes across as if psychologists discovered sport as a developmental context and are creating a new knowledge base. A section on "highly successful and unique sports-based youth development programs" lacks any scientific evidence that these programs indeed promote youth development. Throughout, the substantial knowledge base established by youth sport scholars over many decades is alarmingly neglected.

Perhaps these contributors and others do not recognize this body of knowledge as a significant prelude to PYD or choose to cite studies only using literal PYD language. They may be unaware of the rich history of youth sport psychology research that preceded the PYD movement. Although these studies were not labeled as "positive youth development," they used conceptual frameworks, explored processes, and assessed developmental outcomes similar to the PYD approach. Importantly, youth sport psychology studies were not only conducted by researchers specifically trained in the sport sciences, but these scholars were also passionate about and personally invested in studying sport based on lived experiences as athletes and coaches. As a result, these earlier studies were designed, conducted, and interpreted based on both a scholarly understanding and deep personal experience of sport as a medium for promoting youth development. Disregarding this historically rich knowledge reflects a disconnect between what is communicated in the literature and what is available from youth sport research. It also translates to disrespect (albeit unintended) for senior scholars who pioneered the study of PYD through sport.

Understanding the historical origins and contributions of youth sport psychology research is important to: (a) properly situate current research on PYD through sport within long-standing research preceding this movement; and (b) giving credit where credit is due to scholars who established the body of knowledge in youth development through sport before the present era of PYD. Developmental psychologists have inspired a strong movement on viewing youth as resources to be developed in many extracurricular activities, but they were not the first to unveil sport as a potentially powerful context in which favorable outcomes occur. In fact, before the emerging focus on organized activities as contexts for youth development, one rarely finds mention of sport as a significant setting in mainstream psychology. By contrast, developmental processes and outcomes such as self-perceptions, moral development, and social relationships abound in the youth sport literature for decades (Gould and Weiss, 1987; Malina and Clark, 2003; Smoll and Smith, 2002; Weiss and Gould, 1986). Thus, my intent is to raise awareness of the historically rich scholarship on sport as a context for youth development, strongly encourage researchers to be inclusive in citing relevant studies, and remind all of us to recognize senior scholars who launched and advanced youth development through sport in a significant way.

I purposely titled my chapter, "Old Wine in a New Bottle" to suggest that nearly a century of research on youth development through sport ("old wine") was a prelude to the contemporary PYD framework ("new bottle"). I reflect on how PYD is not an entirely new idea for the *sport* domain, given the scientific tradition of youth sport psychology studies. By the same token, I highlight that PYD assets, processes, and outcomes inform sport researchers to go beyond descriptive studies to envision intervention and evaluation designs that reveal processes and mechanisms of change. I conclude by reflecting on how "old wine" and "new bottle" approaches collectively inform us about what we know, what we do not know, and what we need to know to maximize the benefits of youths' experiences in sport.

Preludes to PYD: historical origins of youth sport psychology research

In the 75th anniversary issue of *Research Quarterly for Exercise and Sport*, Weiss and Gill (2005) reviewed volumes from 1930–2004 to determine research trends on psychosocial aspects of sport. They discovered frequently studied topics early on were still popular 75 years later—moral development, social relationships, self-perceptions, motivation, observational learning, and achievement orientations. Ten years later in 2015, these topics continue to reflect constructs and processes central to understanding youth development through sport. For example, McCloy (1930) wrote a classic paper on character building through physical activity and stated, "Physical educators have for years claimed to be builders of character ... the evidence has not been impressive" (p. 41). His provocative article raised important issues as to what character is and how programs should be structured to achieve this desired objective. The issues he raised remain highly relevant today in the youth sport psychology literature (Weiss et al., 2012).

Another prevalent research topic in youth sport psychology has been social development, such as peer acceptance, close friendships, and leadership qualities, as well as social interactions and relationships with parents and coaches (Weiss et al., 2012). The earliest studies can be traced to the 1940s in which athletic participation was linked with social status, feelings of belonging, and making friends—findings that reverberate today in research on sport participation and group acceptance, friendship quality, and athlete leadership (Smith, 2003).

With a shift to adult-controlled youth sport programs (Wiggins, 2013), and increased interest in coaches' influence on children's experiences, Smith and Smoll's (2007) research on coaching behaviors, starting in the 1970s and enduring for five decades, laid the foundation for programmatic studies. Robust findings showed that behaviors in response to performance attempts characterized by greater reinforcement, instruction, and encouragement, and lower criticism and punishment, are associated with greater confidence, enjoyment, and motivation, and lower anxiety and dropout among youth athletes. They translated their research to create a successful coaching education program and inspired numerous studies on effective leadership behaviors that effect positive change in youths' personal and interpersonal attributes (Horn, 2008).

Similarly, interest in parental influence has escalated over time. As Brustad (1992, p. 72) lamented, "Everybody talks about parents in sport, but nobody does any research on them!" He outlined a course of theory-driven research to study parental beliefs and behaviors on children's experiences. Over the last 25 years, knowledge proliferated on mechanisms of parental influence on children's self-perceptions, emotional responses, and motivational orientations. Robust findings show that parents who hold favorable ability beliefs for their child, value sport as an achievement domain, exhibit positive modeling behaviors, and encourage their child's mastery attempts regardless of outcome, are associated with children who experience beneficial outcomes from their involvement (Horn and Horn, 2007). In this section I presented just a broad brushstroke of long-standing research devoted to understanding youth development through sport. Readers are directed to anthologies and reviews for in-depth discussion on historically enduring topics (Gould and Weiss, 1987; Horn, 2004; Weiss, 2004; Weiss et al., 2012).

Developmental sport psychology: a guiding theoretical perspective

Most of the early work in youth sport psychology was descriptive, examining issues such as reasons for participating in and dropping out of sport. In 1982, Gould published a visionary review of the status, direction, and challenge in youth sport research. He advocated that future research focus on testing and developing theory, employ multiple methods, and conduct a series of interrelated rather than single, isolated studies. Twenty years later, Weiss and Raedeke (2004) performed a content analysis of youth sport research and reported significant progress in testing theory, conducting interrelated studies, and using mixed methods. Areas that did not show similar strides were conducting intervention studies to determine causal relationships and evaluation research to test program effectiveness.

What I believe catapulted the quality of youth sport research following Gould's (1982) recommendations was emergence of social–cognitive frameworks during the 1970s and 1980s that inspired a shift from descriptive to theory-driven studies (Horn, 2004; Weiss and Raedeke, 2004). These included competence motivation theory, self-determination theory, social learning theory, achievement goal theory, expectancy-value theory, and moral development theories. Essays elaborating on processes and mechanisms affecting psychosocial outcomes underwent several iterations over the next ten to twenty years, and youth sport researchers kept pace by testing theory-driven questions on the relationship between sport participation and cognitive, social, emotional, and behavioral outcomes (Horn, 2004).

Guided by social–cognitive theories, Weiss and Bredemeier (1983) highlighted the need to ask research questions, design studies, and interpret findings that consider children's cognitive, social, emotional, and physical maturity. Using examples from observational learning, moral development, and motivational orientations, they demonstrated the utility of adopting a developmental theoretical perspective that considers personal, interpersonal, and social influences on youth development. Others reinforced the benefit of a developmental orientation in youth sport research to understand intra- and inter-individual change in perceptions and behaviors (Duda, 1987; Garcia Bengoechea, 2002).

Twenty years after Gould's (1982) and Weiss and Bredemeier's (1983) recommendations, major progress in developmental theory, methods, and lines of research was documented in a book edited by Weiss (2004), which contained a series of reviews on major content areas. These included self-perceptions, parental influence, peer relationships, emotional experiences, motivational processes, and moral development. Each chapter addressed developmental variations in conceptions of and relationships with behavioral and psychosocial variables, and described the substantive body of knowledge on theory-driven processes and mechanisms by which sport has the potential to promote youth development. This knowledge generated from researchers trained in the sport sciences and who identified with sport through lived experiences reinforced Weiss' (2004, p. xv) own personal experiences as a youth sport coach:

> There, on the volleyball court and softball field, the principles of developmental psychology were illuminated. Sport was a unique social context in which physical, social, and psychological growth and development had the potential to flourish. Children learned and improved specific sport skills and strategies; they learned to cooperate with teammates to maximize the benefits of competition; and they disagreed with and got mad at each other—from which they learned to resolve conflicts and sustain relationships … as a result of positive experiences with caring and competent parents and coaches, these young participants sustained a "love of the game" and the "joy of physical movement."

Programmatic lines of research over the past 40 years provide meaningful contributions to understanding individual, social, and environmental factors that influence youth development through sport. Besides Smith and Smoll on coaching behaviors, research lines include Horn on perceived competence; Duda on motivational climate; and others that align with PYD constructs (see Horn, 2004; Weiss, 2004).

Integrating theory, research, and application through interventions

In 2011 I had the honor of giving the Albert V. Carron Distinguished Lecture at the Société Canadienne D'Apprentissage Psychomoteur et de Pyschologie du Sport/Canadian Society for Psychomotor Learning and Sport Psychology conference in Winnipeg, Manitoba (Canada). To pay homage to Carron's legacy of research in group cohesion and visionary ideas about how sport psychology research can make an impact on real-world practices, I translated his concepts (Carron, 1993) on integrating theory, research, and application to youth development studies that used theory to guide interventions for effecting positive change in social, psychological, and physical outcomes. Integrating theory, research, and application through intervention studies is important from a historical perspective—not only the past but also the present and future. I briefly outline three studies that draw a clear link between developmental sport psychology research and the PYD framework.

Gibbons et al. (1995) utilized social learning and structural developmental theories of moral development to design a study evaluating the Canadian *Fair Play for Kids* program. This included a curriculum of activities that promoted respecting the rules, providing individuals with an equal chance to participate, and maintaining self-control. Grade 4 through 6 classrooms were randomly assigned to *Fair Play for Kids* in PE only, *Fair Play for Kids* in all classes, and a control group (regular PE curriculum). Teaching strategies included modeling and reinforcement (social learning theory) and dilemma, dialogue, and balance concepts (structural developmental theory). Trained teachers implemented the protocol for seven months, with indices of moral judgment, reasoning, intention, and behavior assessed prior to and following the intervention. Both treatment groups showed significantly higher scores on all indices at post-intervention than the control group, and effect sizes were large. Findings suggest that an intentional curriculum of activities delivered by trained teachers is effective for enhancing moral cognitions and prosocial behaviors.

Weiss et al. (1998) designed an intervention based on social–cognitive–developmental theories to assess the influence of peer models on swim skills, self-efficacy, and fear among five- to seven-year-old children. Youth were randomly assigned to peer coping, peer mastery, or control groups that entailed watching a videotape followed by a swim lesson. Children were assessed at pre- and post-intervention and four-day follow-up on outcome variables. Findings revealed that both intervention groups recorded significantly and meaningfully better swim skills, higher self-efficacy, and lower fear than the control group, suggesting that a peer model plus swim lessons is more effective for improving physical and psychological skills than swim lessons alone for fearful youth.

Theeboom et al. (1995) implemented an intervention within a summer sport program based on achievement goal theory. Using a novel martial arts form unfamiliar to eight- to twelve-year-old participants, researchers examined the effect of a mastery- versus performance-oriented climate on motor skill learning, perceived competence, enjoyment, and intrinsic motivation. After a three-week daily protocol, mixed methods revealed that youth in the mastery climate group demonstrated better physical skills and reported greater enjoyment, perceived competence, and motivation than the performance climate group. Findings suggest that a learning environment focused on effort, improvement, and mastery rather than social comparison is superior for instilling positive psychosocial and skill outcomes among youth.

Carron (1993) was passionate about the need to integrate theory, research, and application through intervention studies to advance the field of sport psychology. He used his research on coach–athlete dyads and group cohesion to showcase the interdependence of theory, research, and intervention. I took a parallel route in describing intervention studies in youth sport psychology that were guided by developmental theories and translated to favorable youth outcomes in applied settings. Given the social-contextual features of these interventions (e.g. intentional strategies, trained instructors) and positive change in competencies (e.g. physical skills, self-confidence, prosocial behaviors), the compatibility of these studies in youth sport psychology with the PYD framework is unmistakable. Importantly, Carron's advocacy for integrating theory, research, and application through interventions extends the historical conversation that youth sport researchers have been doing PYD work for quite a while.

Mapping youth sport psychology research onto the PYD framework

My review reveals that long-standing youth sport research examined developmental issues using appropriate theories, but these theories and studies were not labeled as PYD. In 2005, Petitpas et al. introduced a framework that integrated youth sport research with concepts from the PYD framework. They defined *context* as an intrinsically motivating activity within a psychologically safe environment; *external assets* as caring and compassionate adults, peers, and community; and *internal assets* as learned skills important for successfully coping with situations in multiple contexts (life skills). They provided examples from the youth sport psychology literature to support these aspects—motivational climate (context), coach behaviors (external assets), emotion management skills (internal assets), and self-esteem (developmental outcomes).

In framing youth sport research alongside the PYD framework, Petitpas et al. differentiated youth *sport* from youth *development* programs, the former referring to traditional teaching of sport skills to improve performance and the latter referring to those with a deliberate curriculum of skill-building activities; coaches trained to effectively deliver the curriculum; a focus on defining success as mastering skills rather than favorable comparison to others; and an evaluation component to determine program effectiveness. This distinction in program terminology is important because many youth sport programs claim in their mission statements that they focus on teaching life skills, but most lack the essential ingredients of a youth development program.

Following Petitpas et al.'s (2005) integration of youth sport research and PYD concepts, Weiss et al. (2012) published an extensive review of research on PYD through sport by situating the scholarly literature within the *Five Cs* framework (Lerner and Lerner, 2006). Their rationale was that the *Five Cs* of competence, confidence, connection, caring, and character was an accurate and intuitive way of linking youth sport research with the PYD framework. Research on *social assets* included peer group acceptance, friendship quality, and moral development as well as beliefs and behaviors by peers, parents, and coaches. Research on *psychological assets* included global and domain-specific self-conceptions, positive and negative emotions, and motivational orientations and behaviors. Weiss et al. also importantly included *physical assets*—fundamental motor skills, sport-specific skills, physical fitness, physical activity, and physical health—as critical outcomes of effective sport programs in promoting a physically active lifestyle. Physical assets are part and parcel of PYD programs in school and community physical activity contexts, whereas the broader PYD literature focuses on other social contexts (e.g. school, family) and does not adequately address physical competencies. For example, the often-used Youth Experiences Survey (Hansen and Larson, 2005) contains a single item on physical skills. Other scholars (Hellison, 2011; Weiss and Wiese-Bjornstal, 2009) also accentuated physical assets through physical education and other school and community activity programs. Melding youth sport psychology research within the PYD framework provides an inclusive, integrative, and evaluative approach to a long tradition of research on sport as a developmental context.

Coming full circle: current and future studies based on the PYD framework

In reviewing preludes to PYD and trends in theory and research, my intent is to raise awareness of the significance of this work and for citing relevant studies. I now turn to recent research on youth development through sport that was explicitly grounded in the PYD framework. PYD through sport studies emerged in and around publication of key conceptual articles on PYD in the psychology literature (Benson, 2006; Eccles and Gootman, 2002; Larson, 2000; Lerner and Lerner, 2006). This research trend resembles the advancement of theory-driven studies that followed the emergence of social–cognitive frameworks in the 1970s.

I digress a moment to encourage using the term *physical activity* rather than sport, as well as for *physical activity-based PYD* (PA–PYD) rather than sport-based PYD. My reasoning is that physical activity is an overarching term for many forms of activity—structured activities include organized sport, physical education, motor development programs, and outdoor recreation, among others. Positive youth development is most likely to occur in any *structured* activity contexts—a feature of effective youth development programs where rules and expectations are provided and monitored under adult guidance (Eccles and Gootman, 2002).

Many studies on PA–PYD use interviews to elicit athletes' (e.g. Fraser-Thomas and Côté, 2009) or coaches' (e.g. Gould et al., 2007) perceptions of experiences. These studies are important to establish the fit of the PYD framework to the sport context. In my review of PA–PYD research in the last few years, many studies are still conducting interviews, often with small numbers of selected athletes *or* coaches (often elite-level) and asking similar questions as earlier studies (e.g. Falcão et al., 2012). As Horn (2011) suggests in her essay on multiple pathways to knowledge generation, qualitative methods in early phases of research on a topic can guide future questions and methods that go beyond description to test theory, validate hypotheses, and provide explanatory processes for change in outcomes. Applied to PYD, this means advancing knowledge by not solely using qualitative methods but examining, for example, the effectiveness of coaching behaviors on developmental outcomes using mixed methods with *both* coaches and athletes (i.e., process-product approach; Horn, 2008). Over 30 years ago Gould (1982) encouraged youth sport researchers to consider alternatives to quantitative methods; ironically the pendulum may have swung too far in the other direction.

Other studies used correlational designs and survey methods rather than focus groups and individual interviews. Examples include studies of the relationship between perceived coaching behaviors and developmental assets (e.g. Gould and Carson, 2011) and between perceptions of a caring climate and prosocial behaviors (e.g. Gano-Overway et al., 2009). These types of designs are able to quantify associations between social-environmental and athlete variables but, mirroring my critique of qualitative studies, correlational designs are unable to determine causal relationships. Thus, longitudinal and experimental designs are needed to untangle mediators and moderators as well as explanatory processes of relationships among variables.

Some short-term intervention studies with small samples have been conducted in physical activity settings with targeted outcomes such as respect, responsibility, initiative, and goal setting (e.g. Coatsworth and Conroy, 2009; Wright and Burton, 2008). Intervention designs are beneficial for determining causal relationships and the mechanisms explaining change in outcomes. This reinforces my coverage of intervention studies conducted 20 years ago that integrated theory, research, and application. PA–PYD intervention studies were thus a step in the right direction but many are limited by small samples, brief protocols, and not assessing whether positive change endured once the intervention ended. Intervention studies that address these limitations are needed to test theory and offer practical applications for youth sport professionals.

Evaluation research is common in broader PYD but not so in PA–PYD. The sparse number of studies evaluating PA–PYD programs is surprising, given Petitpas et al.'s (2005) emphasis that such designs are necessary to determine whether programs are achieving intended goals and determining where improvements can be made. As the PYD framework has increased in appeal, evaluating the impact of PA–PYD programs in teaching life skills and core values is important for testing theory and providing evidence-based best practices for administrators, coaches, and parents. Thus, an encouraging sign is the emergence of program evaluation studies. Most have used interview methods or pre-post designs without a comparison group (e.g. Anderson-Butcher et al., 2014; Ullrich-French et al., 2012). Studies report positive change in developmental outcomes from pre- to post-program, but definitive conclusions about effectiveness cannot be made without a comparison group (i.e. pre-post change can be due to physical maturity, situational factors, etc.). With pre-post designs it is also unknown whether a "glow effect" occurred from participating in the program without a follow-up assessment. Few studies have measured program effects after immediate post-assessment (Gabriel et al., 2011) or whether skills learned within a program were successfully transferred to other life domains (Walsh et al., 2010) as the PYD framework suggests. As a step toward addressing these issues, my colleagues and I conducted evaluation research with *The First Tee*, a PA–PYD program using golf as the vehicle for teaching life skills and core values (Weiss, 2008; Weiss et al., 2013, 2014, 2015).

In the first phase (Weiss et al., 2013), we conducted focus group and individual interviews with youth, coaches, and parents to assess their understanding of the curriculum, coaching methods to convey life skills, and evidence of generalizing life skills learned in the program to other domains. Evidence and sources of program effectiveness emerged through converging information by all three sources on interpersonal and emotion management skills. In the second phase (Weiss et al., 2014), qualitative findings from phase 1 were used to develop and validate a quantitative measure of life skills transfer in three studies, including tests for construct validity and longitudinal factorial invariance. The third phase (Weiss et al., 2015) entailed: (a) comparing youth in *The First Tee* with youth in other organized activities on life skills transfer and developmental outcomes; and (b) determining stability or change in life skills transfer over three years among participants in *The First Tee*. This phase explicitly addressed the need for a comparison group and longitudinal design to make conclusive statements about program impact. Findings revealed that: (a) participants in *The First Tee* compared favorably to youth in other activities on most dimensions of life skills transfer (e.g. managing emotions) and developmental outcomes (e.g. responsibility); and (b) scores on life skills transfer dimensions improved or remained stable over three years, showing sustained effects of program impact.

I encourage PA–PYD researchers to engage in more longitudinal, intervention, and evaluation designs to determine whether programs are achieving their goal of promoting positive youth development. Appropriate measures are available for employing quantitative *and* qualitative approaches, and many youth programs are keen to demonstrate credible evidence of effectiveness to families, coaches, funders, and community members.

Conclusion

Sport scientists have always valued sport as a context for developing youth physically, socially, and psychologically. As a result, research on youth development through sport has enjoyed a long and productive history for nearly a century. Although theories used to guide studies and the studies themselves were not tabbed as "positive youth development," they entail similar constructs, processes, and mechanisms. I contend that "old wine" in the form of historically rich studies of sport as a developmental context is a meaningful prelude to and compatible with the "new bottle" of the PYD framework.

Over the past few years, PA–PYD research has continued on a course of studies using qualitative designs but has also progressed to conducting more intervention and program evaluation studies. Continued efforts employing longitudinal, intervention, and evaluation designs with comparison groups, and using mixed methods with diverse populations (not just high-level athletes), are essential to advance the knowledge base. These designs and methods will enable researchers to test theory and assist community programs in designing curricula of skill-building activities, making recommendations for coach and parent education, and interpreting findings to enhance positive youth outcomes. Evidence-based best practices stemming from carefully designed PA–PYD studies benefit youth sport stakeholders ranging from administrators to coaches to the participants themselves.

In taking this historical journey down memory lane, I provided evidence of a scientific tradition of youth sport research that has informed current theory, research, and application. I urge PA–PYD researchers to extensively review and cite relevant studies and to recognize the scholars who contributed substantial knowledge on youth development through sport. Let us honor the legacy of a century of youth sport research ("old wine") by giving credit where credit is due, while also integrating the valuable contributions by and inspiration of the contemporary PYD framework ("new bottle").

References

Anderson-Butcher, D., Riley, A., Amorose, A., Iachini, A., and Wade-Mdivanian, R. (2014). Maximizing youth experiences in community sport settings: The design and impact of the LiFE sports camp. *Journal of Sport Management, 28,* 236–249.

Benson, P. L. (2006). *All Kids Are Our Kids: What Communities Must Do to Raise Caring and Responsible Children and Adolescents* (2nd ed.). San Francisco, CA: Jossey-Bass.

Brustad, R. J. (1992). Integrating socialization influences into the study of children in sport. *Journal of Sport & Exercise Psychology, 14,* 59–77.

Carron, A. V. (1993). Toward the integration of theory, research, and practice in sport psychology. *Journal of Applied Sport Psychology, 5,* 207–221.

Coatsworth, J. D., and Conroy, D. E. (2009). The effects of autonomy-supportive coaching, need satisfaction, and self-perceptions on initiative and identity in youth swimmers. *Developmental Psychology, 45,* 320–328.

Duda, J. L. (1987). Toward a developmental theory of children's motivation in sport. *Journal of Sport Psychology, 9,* 130–145.

Eccles, J. S., and Gootman, J. A. (2002). Features of positive developmental settings. In J. S. Eccles and J. A. Gootman (Eds.), *Community Programs to Promote Youth Development* (pp. 86–118). Washington, DC: National Academy Press.

Falcão, W. R., Bloom, G. A., and Gilbert, W. D. (2012). Coaches' perceptions of a coach training program designed to promote youth developmental outcomes. *Journal of Applied Sport Psychology, 24,* 429–444.

Fraser-Thomas, J., and Côté, J. (2009). Understanding adolescents' positive and negative developmental experiences in sport. *The Sport Psychologist, 23,* 3–23.

Gabriel, K. P., DeBate, R. D., High, R. R., and Racine, E. F. (2011). Girls on the run: A quasi-experimental evaluation of a developmentally focused youth sport program. *Journal of Physical Activity and Health, 8,* S285–S294.

Gano-Overway, L. A., Newton, M., Magyar, T. M., Fry, M. D., Kim, M., and Guivernau, M. R. (2009). Influence of caring youth sport contexts on efficacy-related beliefs and social behaviors. *Developmental Psychology, 45,* 329–340.

Garcia Bengoechea, E. (2002). Integrating knowledge and expanding horizons in developmental sport psychology: A bioecological perspective. *Quest, 54,* 1–20.

Gibbons, S. L., Ebbeck, V., and Weiss, M. R. (1995). Fair Play for Kids: Effects on the moral development of children in physical education. *Research Quarterly for Exercise and Sport, 66,* 247–255.

Gould, D. (1982). Sport psychology in the 1980s: Status, direction and challenge in youth sports research. *Journal of Sport Psychology, 4,* 203–218.

Gould, D., and Weiss, M. R. (Eds.) (1987). *Advances in Pediatric Sport Sciences, Vol. 2: Behavioral Issues.* Champaign, IL: Human Kinetics.

Gould, D., and Carson, S. (2011). Young athletes' perceptions of the relationship between coaching behaviors and developmental experiences. *International Journal of Coaching Science, 5,* 3–29.

Gould, D., Collins, K., Lauer, L., and Chung, Y. (2007). Coaching life skills through football: A study of award winning high school coaches. *Journal of Applied Sport Psychology, 19,* 16–37.

Hansen, D., and Larson, R. (2005). *The Youth Experience Survey 2.0: Instrument Revisions and Validity Testing.* Unpublished manuscript, University of Illinois at Urbana-Champaign.

Hellison, D. (2011). *Teaching Personal and Social Responsibility Through Physical Activity* (3rd ed.). Champaign, IL: Human Kinetics.

Horn, T. S. (2004). Lifespan development in sport and exercise psychology: Theoretical perspectives. In M. R. Weiss (Ed.), *Developmental Sport and Exercise Psychology: A Lifespan Perspective* (pp. 27–71). Morgantown, WV: Fitness Information Technology.

Horn, T. S. (2008). Coaching effectiveness in the sport domain. In T. S. Horn (Ed.), *Advances in Sport Psychology* (3rd ed., pp. 240–267). Champaign, IL: Human Kinetics.

Horn, T. S. (2011). Multiple pathways to knowledge generation: Qualitative and quantitative research approaches in sport and exercise psychology. *Qualitative Research in Sport, Exercise and Health, 3,* 291–304.

Horn, T. S., and Horn, J. L. (2007). Family influences on children's sport and physical activity participation, behavior, and psychosocial responses. In G. Tenenbaum and R. C. Eklund (Eds.), *Handbook of Sport Psychology* (pp. 685–711). Hoboken, NJ: Wiley.

Larson, R. W. (2000). Toward a psychology of positive youth development. *American Psychologist, 55,* 170–183.

Lerner, R. M., and Lerner, J. V. (2006). Toward a new vision and vocabulary about adolescence: Theoretical, empirical, and applied bases of a "Positive Youth Development" perspective. In L. Balter and C. S. Tamis-LeMonda (Eds.), *Child Psychology: A Handbook of Contemporary Issues* (pp. 445–469). New York: Psychology Press.

Malina, R. M., and Clark, M. A. (2003). *Youth Sports – Perspectives for a New Century*. Monterey, CA: Coaches Choice.

McCloy, C. H. (1930). Character building through physical education. *Research Quarterly, 1*(3), 41–59.

New Directions for Youth Development, Special Issue: Sports-Based Youth Development, Fall *2007*(115), 1–118.

Petitpas, A. J., Cornelius, A. E., Van Raalte, J. L., and Jones, T. (2005). A framework for planning youth sport programs that foster psychosocial development. *The Sport Psychologist, 19*, 63–80.

Smith, A. L. (2003). Peer relationships in physical activity contexts: A road less traveled in youth sport and exercise psychology research. *Psychology of Sport and Exercise, 4*, 25–39.

Smith, R. E., and Smoll, F. L. (2007). Social-cognitive approach to coaching behaviors. In S. Jowett and D. Lavallee (Eds.), *Social Psychology in Sport* (pp. 75–89). Champaign, IL: Human Kinetics.

Smoll, F. L., and Smith, R. E. (2002). *Children and Youth in Sport: A Biopsychosocial Perspective* (2nd ed.). Dubuque, IA: Kendall/Hunt.

Theeboom, M., De Knop, P., and Weiss, M. R. (1995). Motivational climate, psychosocial responses, and motor skill development in children's sport: A field-based intervention study. *Journal of Sport & Exercise Psychology, 17*, 294–311.

Ullrich-French, S., McDonough, M. H., and Smith, A. L. (2012). Social connection and psychological outcomes in a physical activity-based youth development setting. *Research Quarterly for Exercise and Sport, 83*, 431–441.

Walsh, D. S., Ozaeta, J., and Wright, P. M. (2010). Transference of responsibility model goals to the school environment: Exploring the impact of a coaching club program. *Physical Education and Sport Pedagogy, 15*, 15–28.

Weiss, M. R. (2004). *Developmental Sport and Exercise Psychology: A Lifespan Perspective*. Morgantown, WV: Fitness Information Technology.

Weiss, M. R. (2008). "Field of dreams": Sport as a context for youth development. *Research Quarterly for Exercise and Sport, 79*, 434–449.

Weiss, M. R., and Bredemeier, B. J. (1983). Developmental sport psychology: A theoretical perspective for studying children in sport. *Journal of Sport Psychology, 5*, 216–230.

Weiss, M. R., and Gould, D. (Eds.) (1986). *Sport for Children and Youths*. Champaign, IL: Human Kinetics.

Weiss, M. R., and Raedeke, T. D. (2004). Developmental sport psychology: Research status on youth and directions toward a lifespan perspective. In M. R. Weiss (Ed.), *Developmental Sport and Exercise Psychology: A Lifespan Perspective* (pp. 1–26). Morgantown, WV: Fitness Information Technology.

Weiss, M. R., and Gill, D. L. (2005). What goes around comes around: Reemerging themes in sport and exercise psychology. *Research Quarterly for Exercise and Sport, 76*, S71–S87.

Weiss, M. R., and Wiese-Bjornstal, D. M. (2009). Promoting positive youth development through physical activity. *President's Council on Physical Fitness & Sports Research Digest, 10*(3), 1–8.

Weiss, M. R., McCullagh, P., Smith, A. L., and Berlant, A. R. (1998). Observational learning and the fearful child: Influence of peer models on swimming skill performance and psychological responses. *Research Quarterly for Exercise and Sport, 69*, 380–394.

Weiss, M. R., Kipp, L. E., and Bolter, N. D. (2012). Training for life: Optimizing positive youth development through sport and physical activity. In S. M. Murphy (Ed.), *The*

Oxford Handbook of Sport and Performance Psychology (pp. 448–475). New York: Oxford University Press.

Weiss, M. R., Stuntz, C. P., Bhalla, J. A., Bolter, N. D., and Price, M. S. (2013). 'More than a game': impact of *The First Tee* life skills programme on positive youth development: project introduction and Year 1 findings. *Qualitative Research in Sport, Exercise, and Health, 5,* 214–244.

Weiss, M. R., Bolter, N. D., and Kipp, L. E. (2014). Assessing impact of physical-activity-based youth development programs: Validation of the Life Skills Transfer Survey (LSTS). *Research Quarterly for Exercise and Sport, 85,* 263–278.

Weiss, M. R., Bolter, N. D., and Kipp, L. E. (2015). Evaluation of *The First Tee* in promoting positive youth development: Group comparisons and longitudinal trends. Manuscript submitted for publication.

Wiggins, D. K. (2013). A worthwhile effort? History of organized youth sport in the United States. *Kinesiology Review, 2,* 65–75.

Wright, P. M., and Burton, S. (2008). Implementation and outcomes of a responsibility-based physical activity program integrated into an intact high school physical education class. *Journal of Teaching in Physical Education, 27,* 138–154.

2

POSITIVE YOUTH DEVELOPMENT THROUGH SPORT

Myths, beliefs, and realities

Jay Coakley

A widely used statement to demonstrate the value of sport is, "The battle of Waterloo was won on the playing fields of Eton." It is unclear when, where, and by whom this statement was made, but over time the elites in England used it to claim that young men attending exclusive, high cost schools such as Eton College experienced important forms of positive development because they participated in rigorous, rule-governed, and competitive sports as part of their education. Although this nineteenth-century claim was used to reproduce a tradition-based status hierarchy in England, it was modified during the Progressive Era in the United States where "properly organized" youth sports were believed to create in young men the energy, nationalism, achievement orientation, and competitive spirit that would sustain personal health, fuel industrial expansion, and create American military power. Programs in selected team sports were also used to Americanize immigrant children, convert unruly boys in crowded tenements into efficient and compliant workers, foster good health through outdoor activities, prepare boys to be fit and willing soldiers, and masculinize middle-class boys who were being socialized in female-dominated households and seen as lacking the assertive and competitive character to become political and economic leaders.

Fueled by anecdotal evidence, the personal testimonies of athletes, stories circulated through popular culture, and the pronouncements of physical educators and coaches, the belief that sport participation produced positive development among youth became a taken-for-granted cultural truth in most Western societies. This belief has gone hand-in-hand with the assumption, often made and seldom questioned, that sport is essentially pure and good and that all who participate in it share in that purity and goodness (Coakley, 2015). Today, people worldwide accept this essentialist belief to the point that they have unlimited expectations for what "sport," as they imagine it, can do for individuals, communities, and societies (Wolff, 2011). Accordingly, parents, educators, community leaders, and political officials have allocated vast amounts of public and private resources to sports. When these resources are directed toward youth sports, the expectation is that positive development will occur.

The purpose of this chapter is to examine positive youth development (PYD) in the social, cultural, and historical context in which it has emerged and been linked with sports. The following sections will also focus on the particular approach to development commonly associated with PYD, why sport is seen as an appropriate context for PYD, the challenges of integrating PYD into existing youth sport programs, and the prospects for using sports as sites for fostering PYD.

The neoliberal boost for positive youth development

The belief that sport participation leads to PYD received a major boost in the 1980s as neoliberal ideology increasingly informed national economic doctrine and political policy in many societies. In this context, parents sought for their children activities that were culturally valued and organized to produce useful skills and quantifiable achievements leading to social and economic success. Youth sport entrepreneurs responded with exclusive leagues, clubs, and teams emphasizing excellence in coaching, performance, and competitive challenges.

More than building character, youth sports came to be seen by upper-middle-class parents as sites for preserving their privilege into the next generation, and by less advantaged others as pipelines for a child's upward mobility. Overall, the movement to promote PYD—centered in, but not limited to the United States—was associated with a worldwide increase in sport programs sponsored primarily by private and nonprofit funders in Western societies. Sports, claimed the authors of uncounted proposals, would alter the lives of young people through the inherent lessons they provided, or they would serve as hooks to recruit and retain young people in programs fostering personal growth and development.

Supporters of these programs infused into popular culture wide-ranging statements about the developmental outcomes that sport participation *could* produce. Many of these have been identified and critiqued in other sources, so they are not all listed here (see Sukarieha and Tannock, 2011). To more fully understand the context out of which these statements emerged and were used to guide the allocation of public and private resources, the next section deals with changes in the ways that "development" has been defined over the past half century.

Shifting definitions of "development"

During the late 1960s and early 1970s "development" was linked with community organization and coordinating local political and economic resources to achieve civil rights, social justice, and the "common good." Social and cultural changes were the ultimate goal. Organizing previously marginalized and underserved communities was a common strategy used to foster social responsibility and progressive change. Underlying this strategy was the assumption that creating strong communities maximized opportunities for positive development among people of all ages. Individual development was not ignored during these years, but it was often seen as a process facilitated within a collective setting organized to support everyone in the community. This approach to development is outlined on the left-hand side of Figure 2.1.

Opposition to this definition of development existed in the United States and other societies in which individualism was highly valued. As outlined on the right-hand side of Figure 2.1, proponents of this approach focused on developing individuals and strengthening families. It was assumed that strong families and young people with positive attributes constituted the foundation for viable communities as well as moral order and social progress in society (Lerner et al., 2000).

This latter definition of development—one that focused on developing individuals through family-based socialization—gained global prominence during the 1980s as Margaret Thatcher was prime minister of the United Kingdom and Ronald Reagan was president of the United States. President Reagan and his administration tapped into the growing popular belief in the United States that *government was the problem, not the solution* to national and global problems. Margaret Thatcher, Reagan's closest political ally, declared that the only way to solve problems facing the United Kingdom and the world was to make families responsible for personal and moral development and make individuals responsible for themselves. To paraphrase Thatcher's belief: *There is no society, there are only individuals and families.*

These two ideas—*government is the problem* and *there is no society*—served as the basis for a neoliberal policy orientation that had implications far beyond the United States and the United Kingdom during the 1980s and subsequent decades. As summarized in critiques by Bourdieu (1998) and Harvey (2005), among others, policies in these and other Western nations increasingly reflected the following ideological assumptions:

DEFINING DEVELOPMENT

Mid-twentieth century to 1980s	**1980s to present**
• Emphasize civil rights, social justice, fair laws and policies • Focus on developing marginalized and underserved communities • Organize communities to mobilize political and economic power. *Assumption:* Creating strong communities will support positive development opportunities for all.	• Emphasize personal growth, responsibility, and success. • Focus on developing individuals through family-based socialization. • Develop positive attributes, especially among young people. *Assumption:* Positive individual development is the foundation for creating viable communities.

Today: Definitions of development focus on individual and economic growth; they seldom focus on transforming communities or societies.

FIGURE 2.1   Different approaches to defining 'development'

1. The primary foundation of social order is personal responsibility.
2. The most effective source of economic growth is unregulated pursuit of self-interest.
3. People are motivated by competition and the resulting inequalities of income and wealth.
4. Competitive reward structures are the most effective means of allocating resources and creating progress in society.

As neoliberal ideology was increasingly manifested in the political, economic, cultural, and social spheres of society, there also was an emphasis on intervening in the lives of young people to make them personally responsible and keeping them out of trouble at the same time. Teen pregnancy, drugs, rising youth crime rates, single parent households, and morally suspect trends in popular culture led to an emphasis on restraint and prevention during the 1980s and most of the 1990s. The anti-drug slogan, "Just say no," was presented to young people as a primary guide for all aspects of their lives.

It was in this context that youth sports came to be seen by many people as a tool for teaching dominant values, controlling boys identified as "at risk" (for engaging in deviance), and socializing young people to become personally responsible, physically healthy, self-confident, and motivated to be successful. Sports were also seen as apolitical and non-disruptive, which was attractive to political officials and community leaders as well as private and nonprofit sponsors of leagues, clubs, and teams.

Although the scholarly literature on sport and PYD sometimes mentioned the importance of linking individual development with community development as a means of activating young people as assets and resources, youth sport programs, even those formally committed to PYD, tended to ignore the larger community context in which young people lived. Instead, they focused on the immediate social contexts that influenced sport participation, such as family, friends, and school (Guest, 2013; Rauscher and Cooky, 2015).

When young people were defined as assets and resources, coaches and parents conceptualized development in terms of the strengths and skills acquired by young people. This approach frames development as an internal, individual process as well as an individual responsibility (Sukarieha and Tannock, 2011). Furthermore, it connects development to the attributes and potential of currently powerless young people, rather than seeing development as a messy, tension-filled, conflict-producing process involving power relations and efforts to change the distribution of opportunities at the community and societal levels.

As others have noted, linking individual development to the larger community and mobilizing power to take action and promote progressive social change has not been a concern in PYD or sport for development programs (Burnett, 2013; Rauscher and Cooky, 2015). Such an approach is more consistent with a community organizing framework focused on actions that give systemically disadvantaged populations more control over their lives and living conditions (Alinsky, 1971; Brown, 2007; Schutz and Miller, 2015).

Another change that accompanied the shift to neoliberal cultural orientations was a revised definition of "the good parent." With a decline in the number of children per family and the inability of most parents to directly advocate for their children in the job market, parents shifted their attention to preparing children to gain the skills and credentials that would bring them future success. As part of that shift, parental moral worth came to be linked with parents' efforts to enlist their children in visible, achievement-oriented, and culturally valued activities. Youth sports fit these requirements, and parents who effectively nurtured the sport dreams of their children were evaluated as morally worthy (Coakley, 2006, 2010). In this sense, neoliberal cultures serve as a context in which there is an obligatory focus on the family and the self. Parents are ultimately responsible for fostering and advocating the development of their children. Community development is no longer seen as essential in this process. The focus is on family and individual development.

Sport as a context for positive youth development

Although youth sports have long been assumed to produce positive developmental outcomes, this assumption was formally endorsed on a global scale when the United Nations declared 2005 as the International Year of Sport and Physical Education (IYSPE). In addition to connecting sport with the Millennium Development Goals (MDGs),[1] the United Nations statement described sport as "an entry point ... to help youth promote health, education and development in order to reach the MDGs and for communicating values, such as respect for rules and cooperation, to help build peace" (United Nations, 2005, p. 291).

The UN's IYSPE focused primarily on expectations for how sport *could* improve quality of life in regions of the world with high concentrations of people living in poverty or near poverty conditions. But the spirit of its message and underlying assumptions about the power of sport also inspired a connection between sport and the PYD movement in wealthy industrialized societies. For example, it was in 2005 when Fraser-Thomas et al. published their influential article, "Youth sport programs: An avenue to foster positive youth development." Like the UN's description of the IYSPE, Fraser-Thomas and her colleagues from Queen's University in Ontario, Canada outlined the developmental potential of youth sports. Unlike the UN statement, they acknowledged that youth sports, if not organized around a sound pedagogical approach, could produce negative developmental outcomes. In light of this, they and others called for research to identify the conditions under which selected developmental outcomes were most likely to occur (Petipas et al., 2005).

When the first edition of this book was published (Holt, 2008), it contained state-of-the-art discussions and research on youth development through sport. These focused primarily on North America and the United Kingdom with an emphasis on the use of sports to develop positive attributes among young people. The emphasis reflected a continuing tendency for PYD to be organized around producing two sets of outcomes (Holt and Neely, 2011). One was the 5Cs (*competence, confidence, caring/compassion, character,* and *connection*) identified by Lerner and colleagues (2000). Implicit in this approach was that sport participation produced young people who would then *contribute*—the "6th C"—to the community. A similar approach was organized around activating 40 external and internal developmental assets that research identified as the attributes of personally and socially responsible adolescents (Benson, 1997; Scales and Leffert, 1999).

A key aspect of both PYD approaches was to include young people as full partners "in the community–child relation, bearing a full share of rights and responsibilities" (Damon, 2004, p. 19). Among the internal assets proposed by Benson (1997) were "caring, equality and social justice," and Lerner and Benson (2003) stated that "development" was manifested ultimately through a young person's ability to make "positive, healthy contributions to family, community, and civil society" (p. 7). However, from my reading of the literature, this aspect of PYD—the social agency of young people, apart from encouraging them to engage others in their immediate social world—has seldom been given more than lip-service in most sport-based programs claiming to focus on youth development.

Most PYD projects, influenced by neoliberal cultural orientations, tend to be "excessively child-centered" and do little to hold "children to anything resembling objective standards" (Damon, 2004, p. 21). Instead, they focus on internal assets and subjective indicators of development, such as self-esteem, self-confidence, and making choices leading to personal success and upward social and economic mobility. This appears to be a continuing emphasis in youth development through sport.

Sport-based development programs have also deviated from the original conceptions of PYD in cases involving young people in poor and ethnic minority communities, including those in the developing world. PYD is based on the central assumption, regardless of context, that young people are not to be seen or treated in terms of their deficits or as "at risk" when it comes to their social and moral characteristics (Damon, 2004). But sport-based programs dealing with young people from underserved and marginalized communities often use a deficit-reduction and social control approach (Coakley, 2002). Decision-makers in governments, NGOs, and corporate social responsibility departments have favored programs with underlying evaluative and corrective agendas built into the selection, delivery, and implementation processes (Burnett, 2013; Chawansky, 2012; Coalter, 2010; Darnell, 2010; Spaaij and Jones, 2013; Stenling, 2015; Szto, 2015).

These observations are *not* meant as a criticism of the psychologists, educators, and child development experts who have produced useful knowledge on the connections between sport participation and individual development among young people. My point is that most sport-based programs claiming a concern with youth development have seldom focused on community development and social change as necessary features in a process of creating sustainable development opportunities for young people. Nor have they focused on how sports could be designed to create among young people critical awareness and action strategies linking them to efforts to foster equality, social justice, and other external assets of a progressive nature.

The challenge of integrating positive youth development into sports

Positive youth development is a specific project with an identifiable origin, operational definitions, and research history (Catalano et al., 2002, 2004; Damon, 2004). However, most sport-based projects do not include important components of PYD as originally conceived. For example, a major challenge faced when attempting to integrate PYD into existing youth sport programs, especially in North America, has been a near universal belief that sport participation automatically produces positive developmental outcomes for participants. As a result, the adults who control programs and teams have not felt that specific intervention strategies or new pedagogies were needed to achieve developmental goals. In their minds, good character and good choices led to success, and playing competitive sports led to good character and good choices.

The point here is that existing youth sport programs are controlled by people and organized in ways that resist new pedagogical approaches. This is confirmed by Swedish researcher Cecelia Stenling (2013, 2014a, 2014b, 2015; Stenling and Fahlén, 2014) whose work pulls together knowledge from the sociology of sport, critical sport management, and policy analysis. Her studies of the implementation of new ideas and practices in sport organizations help us understand the challenges faced by any of us wanting to change sport cultures at any level. Her findings stress that established sport programs resist change—like any organizations with institutionalized structures. This means that in a best-case scenario, the pedagogies and practices required to produce PYD will be given meaning, operationalized, and integrated into sport programs in a manner that fits their institutional logic, along with their stated and inferred goals, and the established rationale that guides decision-makers.

On a practical level, institutionalization infers the existence of a relatively integrated set of values, norms, and goals; operational procedures; everyday cultural practices; and methods of assessing success. These influence the actions of adults who manage and coach as well as the perceptions of outsiders who use them as a basis for evaluating programs and making decisions about registering their children and committing family resources to participation. As a result, if and when conceptions of PYD are embraced they will be revised in ways that reaffirm the existing culture and structure of an established program.

The changes required to implement a PYD approach generally challenge the institutional logic and the organizational identity that dominates and defines most competitive youth sport leagues, clubs, and teams today. This creates forms of resistance that are difficult to overcome. And this has even led some advocates to frame PYD as a strategy to produce athletic excellence and competitive success— the stated goals of many youth sport programs. The varying success of efforts to implement PYD into existing leagues and teams reflects the significant differences encountered when innovating in *sport plus* versus *plus sport* programs. The latter may be initiated around the goals and means of PYD, whereas the former are already organized around an institutional logic grounded in a sport culture that uses a performance ethic to evaluate success.

Jim Denison, a professor at the University of Alberta, Canada, and his colleagues (2015), have noted that coach–athlete relationships in most youth sports are structured so that coaches have considerable power over athletes. This undermines the possibility for young people to make choices and develop external assets by engaging the larger community for purposes unrelated to competitive success on the field. It also deepens resistance among coaches (and many parents) to utilize a pedagogy supportive of PYD.

Another challenge faced by PYD advocates is that youth sports have become increasingly privatized with an emphasis on year-round participation and the promise of future benefits, such as scholarships, opportunities to play at elite levels, and personal upward mobility. This leaves them with little leverage when presenting PYD to decision-makers in sport organizations where there are well-established ideas about "who we are and what we do." Appeals to the "common good," which may have resonance in publicly funded and some nonprofit programs, often fail to attract support in private programs.

A straightforward cost–benefit consideration in privatized programs also creates resistance to changes that are inconsistent with the prevailing logic of competitive sport and the organizational identity of the programs. According to Stenling's findings, even state-funded sport programs that exist professedly for the "common good" tend to resist the implementation of specific developmental policies and practices, even when they are supported by research and theory (Stenling, 2015).

An added challenge to accepting and implementing PYD in the United States in particular is the lack of systematic coaching education programs through which PYD could be introduced and explained. Although it is possible for some local park and recreation departments to use "the power of the permit" to mandate coaching education and an explicit PYD approach for leagues, clubs, and teams that seek to use public facilities and fields, this strategy is overlooked or seen as too contentious.

Another issue that continues to be difficult to resolve for PYD advocates is that the young people who could benefit most from sports organized around the principles and practices of PYD are often those who have already rejected adult-controlled sport participation or cannot afford the costs associated with it. Again, it may be that low-cost and well-marketed *plus sport* programs are the most effective way to attract these young people; research is needed to explore this possibility and the funding sources that might support it.

The future of positive youth development through sport

Many of us who have viewed or tried to use youth sports as a hook, vehicle, or site for positive development have underestimated the complexity of our task. The culture of youth sport programs is grounded in strongly held beliefs and an institutional logic to which coaches, administrators, and parents are deeply committed. Implementing changes under these conditions is a major undertaking—one that gives new meaning to "the power of sport." This does not mean that youth sports cannot be changed to include a meaningful implementation of PYD, but it calls on us to understand the magnitude of the challenge faced and the persistence required.

As I have worked with youth sports over the past four decades I have wavered between cautious optimism and skepticism about the possibility of integrating the pedagogy and practices of PYD into existing programs. My sociological perspective has led me to set my sights on fostering cultural and structural changes that would make PYD a reality. Successes have been few and far between, and they have often been followed by gradual reversion to traditional performance-based approaches aimed at producing competitive success. This, along with the growing connection between youth sports and structural inequalities and power relations at the level of funding and implementation, has made me (and sociology of sport colleagues) wonder why sports continue to be a preferred site for youth development projects.

For those of us who continue to work on this project, it is important to accept the merits of incremental change and to understand the complexity of any youth development project. In light of this, I raise the following five points about PYD.

First, PYD is a social process that goes beyond specific outcomes for individual participants. To say that positive personal attributes have been created or that changes have occurred in connection with a sport-focused development program is naïve until longitudinal research tells us otherwise. Meaningful development does not occur unless it involves action and is sustainable over time and beyond sports, and we lack knowledge about the conditions under which this is most likely.

Second, PYD involves more than merely expanding the status quo; instead, it involves the social agency of young people as they engage their community. Such actions create tension and conflict because they threaten vested interests, confront people with power, and require resources (Pieterse, 2001). Therefore, they are very rare, despite the learning experiences they create for young people.

Third, PYD does not guarantee future collective or community development. Contributing to a community requires strategies, organizational knowledge, and coalition-building skills seldom taught, or even considered, by coaches and sport program managers. Preparing young people to *contribute*—the 6th C identified by Lerner at al. (2000)—requires relationships, experiences, and identities that transcend sports and sport-related contexts. To say that sport develops young people as assets and resources begs the question of how and where young people can have an impact that goes beyond personal growth and success as individuals.

Fourth, PYD work is inherently ideological. It raises the question, "Development for whom and to what end?" At a time when social and economic inequality, and associated forms of poverty, have reached oppressive and potentially disruptive levels in nations worldwide, those doing development through sport work must ask who they are working for and if their projects reproduce or reduce inequality.

To claim no connection with inequality suggests that the character and direction of developmental processes have not been fully considered.

Fifth, PYD occurs in context. Understanding the larger historical, social, cultural, political, and economic contexts in which sport participation occurs is a prerequisite for success. Development cannot be imposed on or wished into individuals or communities. Unless development workers do detailed homework on the contexts in which they want to foster development and on the realities faced by the young people with whom they will work, they may inadvertently reproduce conditions that ultimately undermine possibilities for sustainable development for individuals or communities (Nicholls et al., 2011; Spaaij and Jones, 2013).

Even though there is growing awareness that youth sports do not do all of what people have claimed they do for young people, translating this awareness into transformative actions requires strategies that take into account the institutionalized structures of youth sport programs and the organizational identities developed around them. This is no easy task, and it calls for actions designed to produce particular developmental outcomes that may not be related to age-group competitive success. Such strategies are most likely to exist in *plus sport* programs organized around values and norms that are seldom prioritized in current youth sport culture.

Consider the example of youth empowerment as a manifestation of positive development. Empowerment in a neoliberal context is generally defined as a young person's ability to transform the self in a quest for personal success. But the original conceptions of PYD suggested that empowerment constituted an ability to critically assess and transform structures that unfairly disadvantage some people and privilege others. This latter approach to empowerment is rarely used by coaches, except in a few cases where they work with young people in high-poverty, resource-deprived areas (Richardson, 2012).

In sociological terms, empowerment is a process that exists at the intersection of human actors and the context in which they live. It is neither a transcendent attribute of a person nor the result of personal choices. Therefore, to feel and be empowered in a sport context with its unique status hierarchy, norms, choices, and challenges is different from feeling and being empowered in community contexts unrelated to sports. This is especially the case when the legacy of racism and/or colonialism exists, the range of choices is narrow, allies are few, advocates are absent, physical danger is ever present, and law enforcement is perceived as untrustworthy. This means that PYD ultimately requires actions that engage and change the community. Such actions do not occur simply as a result of sport participation. They must be carefully planned and facilitated by those who manage and coach youth sports. This calls for awareness and commitment rarely seen in connection with sports at any level. Developing this awareness and commitment appears to be a never-ending challenge for advocates of PYD through sports.

Note

1   These eight goals included the following: (1) eradicate extreme poverty and hunger; (2) achieve universal primary education; (3) promote gender equality; (4) reduce child mortality; (5) improve maternal health; (6) halt the spread of HIV/AIDS; (7) ensure environmental sustainability; and (8) develop a global partnership for development.

References

Alinsky, S. (1971). *Rules for Radicals*. New York: Vintage Books.

Benson, P. L. (1997). *All Kids Are Our Kids: What Communities Must Do to Raise Caring and Responsible Children and Adolescents*. San Francisco, CA: Jossey-Bass.

Bourdieu, P. (1998). The essence of neoliberalism (trans. by Jeremy J. Shapiro). *Le Monde diplomatique*. Available from http://mondediplo.com/1998/12/08bourdieu

Brown, M. J. (2007). *Building Powerful Community Organizations: A Personal Guide to Creating Groups that Can Solve Problems and Change the World*. Arlington, MA: Long Haul Press.

Burnett, C. (2013). The uptake of a sport-for-development programme in South Africa. *Sport, Education and Society, 20*, 819–837.

Catalano, R. F., Berglund, M. L., Ryan, J. A. M., Lonczak, H. S., and Hawkins, J. D. (2002). Positive youth development in the United States: Research findings on evaluations of positive youth development programs. *Prevention & Treatment, 5*, 98–124.

Catalano, R. F., Berglund, M. L., Ryan, J. A. M., Lonczak, H. S., and Hawkins, J. D. (2004). Positive development: Realizing the potential of youth. *Annals of the American Academy of Political and Social Science, 591*, 202–220.

Chawansky, M. (2012). Good girls play sports: International inspiration and the construction of girlhood. *Feminist Media Studies, 12*, 473–476.

Coakley, J. (2002). Using sports to control deviance and violence among youths: Let's be critical and cautious. In M. Gatz, M. A. Messner, and S. B. Rokeach (Eds.), *Paradoxes of Youth and Sport* (pp. 13–30). Albany, NY: State University of New York Press.

Coakley, J. (2006). The good father: Parental expectations in youth sports. *Leisure Studies, 25*, 153–163.

Coakley, J. (2010). The "logic" of specialization: Using children for adult purposes. *Journal of Physical Education, Recreation and Dance, 81*, 16–18.

Coakley, J. (2015). Assessing the sociology of sport: On cultural sensibilities and the great sport myth. *International Review for the Sociology of Sport, 50*, 402–406.

Coalter, F. (2010). *Sport-for-Development Impact Study. A research initiative funded by Comic Relief and UK Sport and managed by International Development through Sport*. Stirling, Scotland: University of Stirling.

Damon, W. (2004). What is positive youth development? *Annals of the American Academy, 591*, 13–24.

Darnell, S. C. (2010). Power, politics and "sport for development and peace": Investigating the utility of sport for international development. *Sociology of Sport Journal, 27*, 54–75.

Denison, J., Mills, J. P., and Konoval, T. (2015). Sports' disciplinary legacy and the challenge of "coaching differently." *Sport, Education, and Society*. Pre-publication available from doi: 10.1080/13573322.2015.1061986

Fraser-Thomas, J. L., Côté, J., and Deakin, J. (2005). Youth sport programs: An avenue to foster positive youth development. *Physical Education and Sport Pedagogy, 10*, 19–40.

Guest, A. M. (2013). Sport psychology for development and peace? Critical reflections and constructive suggestions. *Journal of Sport Psychology in Action*, *4*, 169–180.

Harvey, D. (2005). *A Brief History of Neoliberalism*. New York: Oxford University Press.

Holt, N. L. (2008). *Positive Youth Development through Sport*. London: Routledge.

Holt, N. L., and Neely, K. C. (2011). Positive youth development through sport: A review. *Revista de Iberoamericana de Psicologia del Ejercico y Deporte*, *6*, 299–316.

Lerner, R. M., and Benson, P. L. (2003). *Developmental Assets and Asset-Building Communities: Implications for Research, Policy, and Practice*. New York: Kluwer Academic/Plenum.

Lerner, R. M., Fisher, C. B., and Weinberg, R. A. (2000). Toward a science for and of the people: Promoting civil society through the application of developmental science. *Child Development*, *71*, 11–20.

Nicholls, S., Giles, A. R., and Sethna, C. (2011). Perpetuating the "lack of evidence" discourse in sport for development: Privileged voices, unheard stories and subjugated knowledge. *International Review for the Sociology of Sport*, *46*, 249–264.

Petitpas, A. J., Cornelius, A. E., Van Raalte, J. L., and Jones, T. (2005). A framework for planning youth sport programs that foster psychosocial development. *The Sport Psychologist*, *19*, 6–80.

Pieterse, J. N. (2001). *Development Theory: Deconstructions/Reconstructions*. London: Sage.

Rauscher, L., and Cooky, C. (2015). Ready for anything the world gives her? A critical look at sports-based positive youth development for girls. *Sex Roles*. Advance online publication.

Richardson Jr., J. B. (2012). Beyond the playing field: Coaches as social capital for inner-city adolescent African-American males. *Journal of African American Studies*, *16*, 171–194.

Scales, P., and Leffert, N. (1999). *Developmental Assets: A Synthesis of the Scientific Research on Adolescent Development*. Minneapolis, MN: Search Institute.

Schutz, A., and Miller, M. (2015). *People Power: The Community Organizing Tradition of Saul Alinsky*. Nashville, TN: Vanderbilt University Press.

Spaaij, R. and Jones, R. (2013). Education for social change? A Freirean critique of sport for development and peace. *Physical Education and Sport Pedagogy*, *18*, 442–457.

Stenling, C. (2013). The introduction of Drive-In Sport in community sport organizations as an example of organizational (non-) change. *Journal of Sport Management*, *27*, 497–509.

Stenling, C. (2014a). The emergence of a new logic? The theorizing of a new practice in the highly institutionalized context of Swedish voluntary sport. *Sport Management Review*, *17*, 507–519.

Stenling, C. (2014b). Sport programme implementation as translation and organizational identity construction: The implementation of Drive-in sport in Swedish sports as an illustration. *International Journal of Sport Policy and Politics*, *6*, 55–69.

Stenling, C. (2015). *The Drive for Change: Putting the Means and Ends of Sport at Stake in the Organizing of Swedish Voluntary Sport*. Umeå, Sweden: Umeå University, Department of Education. Available from http://umu.diva-portal.org/

Stenling, C., and Fahlén, J. (2014). Same, same but different? Exploring the organizational identities of Swedish voluntary sports: Possible implications of sports clubs' self-identification for their role as implementers of policy objectives. *International Review for the Sociology of Sport*. Advance online publication.

Sukarieha, M., and Tannock, S. (2011). The positivity imperative: A critical look at the "new" youth development movement. *Journal of Youth Studies*, *14*, 675–691.

Szto, C. (2015). Serving up change? Gender mainstreaming and the UNESCO–WTA partnership for global gender equality. *Sport in Society: Cultures, Commerce, Media, Politics*. Advance online publication.

United Nations. (2005). *Report on the International Year of Sport and Physical Education, 2005*. Geneva: United Nations Office of Sport for Development and Peace.

Wolff, A. (2011). Sports saves the world. *Sports Illustrated, 115* (September 26), 62–74.

3

POSITIVE YOUTH DEVELOPMENT THROUGH SPORT

A relational developmental systems approach

Jennifer P. Agans, Andrea Vest Ettekal, Karl Erickson, and Richard M. Lerner

Positive youth development (PYD) as a way of thinking about and working with young people, emerged in the 1990s (Lerner et al., 2015) and has a visible presence in sport and physical activity research and practice (Holt, 2008; Holt and Neely, 2011). The PYD perspective is grounded in the idea that all young people have the capacity to thrive when their individual strengths are enhanced by (and in turn contribute to) supportive environments (Damon, 2004; Lerner et al., 2015). This emphasis on both individual strengths and contextual assets moves the PYD perspective away from reductionist approaches to youth development, which emphasize either innate characteristics (nature) or complete malleability (nurture). Instead, PYD aligns with the process-relational paradigm underlying the relational developmental systems (RDS) metatheoretical approach (Overton, 2015). We propose that work promoting PYD through sport should adopt both the general principle that all youth can thrive, and the understanding that development takes place within a system of relations involving young people and all the interrelated contexts in which they are embedded.

The purpose of this chapter is to present an overview of the theoretical underpinnings of PYD and how this approach can be beneficially applied to research on sport contexts. Therefore, we first describe one model of PYD (i.e. the Lerner and Lerner "Five Cs" model; Lerner et al., 2009) and present the metatheoretical assumptions that guide the application of this model to both research and practice. In particular, we focus on the ways in which this approach can contribute to the promotion of PYD through sport, with sport representing one portion of a complex, interrelated system of contexts in which youth engage (e.g. family, school, neighborhood, cultural, and historical context). Although the present approach to PYD has been more widely applied in youth development programs than in sport, we emphasize its applicability to sport and its synergy with existing sport research and practice.

The "Five Cs" model of PYD

Built on the understanding that individuals have the potential to systematically change across the human life span (a concept known as plasticity), the PYD perspective asserts that the characteristics of young people should be seen as strengths that can, in combination with contextual assets, help youth to thrive (Lerner et al., 2012). The PYD perspective recognizes that all contexts have assets, although in some communities these assets may be more easily accessed or available than in others (Urban et al., 2009). Therefore, many PYD-oriented sport programs (e.g. Tenacity: Berlin et al., 2007; Girls on the Run: Gabriel et al., 2011) have been designed to provide communities with resources and help young people develop their strengths so that they can use these contextual assets to thrive.

What does it look like when such thriving occurs? The "Five Cs" model of PYD points to competence, confidence, character, caring, and connection as the central elements of a thriving young person, with a "Sixth C" of contribution to community emerging among youth who exhibit high levels of all five of these characteristics (Lerner et al., 2012). In addition, research suggests that there are three important elements of youth programs that can help to foster the Five Cs, including opportunities to build supportive relationships with adults, engage in leadership, and practice life skills (Lerner et al., 2012). Sport programs that provide these "Big Three" contextual assets may therefore be best able to promote PYD.

In understanding the Five Cs model with respect to youth sport participation, several considerations arise. Even when sport does provide contextual assets (and not all sport settings do; Fields et al., 2010), young people are also embedded in other contexts, including family, school, community, and culture, all of which play an integral role in influencing development (Lerner, 2006). Youth sport cannot be isolated; it is one aspect of a system of interrelated contexts within which youth development occurs. Thus, some sport research has recognized that adopting an ecological approach to youth sport participation can be useful (e.g. Strachan et al., 2009). Furthermore, youth play an active role in their own development (Overton, 2015), and this process has not often been taken into account in youth sport research (Erickson and Gilbert, 2013). RDS metatheory can be a useful way to understand the relations among individuals and their contexts, as well as the processes through which these relations can promote PYD.

Relational developmental systems metatheory

The RDS metatheoretical perspective is based on the understanding that all elements of a system are fused and should be examined in relation to each other, whereas reductionist perspectives view a whole as being made up of separate parts (Overton, 2015). For sport research, adopting an RDS metatheoretical perspective means that studies of one aspect of participation should be viewed not as a discrete piece of a puzzle that can be added together with other pieces to understand the whole. Instead, knowledge develops through "moments of analysis" (Overton, 2015) where one aspect of a complex system is examined while maintaining awareness of its essential interconnectedness or fusion with other aspects of the system. This process-relational view is fundamental to the PYD perspective, where the positive development of young people is understood to be the result of mutually influential relations among individuals and their contexts (Lerner et al., 2015). For example, athletes are influenced by the interaction style of their coaches (Erickson et al., 2011), the team climate (Duda and Ntoumanis, 2005), and other aspects of the sport context. In turn, athletes also influence the sport context through their behavior, attitudes, and skills (Shields et al., 2007). These mutually influential relations, rather than the characteristics of the individual or the context alone, are the focus of analysis for RDS-based research.

It is also important to note that within RDS metatheory, individuals are understood to be active agents in their own development (Lerner, 1982). Although individual plasticity is not infinite, the potential for systematic change exists across the life span and reflects individuals' ability to adapt to their contexts, and to work towards adapting the context to meet their needs (Overton, 2015). These actions take place within the fused system, such that contexts also respond and adapt and, through the integration of individual and contextual regulations, the system itself develops toward increasing complexity and adaptation. This concept of active individuals and adaptive systems reflects the PYD notion of youth as agentic and engaged in their own development rather than as passive recipients of contextual influence or the results of genetic predetermination.

Time is also a key element in RDS metatheory (Overton, 2015). Development is a concept that necessarily includes time, but time is also part of the relational developmental system, integrated with all aspects of individuals (e.g. through age-related changes, prior experiences) and contexts (e.g. through the influence of history on culture, social norms). Thus, research studies all take place in particular moments within the developmental time of participants and the historical time of their societies. RDS metatheory provides a framework for understanding the fused and reciprocal relations among all aspects of the developmental system (including time, characteristics of individuals, and features of contexts), and the process of mutually influential active engagement that leads to the development of this system (Bronfenbrenner and Morris, 2006).

The Five Cs model of PYD (Lerner et al., 2009) is nested under the RDS metatheoretical perspective, and thus incorporates these concepts to understand PYD as a developmental process. Given that PYD is the result of the fused relations among individuals and contexts, young people develop competence, confidence, character, caring, and connection as a result of their engagement with the assets in their communities (Lerner et al., 2012). The development of PYD in young people is a reflection of the relative plasticity of human development, such that all young people have the potential for positive development when contextual assets are available to support them (Lerner et al., 2012). In addition, these relations are reciprocal and can be mutually beneficial, because with contextual support for their positive development young people can contribute to their communities (Lerner et al., 2009).

These elements of RDS metatheory are applicable to the sport context, where PYD can be fostered and supported. Therefore, in the following sections we first examine sport as a context within a relational developmental system, then focus in on the ways in which sport contexts can serve as an illustrative microsystem for understanding fused relations within RDS. Finally, we explore the development of PYD through sport using the RDS perspective.

Sport in the relational developmental system

As previously stated, sport contexts are part of a larger system in which young people are embedded, which has a combined effect on development that is different from the sum of its parts. For example, research on youth participation in a variety of activity contexts suggests that young people who are involved in both a youth development program and a sport are more likely to show high levels of PYD than youth who only play sports (Forneris et al., 2015; Zarrett et al., 2009). Youth who participate in more than one activity have opportunities to practice different life skills (Hansen et al., 2010) and to translate these skills across the multiple contexts in which they are involved. Furthermore, if youth are engaged in multiple contexts that share a focus on promoting PYD, the holistic impact of these programs is greater than the additive influence of each program would be (Kubisch et al., 2010), supporting findings that youth who participate in a wide variety of activities have higher PYD than their less-engaged peers (Agans et al., 2014).

Researchers have also noted relations between school contexts and athletic contexts, as part of this system of influences affecting developmental outcomes. For example, athletes often have higher grades and are less likely to drop out of school than their non-athlete peers (McNeal, 1995), but these findings do not necessarily indicate a straightforward connection between sport and academic achievement. In particular, in the United States sport is often school-based and therefore structurally linked to academic achievement through requirements that players maintain certain grades in order to stay on the team (Vidal-Fernández, 2011). Furthermore, youth who play sports not only gain access to the developmental assets present in the athletic context, they may also experience the school context differently due to their athletic participation.

The system of contexts that includes school and extracurricular activities is also inseparably linked with family and cultural factors. These factors can affect whether young people engage in sport at all, especially among cultural groups that place less value on athletic participation (Simpkins et al., 2011) or in families with fewer resources or less access to sport facilities (Moore et al., 2010). Parental beliefs about their children's abilities can shape youth self-perceptions and levels of participation in extracurricular activities including sport (Fredricks and Eccles, 2005), thus influencing both the combination of activities in which youth participate and the ways in which they engage in the activities selected. The multifaceted influence of parents and culture on youth involvement in, and experiences of, activities, and the fundamental interconnectedness of this influence with other aspects of the system (including factors external and internal to the youth), illustrates the RDS conception of a fused system in which young people are embedded. However, in another moment of analysis, sport can also be viewed as a distinct microsystem in which to examine the person–context relations that can lead to PYD.

Sport as a relational developmental system

Narrowing our focus to the context of sport itself (while maintaining an awareness of the other aspects of the larger system) provides an opportunity to examine the mutually influential relations between the various aspects of youth sport programs and the athletes themselves. These relations are interconnected, with all aspects of the sport (e.g. coaching style, peer relations, the type of sport being played) simultaneously contributing to the ways in which the athlete and the sport context influence each other. From an RDS perspective, it is the combined effect of the athlete's relations with the whole system of influences (including other contexts) that contributes to youth development.

Thus, existing research examining particular elements of the youth sport experience in isolation might be integrated through consideration of sport as a relational developmental system. For instance, research on youth sport coaching (see Chapter 11) suggests that coaching styles based on support and instruction are more likely than punitive coaching styles to promote positive developmental outcomes among athletes, and these effects are more pronounced for athletes with initially lower levels of PYD (e.g. lower self-esteem; see review by Erickson and Gilbert, 2013). Within a relational developmental system, these coaching behaviors represent one aspect of the coach–athlete relationship, eliciting responses from athletes that may affect the coach as well and potentially the coach's interactions with other athletes. As a result, supportive coaching styles may affect not only the individual relationships among athletes and coaches, but also contribute to a more warm and encouraging team climate overall (Duda and Ntoumanis, 2005; Weiss and Wiese-Bjornstal, 2009). Resulting environments in which coaches support athletes in working toward self-improvement and mastery also promote positive outcomes such as persistence and enjoyment of the activity (Roberts, 2012), increasing the likelihood of continued participation and reinforcing the mastery-oriented culture of the team.

As part of the relational developmental system, team climate also influences and is influenced by the athletes who comprise the team and their relationships with each other. Many different kinds of social interactions exist within youth sport contexts, from connecting with new players to navigating conflict to learning to work as a team (Holt et al., 2008a). An athlete with a negative attitude can "infect" his or her teammates and change the team context to one marked by discontent (Shields et al., 2007). However, a warm and supportive team climate can also help athletes to become more motivated and encouraging of each other's efforts

(Roberts, 2012). An RDS perspective can provide a framework for integrating these research findings and understanding the ways in which the characteristics of athletes, coaches, and sport contexts mutually influence each other.

From an RDS perspective, the key to promoting PYD through sport is having a good "fit" among the skills and needs of the athlete and the attributes of the sport context. "Fit" refers to the extent to which the individual is able to meet the demands of the context in adaptive ways and the extent to which the context is supportive of the individual's development (Lerner, 1982). Thus, when the characteristics of the individual and the sport context align, young people have opportunities to develop athletic competence, confidence in their abilities, character skills such as leadership, caring for teammates, and connection to their schools and communities—the elements of PYD within the Five Cs model (Lerner et al., 2009).

Applying RDS to promote PYD through sport

The idea of "fit" (or mutually beneficial relations) between individuals and their contexts is key to the promotion of PYD (Lerner, 1984). This concept can be usefully applied to both sport research and practice, and in many cases aligns with current efforts in the field. For example, research examining coach–athlete relationships has mapped the ways in which coach behaviors lead to different athlete responses, which in turn elicit different behaviors from the coaches (Erickson et al., 2011). This research supports an RDS view of mutual influence, indicating that coaches can influence the on-task behavior of their athletes and that, at the same time, athletes can influence coaches' behavior as well. Additional research examining such bidirectional relations in different aspects of the system may help to elucidate not only the factors that contribute to the promotion of PYD through sport, but the processes through which these factors interrelate. Such future work will necessarily require shifting the focus of analysis from individual aspects of the system as variables in isolation to relations among elements of the system as the fundamental units of analysis (see Poczwardowski et al., 2006).

The concept of mutually beneficial relations is also important when considering the extent to which particular sport programs contribute to the positive development of athletes. It is clear from reports of disrespectful and violent behavior at youth sporting events (e.g. Fields et al., 2010) that these contexts may not always be supportive, or even safe. However, there are also many examples of youth sport programs that actively work to promote PYD (e.g. Berlin et al., 2007; Gabriel et al., 2011), and these programs can provide opportunities for youth to understand their potential to contribute to the sport context. Such contribution (the "Sixth C") demonstrates the extent to which these sport programs have fostered PYD among their athletes. This notion of contribution to the wider community makes explicit the linkages across contexts that are a fundamental aspect of PYD when considered from an RDS perspective. However, these cross-contextual long-term social outcomes have received comparatively little empirical examination in youth sport research (Gould and Carson, 2008).

Although in practice, developing good "fit" with every athlete may be a utopian dream, coaches may work toward such fit by aligning their interaction styles to the athlete (e.g. providing kind encouragement to one athlete while pushing another to increase his or her effort). By adapting to the personalities, motivations, and needs of individual athletes, coaches can help to support the positive development of the diverse players on their teams (Becker, 2009). This individualized approach is already espoused by many great coaches, including National Basketball Hall of Fame coach John Wooden (Gallimore and Tharp, 2004), and aligns with research on the important role that adult mentors can play in promoting PYD (Bowers et al., 2012).

In addition, as the RDS approach to PYD emphasizes that all aspects of the relational developmental system are interconnected, there is a need for holistic approaches as well as moments of analysis examining particular portions of the system (Overton, 2015). Research bringing an ecological perspective to the study of physical activity has already begun to examine the influences of these complex, multilevel relations (Sallis et al., 2008). For example, in a meta-study on children's active free play, Lee and colleagues (2015) brought together qualitative research findings representing different moments of analysis (assessing factors ranging from child characteristics to parental safety concerns to neighborhood and policy issues), and synthesized these findings into a holistic ecological model. The first edition of this book also featured chapters examining the application of an ecological or systems approach to the promotion of PYD through sport (e.g. Côté et al., 2008), as have other publications in the field (e.g. Holt et al., 2008b; Riley and Anderson-Butcher, 2012). Continuing to examine the interconnected influence of multiple levels of the relational developmental system and the mutual influence of these levels on each other (including bidirectional relations among athletes and the various aspects of the contexts in which they are embedded) will enable a better understanding of how to effectively promote PYD through sport.

Moreover, practical application of these concepts is key if our knowledge of positive development is to make an impact. Programs designed to promote PYD through sport should therefore focus on building mutually beneficial relations among athletes and the athletic context through, for example, instructive coaching (Erickson and Gilbert, 2013), supportive team climates (Gould et al., 2012), and opportunities for young people to practice life skills and leadership (Gould and Voelker, 2010)—with an emphasis on facilitating good "fit" between individual athletes and these modifiable elements of the youth sport context. In addition, programs that address multiple levels of the system, including athletes, coaches, parents, and community leaders (e.g. Positive Coaching Alliance; see Thompson, 2010), or engage in community collaboration (e.g. Kubisch et al., 2010), may be especially important for promoting PYD across the many contexts in which young people develop.

Conclusion

The RDS metatheoretical approach that frames the Five Cs model of PYD (Lerner et al., 2009) may prove useful for researchers and practitioners alike, enhancing efforts to promote positive development among youth. In addition, research and practice applying RDS concepts to the promotion of PYD through sport can help to further the scientific understanding of relational developmental systems and developmental processes more generally; a mutually beneficial relation at the level of science that can also enhance the lives of youth.

Future research should therefore focus not only on factors associated with higher levels of PYD among youth sport participants, but on the relations among various aspects of the developmental system that may contribute to thriving. For example, studies examining factors associated with good "fit" between athletes and sport context, and longitudinal evaluations of how youth translate life skills from the sport context to other areas of their lives, will be useful to advance knowledge about PYD through sport. In addition, the field must maintain a clear focus on the application of research findings to youth sport contexts, and work with practitioners and policy makers to ensure that research findings on best practices for promoting PYD can be applied and that studies address the important questions coaches grapple with in their programs.

The RDS metatheoretical approach to PYD provides a useful framework for examining the ways in which sport participation may contribute to positive outcomes among youth, and points to important questions for future research. In addition, by synthesizing findings regarding various aspects of the relational developmental system examined in different moments of analysis, a holistic view of the interrelations among athletes, sport contexts, and the rest of the system may emerge, allowing for enhancements in the promotion of PYD through sport. Such work is necessary to continue to advance the field and to enable youth sport programs to most effectively promote thriving among the youth they serve.

Acknowledgment

The preparation of this chapter was supported in part by grants from the John Templeton Foundation.

References

Agans, J. P., Champine, R. B., DeSouza, L. M., Mueller, M. K., Johnson, S. K., and Lerner, R. M. (2014). Activity involvement as an ecological asset: Profiles of participation and youth outcomes. *Journal of Youth and Adolescence, 43*, 919–932.

Becker, A. J. (2009). It's not what they do, it's how they do it: Athlete experiences of great coaching. *International Journal of Sports Science and Coaching, 4*, 93–119.

Berlin, R. A., Dworkin, A., Eames, N., Menconi, A. and Perkins, D. F. (2007). Examples of sports-based youth development programs. *New Directions for Youth Development, 115*, 85–106.

Bowers, E. P., Geldhof, G. J., Schmid, K. L., Napolitano, C. M., Minor, K., and Lerner, J. V. (2012). Relationships with important nonparental adults and positive youth development: An examination of youth self-regulatory strengths as mediators. *Research in Human Development*, *9*, 298–316.

Bronfenbrenner, U., and Morris, P. A. (2006). The bioecological model of human development. In R. M. Lerner (Ed.), *Handbook of Child Development: Vol. 1. Theoretical Models of Human Development* (6th ed., pp. 793–828). Hoboken, NJ: Wiley.

Côté, J., Strachan, L., and Fraser-Thomas, J. (2008). Participation, personal development and performance through youth sport. In N. L. Holt (Ed.), *Positive Youth Development through Sport* (pp. 34–46). London: Routledge.

Damon, W. (2004). What is positive youth development? *Annals of the American Academy of Political and Social Science*, *591*, 13–24.

Duda, J. L., and Ntoumanis, N. (2005). After-school sport for children: Implications of a task-involving motivational climate. In J. L. Mahoney, R. Larson, and J. Eccles (Eds.), *Organized Activities as Contexts of Development: Extracurricular Activities, After-School and Community Programs* (pp. 311–330). Mahwah, NJ: Erlbaum.

Erickson, K., and Gilbert, W. (2013). Coach–athlete interactions in children's sport. In J. Côté and R. Lidor (Eds.), *Conditions of Children's Talent Development in Sport* (pp. 139–156). Morgantown, WV: Fitness Information Technology.

Erickson, K., Côté, J., Hollenstein, T., and Deakin, J. (2011). Examining coach–athlete interactions using state space grids: An observational analysis in competitive youth sport. *Psychology of Sport and Exercise*, *12*, 645–654.

Fields, S. K., Collins, C. L., and Comstock, R. D. (2010). Violence in youth sports: Hazing, brawling and foul play. *British Journal of Sports Medicine*, *44*, 32–37.

Forneris, T., Camiré, M., and Williamson, R. (2015). Extracurricular activity participation and the acquisition of developmental assets: Differences between involved and noninvolved Canadian high school students. *Applied Developmental Science*, *19*, 47–55.

Fredricks, J. A., and Eccles, J. S. (2005). Developmental benefits of extracurricular involvement: Do peer characteristics mediate the link between activities and youth outcomes? *Journal of Youth and Adolescence*, *34*, 507–520.

Gabriel, K. K. P., DeBate, R. D., High, R. R., and Racine, E. F. (2011). Girls on the Run: A quasi-experimental evaluation of a developmentally focused youth sport program. *Journal of Physical Activity and Health*, *8*, S285–S294.

Gallimore, R., and Tharp, R. (2004). What a coach can teach a teacher, 1975–2004: Reflections and reanalysis of John Wooden's teaching practices. *The Sport Psychologist*, *18*, 119–137.

Gould, D., and Carson, S. (2008). Life skills development through sport: Current status and future directions. *International Review of Sport and Exercise Psychology*, *1*, 58–78.

Gould, D., and Voelker, D. K. (2010). Youth sport leadership development: Leveraging the sports captaincy experience. *Journal of Sport Psychology in Action*, *1*, 1–14.

Gould, D., Flett, R., and Lauer, L. (2012). The relationship between psychosocial developmental and the sports climate experienced by underserved youth. *Psychology of Sport and Exercise*, *13*, 80–87.

Hansen, D. M., Skorupski, W. P., and Arrington, T. L. (2010). Differences in developmental experiences for commonly used categories of organized youth activities. *Journal of Applied Developmental Psychology*, *31*, 413–421.

Holt, N. L. (Ed.) (2008). *Positive Youth Development through Sport*. London: Routledge.

Holt, N. L., and Neely, K. C. (2011). Positive youth development through sport: A review. *Revista Iberoamericana de Psicología del Ejercicio y el Deporte, 6,* 299–316.

Holt, N. L., Black, D. E., Tamminen, K. A., Mandigo, J. L., and Fox, K. R. (2008a). Levels of social complexity and dimensions of peer experience in youth sport. *Journal of Sport and Exercise Psychology, 30,* 411–431.

Holt, N. L., Tink, L. N., Mandigo, J. L., and Fox, K. R. (2008b). Do youth learn life skills through their involvement in high school sport? A case study. *Canadian Journal of Education/Revue Canadienne de l'éducation, 31,* 281–304.

Kubisch, A. C., Auspos, P., Brown, P., and Dewar, T. (2010). Community change initiatives from 1990–2010: Accomplishments and implications for future work. *Community Investments, 22,* 8–13.

Lee, H., Tamminen, K. A., Clark, A. M., Slater, L., Spence, J. C., and Holt, N. L. (2015). A meta-study of qualitative research examining determinants of children's independent active free play. *International Journal of Behavioral Nutrition and Physical Activity, 12,* 1–12.

Lerner, J. V. (1984). The import of temperament for psychosocial functioning: Test of a "goodness of fit" model. *Merrill-Palmer Quarterly, 30,* 177–188.

Lerner, R. M. (1982). Children and adolescents as producers of their own development. *Developmental Review, 2,* 342–370.

Lerner, R. M. (2006). Developmental science, developmental systems, and contemporary theories of human development. In W. Damon and R. M. Lerner (Eds.), *Handbook of Child Psychology* (pp. 1–17). New York: Wiley.

Lerner, R. M., von Eye, A., Lerner, J. V., and Lewin-Bizan, S. (2009). Exploring the foundations and functions of adolescent thriving within the 4-H study of positive youth development: A view of the issues. *Journal of Applied Developmental Psychology, 30,* 567–570.

Lerner, R. M., Bowers, E. P., Geldhof, G. J., Gestsdóttir, S., and DeSouza, L. (2012). Promoting positive youth development in the face of contextual changes and challenges: The roles of individual strengths and ecological assets. *New Directions for Youth Development, 135,* 119–128.

Lerner, R. M., Lerner, J. V., Bowers, E. P., and Geldhof, G. J. (2015). Positive youth development and relational-developmental-systems. In W. F. Overton and P. C. Molenaar (Eds.), *Handbook of Child Psychology and Developmental Science. Vol. 1: Theory and Method* (7th ed., pp. 607–651). Hoboken, NJ: Wiley.

McNeal Jr, R. B. (1995). Extracurricular activities and high school dropouts. *Sociology of Education, 68,* 62–80.

Moore, J. B., Jilcott, S. B., Shores, K. A., Evenson, K. R., Brownson, R. C., and Novick, L. F. (2010). A qualitative examination of perceived barriers and facilitators of physical activity for urban and rural youth. *Health Education Research, 25,* 355–367.

Overton, W. F. (2015). Processes, relations, and relational-developmental-systems. In W. F. Overton and P. C. Molenaar (Eds.), *Handbook of Child Psychology and Developmental Science. Vol. 1: Theory and Method* (7th ed., pp. 9–62). Hoboken, NJ: Wiley.

Poczwardowski, A., Barott, J. E., and Jowett, S. (2006). Diversifying approaches to research on athlete–coach relationships. *Psychology of Sport and Exercise, 7,* 125–142.

Riley, A., and Anderson-Butcher, D. (2012). Participation in a summer sport-based youth development program for disadvantaged youth: Getting the parent perspective. *Children and Youth Services Review, 34,* 1367–1377.

Roberts, G. C. (2012). Motivation in sport and exercise from an achievement goal theory perspective: After 30 years, where are we? In G. C. Roberts and D. C. Treasure (Eds.), *Advances in Motivation in Sport and Exercise* (pp. 5–58). Champaign, IL: Human Kinetics.

Sallis, J. F., Owen, N., and Fisher, E. B. (2008). Ecological models of health behavior. *Health Behavior and Health Education: Theory, Research, and Practice, 4,* 465–486.

Shields, D. L., LaVoi, N. M., Bredemeier, B. L., and Power, F. C. (2007). Predictors of poor sportspersonship in youth sports: Personal attitudes and social influences. *Journal of Sport and Exercise Psychology, 29,* 747–762.

Simpkins, S. D., Vest, A. E., and Price, C. D. (2011). Intergenerational continuity and discontinuity in Mexican-origin youths' participation in organized activities: Insights from mixed-methods. *Journal of Family Psychology, 25,* 814–824.

Strachan, L., Côté, J., and Deakin, J. (2009). An evaluation of personal and contextual factors in competitive youth sport. *Journal of Applied Sport Psychology, 21,* 340–355.

Thompson, J. (2010). *The Power of Double-Goal Coaching.* Portola Valley, CA: Balance Sports Publishing.

Urban, J. B., Lewin-Bizan, S., and Lerner, R. M. (2009). The role of neighborhood ecological assets and activity involvement in youth developmental outcomes: Differential impacts of asset poor and asset rich neighborhoods. *Journal of Applied Developmental Psychology, 30,* 601–614.

Vidal-Fernández, M. (2011). The effect of minimum academic requirements to participate in sports on high school graduation. *The B.E. Journal of Economic Analysis and Policy, 11,* 1–19.

Weiss, M., and Wiese-Bjornstal, D. (2009). Promoting positive youth development through physical activity. *President's Council on Physical Fitness and Sports Research Digest, 10*(3), 1–8.

Zarrett, N., Fay, K., Li, Y., Carrano, J., Phelps, E., and Lerner, R. M. (2009). More than child's play: Variable- and pattern-centered approaches for examining effects of sports participation on youth development. *Developmental Psychology, 45,* 368.

4

LIFE SKILLS AND BASIC PSYCHOLOGICAL NEEDS

A conceptual framework for life skills interventions

Ken Hodge, Steven Danish, Tanya Forneris, and Adam Miles

The purpose of this chapter is to move beyond descriptive evaluations to conceptually driven investigations of life skills programs focused on positive youth development (PYD). Accordingly, we outline a comprehensive conceptual framework for life skills interventions developed by Hodge et al. (2012), and we report some preliminary findings regarding the usefulness of the model for PYD. Hodge et al. advocated the integration of: (a) the three basic psychological needs of autonomy, competence, and relatedness; and (b) the need-supportive motivational climate from Basic Needs Theory (BNT) into the Life Development Intervention (LDI) framework. When these basic psychological needs are satisfied people experience positive psychological development and optimal psychological well-being—the stated outcome goals of most PYD-focused life skills programs. By developing this framework, Hodge and colleagues sought to identify and articulate the key underlying psychological mechanisms (i.e. basic needs) that contribute to optimal human functioning and positive psychosocial development in all PYD-focused life skills programs.

Life Development Intervention (LDI) focuses on self-directed change, being goal-directed, and focusing on the future, with an understanding of what needs to be done in the present to reach one's best possible future. The specific goal of LDI is to increase the likelihood of success by enhancing personal competence through the teaching of *life skills* (Danish and Forneris, 2008). One of the key challenges in developing a conceptual framework for life skills is that there are multiple definitions of life skills. For example, the World Health Organization (WHO) (1999) identified five basic areas of life skills that they deemed were applicable across cultures: (a) decision-making and problem-solving; (b) creative thinking and critical thinking; (c) communication and interpersonal skills; (d) self-awareness and empathy; and (e) coping with emotions and stress. Life skills education, according to WHO, "is aimed at facilitating the development of psychosocial skills that are required to deal with the demands and challenges of everyday life" (1999, p. 1). Furthermore, Gould and Carson (2008) defined sport-based life skills as "those internal personal assets, characteristics and skills such as goal setting, emotional control, self-esteem, and hard work ethic that can be facilitated or developed in sport and are transferred for use in non-sport settings" (p. 60). Life skills can be "behavioral (communicating effectively with peers and adults) or cognitive (making effective decisions); interpersonal (being assertive) or intrapersonal (setting goals)" (Danish et al., 2004, p. 40).

Several points stand out as a result of these varied definitions. First, what constitutes life skills has multiple meanings, and how we define life skills significantly affects both the kinds of interventions developed and how we measure whether we have successfully taught these skills. Second, we are considering life skills to be psychosocial characteristics rather than isolated behaviors, such as learning to manage money, balancing a checkbook, or cooking a meal. Third, we have chosen to focus on the term "life skills" because we are concentrating on the teaching of *skills*. Fourth, to date, interventions to teach or enhance life skills have primarily focused on positive youth development (Larson, 2000) with limited focus on adult or elite athletes (e.g. Jones et al., 2011). Finally, the relationship between life skills and PYD is typically viewed as an implicit assumption rather than articulating an explicit relationship. As Holt (2008) observed, mere participation in sport does not automatically produce PYD; rather positive development depends on how sport programs (e.g. sport-based life skills programs) are delivered and experienced. Deliberate teaching/coaching is necessary for PYD outcomes to occur. From our perspective, life skills programs are one concrete way to deliver on those outcomes (Hodge et al., 2012).

Why do we need a life skills model?

The range of life skills taught and the definitions used in interventions limits our ability to make comparisons about the relative effectiveness of these intervention programs. If each life skills intervention program highlights a particular set of life skills then meaningful comparisons and any consensus about the relative worth of such programs becomes problematic. In this chapter, and in our earlier article (Hodge et al., 2012), we argue that one solution to this problem is to utilize a comprehensive conceptual framework/model of life skills development that seeks to articulate the key underlying psychological mechanisms that underpin optimal human functioning and PYD.

Another reason why a comprehensive conceptual model of life skills development is needed is the paucity of empirical research evaluating the *effectiveness* of life skills intervention programs. The life skills literature consists of a number of position papers (e.g. Gould and Carson, 2008; Theokas et al., 2007), reviews of life skills programs (e.g. Danish and Forneris, 2008), and descriptions of specific life skills programs (e.g. Danish, 2000, 2002a, 2002b; Petitpas et al., 2004). However, much of this research has not examined the causal effects of life skills interventions. We argue that one explanation for this lack of evaluative research is the absence of a comprehensive conceptual framework of life skills development to inform, guide, and direct such research.

Empirical research on life skills interventions and its limitations

While there is a considerable literature that purports to empirically examine life skills interventions, a number of these studies failed to provide the reader with a detailed explanation of the life skills program, the specific life skills addressed in the program, the content of the life skills program sessions/workshops (i.e. *what* is taught and *how* it is taught), the training of the practitioners who are charged with delivering the life skills program, how the setting where the intervention is conducted affects the outcome, and evidence of intervention fidelity with respect to life skills program delivery. For example, few evaluation studies have analyzed *why* life skills programs are effective or identified what mediating processes may be involved (Botvin and Griffin, 2004). The underlying assumption of the life skills approach is that PYD is aided by the promotion of both general and specific life skills (WHO, 1999). Thus, it is assumed that improvements in intrapersonal and interpersonal competencies contribute to the effectiveness of these life skills prevention programs (Cuijpers, 2002). However, this life skills research has not fully examined, or in some cases identified, the underlying psychological development that may have occurred as an outcome of a life skills intervention.

Nevertheless, despite our previous observation a small number of studies in the sport development literature have provided a detailed examination of both life skills programs and the specific content of these programs (e.g. Petitpas et al., 2004). These studies have ranged from: (a) examining the impact of a summer sport-based life skills program (Anderson-Butcher et al., 2013); (b) assessing the impact of The First Tee golf life skills program on positive youth development (Weiss et al., 2013); (c) exploring the perceived effectiveness of a life skills development program for high-performance athletes (Hardcastle et al., 2015); and (d) investigating sport as a setting for the development and transfer of desirable competencies in a non-Western country (Whitley et al., in press).

Biddle et al. (2008) reviewed the causal effects of eleven sport-based life skills interventions, all of which focused on youth and adolescents (age range: ten to eighteen years), took place in a school environment, community organization, or sports club, and had as its goal positive change in the youth populations (e.g. Goudas and Giannoudis, 2008; Papacharisis et al., 2005). A number of these intervention studies employed a similar quasi-experimental research design, using cluster randomized controlled trials in which participants were assigned to either experimental or control conditions by pre-existing group (e.g. school class) before the life skills intervention was delivered. For example, Papacharisis et al. (2005) adapted the SUPER program (Danish, 2002b) for use with youth (age range: ten to twelve years) volleyball and football (soccer) teams. The experimental groups were taught life skills at the beginning of each training session for eight weeks. The results of the study indicated that students who received the intervention had higher self-beliefs for personal goal setting, problem solving, and positive thinking than those in the control group. In addition, the intervention group demonstrated an increase in program knowledge and improvement in physical skills compared to the control condition.

Although the quasi-experimental design of these studies is critical, because it establishes how teaching life skills can directly result in positive changes in targeted variables, these experimental assessments of life skills programs still have some common limitations. These studies focused solely on increasing knowledge and self-beliefs about life skills such as goal setting, problem solving and positive thinking. There were no indications that either the knowledge can be applied or that the self-beliefs resulted in actual behavior change. Crucially, there was no attempt to verify the actual use of life skills in other life domains. While these studies provide teachers, parents, and coaches with important information, it is difficult to examine their overall effectiveness as these studies did not reveal or even explore the underlying psychological mechanisms that enabled the targeted life skills to be effective.

In addition to being largely atheoretical, most of the empirical studies reviewed above employed superficial or indirect measures of life skills outcomes. These measures are at best only indirect assessments of any underlying psychological development that may have occurred as an outcome of a life skills intervention. To truly assess underlying psychological development that may have occurred as an outcome of a life skills intervention we need direct measures of psychological mechanisms that affect such development. Employing a conceptual model of life skills development allows researchers to examine direct measures of key psychological mechanisms that affect life skills development, which in turn will provide important information about "how" practitioners can adapt, modify, and improve aspects of their life skills intervention program(s).

A LDI/BNT life skills development model

Hodge et al. (2012) sought to develop a strong conceptual framework for life skills development by integrating BNT, a sub-theory within Self-Determination Theory (SDT) (Deci and Ryan, 2000, 2008; Van Petegem et al., 2012), with LDI (see Hodge et al., 2012 for details). Basic Needs Theory includes: (a) the three basic psychological needs of autonomy, competence, and relatedness; and (b) the need-supportive motivational climate (see Figure 4.1; explained in detail later). Autonomy is defined as being the perceived origin of one's own behavior, and having an authentic sense of self-direction and volition (Ryan and Deci, 2000a). Competence refers to individuals feeling effective in their ongoing interactions with the social environment and experiencing opportunities to exercise and express their capacities (Ryan and Deci, 2000a). Relatedness refers to having a sense of belonging both with other individuals and with one's community, feeling connected to others, and caring about and being cared for by others (Ryan and

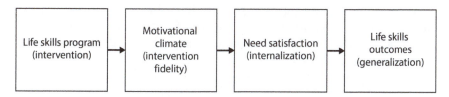

FIGURE 4.1   Conceptual model of life skills development: the LDI/BNT life skills model (adapted from Hodge et al., 2012)

Deci, 2000a). Deci and Ryan (2000) consider the three psychological needs to be "innate psychological nutriments that are essential for ongoing psychological growth, integrity, and well-being" (p. 229) for all individuals regardless of age, gender, or culture. We argue that life skills interventions should be designed to directly support the satisfaction of these three basic psychological needs if we wish PYD to occur.

The context or setting within which life skills programs are delivered is also a crucial factor to consider (O'Hearn and Gatz, 2002). A need-supportive motivational climate is regarded as a fundamental environmental influence for the satisfaction of the three basic needs (Baard et al., 2004). A need-supportive motivational climate refers to the goals and behaviors emphasized with respect to the three basic needs, and the values that are salient in the social environment created by significant others (e.g. life skills leaders/mentors, teachers, coaches, peers, parents; Baard et al., 2004). From a life skills program fidelity perspective, it is essential to assess the influence of not just the "content" of a life skills intervention (e.g. workshops/exercises/activities designed to satisfy autonomy, competence, and relatedness), but also the "context" surrounding the individuals participating in the life skills intervention (see Figure 4.1). Does the implementation of a life skills intervention generate a motivational climate that supports the satisfaction of the three basic needs?

The general goal of LDI is to enhance personal competence (Danish and D'Augelli, 1983). From a LDI perspective, personal competence is defined as the ability to do life planning, be self-reliant, and seek the resources of others with the result that the individual will have the ability to work well, play well, love well, think well, serve well, and be well (Danish, 2000). In other words, competence has interpersonal (e.g. effective in one's ongoing social interactions), as well as intrapersonal (e.g. exercise and express one's capacities; autonomy) dimensions (Danish et al., 1984).

Basic needs with LDI

Considerable research has demonstrated that satisfaction of these three basic needs predicts intrinsic motivation, well-being, and other positive outcomes in various life domains such as work, health (Baard et al., 2004), education (Ferrer-Caja and Weiss, 2000), sport (Hodge and Gucciardi, 2015), and exercise (Wilson and

Rodgers, 2004). In addition, a need-supportive motivational climate has been shown to predict need satisfaction in work (Baard et al., 2004), sport (Reinboth et al., 2004), exercise (Wilson and Rodgers, 2004), and physical education (Taylor and Ntoumanis, 2007) contexts.

Internalization and generalization

A key aspect of BNT is the proposition that adaptive psychological outcomes will result the more that an individual internalizes the basic needs of autonomy, competence, and relatedness (Niemiec and Ryan, 2007; Ryan et al., 2011). Internalization of values is conceptualized as the process by which individuals progressively accept values and integrate them into their sense of self, such that their behavior becomes internally regulated rather than primarily externally controlled (Ryan and Deci, 2000b). Consequently, the more that individuals internalize the basic needs (see Figure 4.1), the more likely they are to develop the ability to "generalize" life skills to a number of life contexts (e.g. school, family, part-time work, job; Ryan and Deci, 2008), and for subsequent PYD to occur.

The integrated LDI/BNT life skills model depicted in Figure 4.1 characterizes life skills development as occurring via the satisfaction of the three basic psychological needs of autonomy, competence, and relatedness. Such life skills development begins with participation in a life skills intervention program (left-hand side of Figure 4.1). The specific content (i.e. workshops, exercises, activities, skills, homework) of a life skills program that follows the LDI/BNT life skills model should be designed to provide opportunities for participants to learn life skills that help satisfy one or more of the psychological needs of autonomy, competence, and relatedness (see Figure 4.1). According to the LDI/BNT conceptual model, the life skills intervention will only be successful in satisfying these three needs if the motivational climate created and nurtured by the life skills instructors/leaders is need-supportive; that is, if the social environment within which the life skills program occurs is specifically engineered to support the three basic psychological needs.

Evaluating the effective provision of a need-supportive motivational climate can also serve as a manipulation check regarding life skills intervention fidelity. If the life skills program and the need-supportive motivational climate are effective then the participant will likely report greater satisfaction of her/his three basic psychological needs; the more these three needs are satisfied the more they become internalized by the participant. Finally, the greater the level of need satisfaction and internalization, the increased likelihood that the participant will report higher levels of markers of optimal psychological well-being such as intrinsic motivation, subjective well-being, less stress, enjoyment, and life satisfaction. According to the LDI/BNT life skills model such an outcome will increase the potential for program participants to be able to generalize their life skills to multiple life domains (right-hand side of Figure 4.1), and to experience PYD.

Empirical investigations of the LDI/BNT life skills model

Although future research is needed to fully test the LDI/BNT model, preliminary findings support the model. Two studies examined whether or not a physical activity-based life skills program was perceived as supporting the three basic psychological needs. In addition, a third study examined whether or not a perceived need-supportive motivational climate predicted perceived life skills outcomes. In all three studies, described below, need-supportive motivational climate was measured with the Learning Climate Questionnaire (LCQ). The LCQ was developed by Standage et al. (2005) and consists of twenty-four items that measure perceptions regarding the degree to which, in this case a program leader, supported their sense of autonomy, competence, and relatedness. The LCQ has good internal consistency (.88–.92) and was used in previous research with youth in a physical activity setting (Standage et al., 2005).

The first study examined whether a physical activity-based life skills program for young females (n = 10 participants; M age = 11.75 years) was perceived by the participants as providing a need-supportive motivational climate (Forneris et al., 2013). The *Girls Just Wanna Have Fun (GJWHF)* program was comprised of thirty-one weekly sessions over nine months. Within each 1.5-hour session the youth learned a life skill and participated in some form of physical activity designed to reinforce the life skill (e.g. teamwork was reinforced with basketball). Scores on the LCQ indicated that the youth believed that the leaders were providing a need-supportive motivational climate. On a six-point Likert scale the mean scores were 5.25, 5.70, and 5.80 for autonomy, competence, and relatedness support respectively. In addition, interviews with the youth further supported the quantitative findings as the following three themes emerged from the analysis: "We got to pick the games we wanted," "It made me feel like I can do it," "They wanted to know how you feel, they care" (Bean et al., 2013).

The second study examined whether *PULSE*, a physical activity-based life skills program, would be perceived as providing a need-supportive motivational climate (Barker, 2014). *PULSE* was designed to provide a developmentally appropriate understanding of resistance and aerobic training and incorporated the teaching of life skills adapted from the Sports United to Promote Education and Recreation program (Danish, 2002b), and the Teaching Personal and Social Responsibility (TPSR) levels (Hellison, 2011). *PULSE* was structured into three phases over the course of five months (participants were three females and thirteen males; M age = 15.5 years). The goal of the program was to have the youth become independent with regard to engaging in physical activity and practicing life skills. As a result the first phase was leader-involved with a greater number of program sessions with the leaders teaching both physical activity and life skills, while the last phase was more youth-driven with leaders being present for brief check-ins if needed. For a full description of the program please see Barker (2014).

As mentioned above, the LCQ was used to measure need-supportive motivational climate, and the results showed that the youth perceived the *PULSE* program as supporting their overall needs with mean scores on a seven-point Likert scale of 6.50 for autonomy, 6.63 for competence, and 6.57 for relatedness (Barker, 2014). Similar to the *GJWHF* program, interviews were conducted with the youth participants and the following four themes emerged: (a) leaders provided choice to facilitate autonomy; (b) leaders facilitated the development of competence in physical activity skills; (c) leaders developed competence to be active independently; and (d) leaders were perceived as supportive, trustworthy and knowledgeable (Barker, 2014).

The third study was designed to examine whether a perceived need-supportive motivational climate predicted perceived life skills development for participants (48 females, 44 males; *M* age = 11.8 years) attending a residential summer camp (Bean et al., 2014). This residential camp focused on the development of life skills through structured sports and recreation programming, team-building, and leadership activities. Again, need-supportive motivational climate was measured using the LCQ and perceived life skills outcomes were measured using the Youth Experiences Survey (YES) 2.0 (Hansen and Larson, 2005). The YES 2.0 was designed to assess the experiences of youth participating in different extra-curricular activities and youth programs. While the YES 2.0 has seventeen subscales, only the subscales relevant to the objectives of the camp were used in this study to minimize participant burden. The subscales included were: Identity Experiences (e.g. tried doing new things), Initiative Experiences (e.g. I set goals for myself), Basic Skills (e.g. improved communication and physical skills), and Interpersonal Relationships (e.g. learned about helping others). In this study Cronbach's alpha for the four YES 2.0 subscales ranged from .72 to .86, showing good internal consistency.

Four hierarchical regressions were conducted to examine whether a need-supportive motivational climate predicted the four perceived life skills outcomes after controlling for age, gender, and years of experience at camp (Bean et al., 2015). All four regressions were significant. Need-supportive motivational climate explained 9 percent of the variance for Identity Experiences (Fchange = 7.360, p < .05), 12 percent of the variance for Initiative Experiences (Fchange = 10.677, p < .05), 16 percent of the variance for Basic Skills (Fchange = 17.010, p < .001) and 18 percent of the variance for Interpersonal Relationships. In addition, in all four hierarchical regression analyses, need-supportive motivational climate made a significant unique contribution to the psychosocial outcomes.

Conclusion

The studies reviewed in this chapter provide preliminary empirical support for the LDI/BNT model. More specifically, these life skills programs appeared to be effective at providing a need-supportive motivational climate and also appeared to support the development of life skills. Likewise, the initial qualitative results indicated that the teaching of life skills may be particularly helpful in providing choice for youth with regard to activities (i.e. autonomy), and developing competence through the learning of a variety of skills, including those that can enhance relationships among peers and between the youth and leaders (i.e.

relatedness). However, further quantitative research is needed to fully examine relationships between need-supportive motivational climate and need satisfaction, within life skills programs; and among need satisfaction, life skills development, and general psychological well-being. In particular, future LDI/BNT research should directly assess need satisfaction and its relation to life skills outcomes. Additional qualitative research is also needed to better understand how the context of a life skills program incorporates a need-supportive climate that leads to need satisfaction (Bean et al., 2015), as well as how life skills programs help support enhanced psychological well-being for youth (i.e. PYD).

Preliminary research evidence using the LDI/BNT life skills model is promising, but more evaluation work needs to be conducted. A key focus for future research should be on the critical issue of actual life skills "transfer" from sport to other life domains (e.g. via data triangulation using multiple data sources and multiple social agents). Does need satisfaction in a sport-based life skills program facilitate/promote life skills "transfer" to other life domains? That is a crucial question that needs a clear-cut answer (Turnnidge et al., 2014; Weiss et al., 2014). A key aspect of BNT is the proposition that adaptive psychological outcomes (e.g. life skills development) will result the more that an individual internalizes the basic needs of autonomy, competence, and relatedness (Niemiec and Ryan, 2007; Ryan and Deci, 2008). The more that an individual internalizes the basic needs, the more likely they are to develop the ability to "generalize" life skills to a number of life domains (e.g. school, family, part-time work, job). Furthermore, when life skills values are central to an individual's sense of self, those values are more likely to motivate life-skills-related actions and the transfer of life skills from one life domain to others; and to realize PYD benefits.

Acknowledgment

We would like to acknowledge the Social Science and Humanities Research Council of Canada for their funding to support the *Girls Just Wanna Have Fun* program and the Ontario Trillium Foundation for their support of the *PULSE* program.

References

Anderson-Butcher, D., Iachini, A., Riley, A., Wade-Mdivanian, R., Davis, J., and Amorose, A. J. (2013). Exploring the impact of a summer sport-based youth development program. *Evaluation & Program Planning, 37,* 64–69.

Baard, P. P., Deci, E. L., and Ryan, R. M. (2004). Intrinsic need satisfaction: A motivational basis of performance and well-being in two work settings. *Journal of Applied Social Psychology, 34,* 2045–2068.

Barker, B. (2014). *The PULSE Program: A life skills based physical activity program for at-risk adolescents* (Unpublished doctoral dissertation). Ottawa, Ontario, Canada: University of Ottawa.

Bean, C. N., Kendellen, K., and Forneris, T. (2013, October). Exploring basic needs satisfaction in a physical activity-based life skills program for female youth: A qualitative case study. Canadian Society for Psychomotor Learning and Sport Psychology (SCAPPS) Conference, Kelowna, British Columbia.

Bean, C. N., Kendellen, K., and Forneris, T. (2014). Does participation in summer camp fulfill youth's basic needs and facilitate life skill development? *Journal of Sports and Exercise Psychology, 36,* S81.

Bean, C. N., Kendellen, K., Halsall, T., and Forneris, T. (2015). Putting program evaluation into practice: Enhancing the Girls Just Wanna Have Fun program. *Evaluation & Program Planning, 49,* 31–40.

Biddle, S., Brown, H., and Lavallee, D. (2008). *The Development of Life Skills in Children Through Golf.* Loughborough: The Institute of Youth Sport, Loughborough University.

Botvin, G. J. and Griffin, K. W. (2004). Life skills training: Empirical findings and future directions. *The Journal of Primary Prevention, 25,* 211–232.

Cuijpers, P. (2002). Effective ingredients of school-based drug prevention programs: A systematic review. *Addictive Behaviors, 27,* 1009–1023.

Danish, S. J. (2000). Youth and community development: How after-school programming can make a difference. In S. J. Danish and T. Gullotta (Eds.), *Developing Competent Youth and Strong Communities Through After-School Programming* (pp. 275–302). Washington, DC: CWLA Press.

Danish, S. (2002a). *Going for the Goal: Leader Manual* (4th ed.). Richmond, VA: Life Skills Center, Virginia Commonwealth University.

Danish, S. (2002b). *SUPER (Sports United to Promote Education and Recreation) Program (3rd ed.): Leader Manual and Student Activity Book.* Richmond, VA: Life Skills Center, Virginia Commonwealth University.

Danish, S. J., and D'Augelli, A. R. (1983). *Helping Skills II: Life Development Intervention.* New York: Human Sciences.

Danish, S. J., and Forneris, T. (2008). Promoting positive development and competency across the lifespan. In S. D. Brown and R. W. Lent (Eds.), *Handbook of Counseling Psychology* (4th ed., pp. 500–517). Hoboken, NJ: Wiley.

Danish, S., D'Augelli, A., and Ginsberg, M. (1984). Life development intervention: Promotion of mental health through the development of competence. In S. D. Brown and R. W. Lent (Eds.), *Handbook of Counseling Psychology* (4th ed., pp. 520–544). Hoboken, NJ: Wiley.

Danish, S. J., Forneris, T., Hodge, K., and Heke, I. (2004). Enhancing youth development through sport. *World Leisure 3,* 38–49.

Deci, E. L., and Ryan, R. M. (2000). The 'what' and 'why' of goal pursuits: Human needs and the self-determination of behavior. *Psychological Inquiry, 11,* 227–268.

Deci, E., and Ryan, R. (2008). Facilitating optimal motivation and psychological well-being across life's domains. *Canadian Psychology, 49,* 14–23.

Ferrer-Caja, E., and Weiss, M. R. (2000). Predictors of intrinsic motivation among adolescent students in physical education. *Research Quarterly for Exercise & Sport, 71,* 267–279.

Forneris, T., Bean, C. N., Danish, S. J., and Fortier, M. (2013). Examining the relationship between Basic Needs Theory and life skills programming for female youth. *Journal of Sport & Exercise Psychology, 35,* S85.

Goudas, M., and Giannoudis, G. (2008). A team-sports-based life-skills program in a physical education context. *Learning & Instruction, 18,* 528–536.

Gould, D., and Carson, S. (2008). Life skills development through sport: Current status and future directions. *International Review of Sport and Exercise Psychology Reviews, 1,* 58–78.

Hansen, D. M., and Larson, R. W. (2005). *The Youth Experience Survey.* Unpublished manuscript, University of Illinois at Urbana-Champaign. Available from http://youthdev.illinois.edu

Hardcastle, S. J., Tye, M., Glassey, R., and Hagger, M. S. (2015). Exploring the perceived effectiveness of a life skills development program for high-performance athletes. *Psychology of Sport and Exercise, 16,* 139–149.

Hellison, D. (2011). *Teaching Personal and Social Responsibility Through Physical Activity.* Champaign, IL: Human Kinetics.

Hodge, K., and Gucciardi, D. (2015). Antisocial and prosocial behavior in sport: The role of motivational climate, basic psychological needs, and moral disengagement. *Journal of Sport and Exercise Psychology, 37,* 257–273.

Hodge, K., Danish, S., and Martin, J. (2012). Developing a conceptual framework for life skills interventions. *The Counseling Psychologist, 41,* 1125–1152.

Holt, N. L. (2008). *Positive Youth Development through Sport.* London: Routledge.

Jones, M. I., Lavallee, D., and Tod, D. (2011). Developing communication and organization skills: The ELITE life skills reflective practice intervention. *The Sport Psychologist, 25,* 35–52.

Larson, R. (2000). Towards a psychology of positive youth development. *American Psychologist, 55,* 170–183.

Niemiec, C., and Ryan, R. (2007). Autonomy, competence, and relatedness in the classroom: Applying self-determination theory to educational practice. *Theory and Research in Education, 7,* 133–144.

O'Hearn, T., and Gatz, M. (2002). Going for the Goal: Improving youth's problem-solving skills through a school-based intervention. *Journal of Community Psychology, 30,* 281–303.

Papacharisis, V., Goudas, M., Danish, S. J., and Theodorakis, Y. (2005). The effectiveness of teaching a life skills program in a sport context. *Journal of Applied Sport Psychology, 17,* 247–254.

Petitpas, A. J., Van Raalte, J. L., Cornelius, A. E., and Presbrey, J. (2004). A life skills development program for high school student athletes. *Journal of Primary Prevention, 24,* 325–334.

Reinboth, M., Duda, J. L., and Ntoumanis, N. (2004). Dimensions of coaching behavior, need satisfaction, and the psychological and physical welfare of young athletes. *Motivation and Emotion, 28,* 297–313.

Ryan, R. M., and Deci, E. L. (2000a). The darker and brighter sides of human existence: Basic psychological needs as a unifying concept. *Psychological Inquiry, 11,* 319–338.

Ryan, R. M., and Deci, E. L. (2000b). Self-determination theory and the facilitation of intrinsic motivation, social development, and well-being. *American Psychologist, 55,* 68–78.

Ryan, R. M., and Deci, E. L. (2008). A self-determination theory approach to psychotherapy: The motivational basis for effective change. *Canadian Psychology, 49,* 186–193.

Ryan, R. M., Lynch, M. F., Vansteenkiste, M., and Deci, E. L. (2011). Motivation and autonomy in counseling, psychotherapy, and behavior change: A look at theory and practice. *The Counseling Psychologist, 39,* 193–260.

Standage, M., Duda, J. L., and Ntoumanis, N. (2005). A test of self-determination theory in school physical education. *British Journal of Educational Psychology, 75,* 411–433.

Taylor, I., and Ntoumanis, N. (2007). Teacher motivational strategies and student self-determination in Physical Education. *Journal of Educational Psychology, 99*, 747–760.

Theokas, C., Danish, S., Hodge, K., Heke, I., and Forneris, T. (2007). Enhancing life skills through sport for children and youth. In N. L. Holt (Ed.), *Positive Youth Development through Sport* (pp. 71–81). London: Routledge.

Turnnidge, J., Côté, J., and Hancock, D. J. (2014). Positive youth development from sport to life: Explicit or implicit transfer? *Quest, 66*, 203–217.

Van Petegem, S., Beyers, W., Vansteenkiste, M., and Soenens, B. (2012). On the association between adolescent autonomy and psychosocial functioning: Examining decisional independence from a self-determination theory perspective. *Developmental Psychology, 48*, 76–88.

Weiss, M. R., Stuntz, C. P., Bhalla, J. A., Bolter, N. D., and Price, M. S. (2013). 'More than a game': Impact of The First Tee life skills program on positive youth development: Project introduction and Year 1 findings. *Qualitative Research in Sport, Exercise and Health, 5*, 214–244.

Weiss, M. R., Bolter, N. D., and Kipp, L. E. (2014). Assessing impact of physical activity-based youth development programs: Validation of the Life Skills Transfer Survey (LSTS). *Research Quarterly for Exercise and Sport, 85*, 263–278.

Whitley, M. A., Hayden, L. A., and Gould, D. (in press). Growing up in the Kayamandi Township: II. Sport as a setting for the development and transfer of desirable competencies. *International Journal of Sport and Exercise Psychology*. Available from http://www.tandfonline.com/doi/abs/10.1080/1612197X.2015.1036095

Wilson, P. M., and Rodgers, W. M. (2004). The relationship between perceived autonomy support, exercise regulations and behavioral intentions in women. *Psychology of Sport and Exercise, 5*, 229–242.

World Health Organization. (1999). *Partners in Life Skills Education*. Geneva: World Health Organization.

5

AN ECOLOGICAL PERSPECTIVE ON HIGH PERFORMANCE SPORT AND POSITIVE YOUTH DEVELOPMENT

Leisha Strachan, Jessica Fraser-Thomas, and Kendra Nelson-Ferguson

Positive youth development (PYD) encompasses various skills that a young person needs to amass to assist with their personal growth in sport and in life (Gould and Carson, 2008). The Developmental Model of Sport Participation (DMSP; Côté and Fraser-Thomas, 2015), one of the most prominent conceptual frameworks of athlete development in the literature (Bruner et al., 2009), proposes three key sport development trajectories. Much research in the field has focused on the first two trajectories of the DMSP—recreational sport through sampling and elite performance through sampling—proposing enhanced psychosocial development as a probable outcome of these paths. However, the DMSP also describes a third trajectory—elite performance through early specialization—outlining probable outcomes of reduced physical health, reduced enjoyment, and reduced positive psychosocial development through this path. In this chapter we extend upon our last contribution to this series (Côté et al., 2008) and focus on an ecological approach to understanding high performance sport and explore new research surrounding PYD and its role in elite sport contexts. The purpose of this chapter is to explore the opportunities and threats within high performance youth sport and how the promotion of PYD within this context could help create an optimal sport experience.

Ecological theory: a guiding framework

In the chapter in the first edition of this book, an ecological approach was suggested to explore PYD in sport with regards to three main outcomes: participation, performance, and personal development (Côté et al., 2008). While research in the field has developed since the last edition, the ecological framework remains an important platform for discussing youth development in sport. This approach is also the base for relational developmental system (RDS) metatheory, which describes mutually influential relationships between the individual and his/her context (Lerner and Overton, 2008). As such, this chapter will draw upon Bronfenbrenner's (1999) Process–Person–Context–Time (PPCT) model to discuss high performance sport as a context for PYD. In the first section on *Process*, we discuss the key propositions of the model, related to "proximal processes," and provide a working definition of high performance youth athletes. In discussing *Person*, we focus on how individual factors influence proximal processes of high performance athletes. *Context* draws upon the ecological theory's five environmental levels: microsystem, mesosystem, exosystem, macrosystem, and chronosystem (Bronfenbrenner, 1977), and we wrap up our discussion of the PPCT model by examining *Time*'s prominent role in athletes' high performance and PYD. We conclude the chapter by outlining potential areas of future research that may further enhance understanding of the complementary (or opposing) objectives of PYD and high performance among youth athletes.

Process: defining development in high performance athletes

At the foundation of Bronfenbrenner's ecological theory are two key propositions related to the processes of development (Bronfenbrenner, 2005; Bronfenbrenner and Morris, 1998). *Proposition 1* suggests that human development involves complex interactions between a person and his/her environment, which are termed "proximal processes." *Proposition 2* outlines that the direction, power, content, and form of these processes vary according to the developmental outcomes sought, the individual characteristics of the person, the environment surrounding the person, and the time period under consideration. These propositions highlight interesting and unique considerations in our exploration of opportunities and threats for PYD among high performance athletes. As detailed through Proposition 2, the "shape" of elite youth athletes' development varies according to such factors as the outcomes sought (i.e. high performance sport goals), athletes' surrounding environment (i.e. social environments including coaches, parents, teammates, and peers, and structural environments including living and training settings). Individuals' characteristics also play a role in shaping athletes' development. During the time under consideration (i.e. late childhood/adolescence), individuals experience extensive and ongoing physiological, psychological, social, and cognitive changes. Bronfenbrenner (2005) also contends that experience, increasing complexity of activities, internalization (i.e. child conforming to the wishes of a parent), and the strong presence of a third party (i.e. another adult) all play key roles in the development of a child.

Although the influence of proximal processes on high performance youth athletes is challenging to study, in part due to the reciprocal nature of these processes, and additionally due to the multiple social agents and settings that generate proximal processes, it becomes particularly important to define the parameters of high performance youth athletes. For the purposes of this chapter, we draw upon constructs from within the DMSP (Côté and Fraser-Thomas, 2015) to build a working definition. More specifically, high performance youth athletes are assumed to meet a high standard of performance, and spend large amounts of time in deliberate practice (i.e. training with the primary goal of improving performance which is high in structure, effort, and concentration; Ericsson et al., 1993). These criteria are in line with Baker and colleagues' (Baker et al., 2015) recently proposed taxonomy of expertise, which suggests state/provincial and national levels of performance within the "transitional" (i.e. youth) period of skill development potentially lead to expert or imminent performance following youth. As such, in this chapter we consider studies of "high performance" youth athletes; however, given that this term is often considered interchangeably with multiple other terms within the literature, we also considered research identifying youth athletes as "elite," "expert," "high investing," "select," "specializing," or "talented."

Person: individual factors in research with high performance youth athletes

In Bronfenbrenner's (1977) work, "the person" is described as an individual's biological, emotional, cognitive, and behavioral characteristics. Bronfenbrenner and Morris (1998) extended conceptualizations of the person by identifying three types of characteristics that are most influential in shaping future development. The authors describe personal dispositions, bioecological resources (i.e. ability, experience, knowledge, and skill), and the demands within the social environment as important considerations in terms of their impact on proximal processes. Each of these characteristics should be considered in terms of development through high performance sport.

Dispositions can "set proximal processes in motion in a particular developmental domain and continue to sustain their operation" (Bronfenbrenner and Morris, 1998, p. 955). Within the field of PYD, a person's inclinations or personality could be manifested through the 40 developmental assets framework, described as the "building blocks" of positive development (Benson, 1997). The 40 assets are divided into two main categories (internal and external), which are further delineated into eight types. The four types of internal assets include: positive identity, social competencies, positive values, and commitment to learning. External assets are represented by support, empowerment, constructive use of time, and boundaries and expectations. While internal assets describe a person's beliefs and values, external assets represent external resources and networks that may facilitate optimal development. Research examining asset possession has discovered that the more assets a person has, the more likely that he/she will develop in a healthy and positive manner (Benson, 2003). Asset possession has also been linked to thriving indicators including academic achievement, prosocial behaviors, and leadership (Scales et al., 2000; Scales et al., 2006).

The developmental assets framework has been suggested as an ideal platform for studying the person in youth sport (Côté et al., 2008; Fraser-Thomas et al., 2005); however, it has been used sparingly in the sport literature. Considering the links between the individual and context (as described in RDS), researchers might be hesitant to explore the individual and positive development independent of context. Nonetheless, research has examined asset possession and links to sport outcomes, namely burnout and enjoyment (Strachan et al., 2009a). In a sample of 123 youth athletes between the ages of twelve and sixteen years, the authors found that three types of assets were closely related to the aforementioned outcomes—positive identity, support, and empowerment. From an applied perspective, maintaining a positive identity (one that is not too closely aligned to sport identity), providing appropriate levels of support, and allowing for choice are important considerations that may be particularly applicable to high performing youth athletes.

Bronfenbrenner and Morris (1998) also suggest that resources which include "ability, experience, knowledge, and skills [are] required for the effective functioning of proximal processes at a given stage of development" (p. 955). These particular resources are often a developmental focus for youth who are highly invested in sport; resources tend to be explained and pursued in the physical domain. As described in the DMSP, youth enter various trajectories throughout sport development, which may affect or encompass the resources described by Bronfenbrenner and Morris (1998). Depending on sport abilities, decisions may be made by young athletes, parents, and/or coaches through sport development that may have an impact on the knowledge and skills gained as well as experiences. One study (Strachan et al., 2009b) found that young "sampler" athletes (i.e. those who developed through the first and second sampling trajectories of the DMSP) had distinct experiences from "specializers" (i.e. those who developed through the third early specialization trajectory of the DMSP). Specifically, "samplers" reported more links to the community, family, and school through sport while the "specializers" reported more diverse peer experiences through their sport participation. This points to the unique nature of the trajectories and the possibility that individual development might vary depending on the sport experience.

Finally, Bronfenbrenner and Morris (1998) note that "there are demand characteristics that invite or discourage reactions from the social environment of a kind that can foster or disrupt the operation of proximal processes" (p. 995). PYD researchers have identified various demand characteristics (i.e. lack of resources, lack of time, lack of support) that may impact development and growth (Fraser-Thomas et al., 2005). Due to the investment of personal time in high performance youth sport, the aforementioned demands may influence overall experiences within sport, while also impacting other relationships (e.g. with peers, within families). Furthermore, the amount of time athletes devote to training and competition may actually detract from psychosocial development (Strachan and Davies, 2015), reducing time spent contributing to community and school, hence leaving some youth feeling isolated. The demands of high performance youth sport could disrupt positive development however, if the context is aligned to a strength-based approach (i.e. enhancing individual assets), then healthy development is indeed possible.

Context: support and high performance youth sport

High performing athletes' development through proximal processes is also contingent upon various supporting contexts. Bronfenbrenner (1977, 1999) suggests five nested levels of environmental influences upon persons' development. Microsystem contexts most commonly influencing children's participation in sport consist of the child, family, coach, and peers (Scanlan and Lewthwaite, 1988). Fewer studies have focused on influences at the mesosystem (e.g. parent–coach interactions), exosystem (e.g. the extent to which coaches are educated), macrosystem (e.g. society's views on the purpose and emphasis placed on development and performance outcomes), and chronosystem (e.g. the increase in opportunities for sport in developing countries) in relation to PYD. However, emerging research highlights how sport structures, community size and birth date may indirectly influence sport developmental outcomes related to performance, psychosocial development, and withdrawal (Fraser-Thomas and Côté, 2009; Fraser-Thomas et al., 2010; Lemez et al., 2014; Turnnidge et al., 2014).

At the microsystem level, research relating to the influence of the coach in youth sport is abundant. One specific study examining high performance sport and links to PYD highlighted the important role of the coach in the promotion of positive youth sport contexts (Strachan et al., 2011). Coaches in this study suggested important psychosocial skills were taught in high performance sport environments, but they also admitted that athletes may lack connections to family, school, and community as a result of their invested involvement in sport. Although appropriate supportive contexts are necessary for PYD through high performance sport, the investment required by youth athletes to compete at a high level has the potential to detract from PYD.

With family influence becoming a more prominent area of research, many key models and conceptual frameworks have emerged examining and accounting for parents' influence on their children's sport development. Various typologies for parental support (Côté and Hay, 2002), classifications of parental involvement (Fredricks and Eccles, 2004), and research exploring specific parenting styles (Holt et al., 2009) have furthered understanding of the complexity of the parent–athlete dyad.

There is some evidence suggesting that parents can negatively influence high performance youth athletes' sport development and participation. For example, high levels of parental involvement and parents' past sport involvement have been associated with negative outcomes, such as withdrawal and burnout (Fraser-Thomas et al., 2008a; Strachan et al., 2009a). Further, Knight et al. (2011) found that young athletes are particularly attuned to parents' non-verbal communication (e.g. disappointed body language), and become frustrated when their parents' non-verbal communication messages are inconsistent with their verbal messages. It is also common for high performing youth athletes to confuse parents' feedback with their coach's advice, often leading to an overload of conflicting information (Knight et al., 2011). Parents can play a major role in facilitating social and personal development, but parents who display and/or accept poor sport behaviors can serve as negative role models to their children (Shields et al., 2007). In a longitudinal observational study, Holt et al. (2008) found parents' behaviors and interactions were often influenced by their perceived knowledge and/or past experiences. Thus, it is evident that parental behaviors can have an impact on elite youth sport participation.

Research investigating good parenting in sport can be broken down into four categories: (1) parents' emotional and informational support (e.g. parents' level of involvement); (2) parents' tangible support (e.g. transportation); (3) parent modeling (e.g. displaying a strong work ethic, leadership); and (4) parents' role in facilitating social and personal development (e.g. instilling core values) (Fraser-Thomas et al., 2013). Additionally, high performance sport serves as a venue for parents to facilitate life skills, such as controlling emotions during stressful circumstances, overcoming obstacles, demonstrating respectful behaviors, and developing resilience (Knight et al., 2011). These findings highlight specific ways in which parents facilitate positive sport development and decrease adverse outcomes, consistent with frameworks of PYD (e.g. Fraser-Thomas et al., 2005). Few studies make an explicit connection between parenting and PYD. Thus, the short- and long-term effects of parenting styles and strategies in sport related to PYD need to be considered.

While much less research has focused on sibling–athlete interactions (Davis and Meyer, 2008) within the microsystem, identifying family dynamics that extend beyond parents is crucial in understanding sustained positive sport participation and development (Côté, 1999). Siblings can serve as sources of emotional and instructional support by displaying pride, providing encouragement, and offering sport-specific advice (Davis and Meyer, 2008). It is also common for older siblings to act as role models by portraying strong work ethics for youth involved in sport (Fraser-Thomas et al., 2008b). Although there have been some positive relationships found, it is common for tensions to arise among siblings in relation to their sport participation. Sulloway (1996) found that younger siblings may compare themselves to the older siblings' achievements, often resulting in jealousy. Further, the existence of a power and/or status differential can exist, as the oldest child tends to possess an authoritative type personality, enabling him/her to provide guidance to their younger sibling (Davis and Meyer, 2008). This can lead to negative implications including pressure to perform, loss of confidence, jealousy, and more competitive sibling relationships (Nelson, 2015). The coexistence of both positive and negative characteristics is consistent with Furman and Buhrmester's (1985) suggestion that sibling relationships are paradoxical in nature; siblings can be an important source of closeness but also sources of conflict and rivalry. The complexity of the athlete–sibling relationship has the potential to detract from PYD. Therefore, exploring sibling influence further may help to uncover ways to structure these interactions to promote PYD, especially for high performance youth athletes who may be at risk due to their extensive devotion to sport.

Another important but minimally studied inter-relationship within the microsystem is between high performance athletes and their peers and/or teammates. Research suggests teammates have the potential to positively influence young athletes' development by serving as models of work ethic and perspective, facilitators of psychological skills learning, and overall emotional supporters (Durand-Bush and Salmela, 2002; Gould et al., 2002; Morgan and Giacobbi, 2006). Given that teammates are also often competitors, sometimes tensions arise. However, problems are usually short-lived, as sport typically requires rapid resolutions, with individuals developing conflict resolution and resiliency skills (Fraser-Thomas and Côté, 2009; Patrick et al., 1999; Weiss et al., 1996). Further exploration is required to unpack the complexity of the athlete–teammate, athlete–peer, and athlete–sibling relationships in high performance sport settings, to offer clearer implications with regard to healthy reciprocal relationships, facilitating optimal sport development, and positive sport experiences.

Time: exploring the relationship of time and high performance sport

Time features prominently in the developmental process, at multiple levels within the ecological theory. As such, Bronfenbrenner (2005) suggested that in order to show that development has indeed occurred, research designs need to take place over an extended period of time. Within the youth development literature, this factor continues to be under-researched (Côté et al., 2008) and non-existent within PYD and sport. In an in-depth report of PYD programs in the United States, Catalano et al. (2002) concluded that longer programs were more effective in facilitating youth development.

When examined through the lens of PYD, some research has highlighted additional benefits of large time investments for promoting positive development. Specifically, a greater length of time spent within an activity (i.e. the number of hours invested per week) as well as greater time given to an activity throughout development (i.e. the number of years an athlete has spent in one sport context) have been associated with higher indications of positive development (Simpkins et al., 2005). However, spending time in other activities (i.e. not one's primary sport) has also been found to positively contribute to youth development (Zarrett et al., 2009; Zarrett et al., 2008). Of additional interest are findings by Zarrett et al. (2009) that show youth who were highly invested in sport along with other activities, were more likely to contribute back to the community, but also reported higher rates of depression. The authors suggested that:

> Although much time spent participating in multiple activities is related to PYD and contribution, factors associated with spending this much time in activities (e.g., the possible pressure from parents, issues of time management) can lead to slightly higher rates of depression during the middle school years for a subset of highly engaged youths.

> *(p. 379)*

This line of research clearly warrants further attention, given the complexities of activity time involvement patterns as youth seek to find an appropriate level of balance to enhance development and identity formation.

Conclusion

For many stakeholders within the high performance context (e.g. coaches, parents, athletes), a belief continues to resonate that personal well-being must be sacrificed in order to attain performance success (Gervis and Dunn, 2004; Stirling and Kerr, 2007). We opened the chapter with the proposition that, although there are potential challenges, high performance youth sport and PYD can be complementary. In this review, we presented evidence to suggest that this is the case; however, many questions remain regarding the circumstances surrounding youths' optimal development through high performance sport. While the DMSP proposes probable negative psychosocial outcomes of elite sport through the early specialization trajectory, further research is needed to determine exactly when and how these outcomes are most (un)likely to occur, and how the complementarity of PYD and high performance in youth can be assured.

In moving this line of research forward, several avenues for investigation have been proposed. First, the bi-directionality of proximal processes in facilitating youths' development is a paramount consideration. The ecological perspective explores the individual as both a product and producer within his/her environment (Bronfenbrenner, 1999). As research has focused primarily on factors that influence young people's development (i.e. framing youth athletes as products of his/her environment), attention should shift to focus to a greater extent on how individuals may be producers of their own development (e.g. youths' influence on parents/guardians, who in turn influence youths' sporting experiences and/or parent/guardian's personal growth). Further, the majority of research in youth sport has focused within the first nested level of the ecological system (the microsystem), with much less understanding offered of other environmental influences (e.g. coach–parent relationships within the mesosystem; sport organizations' policies at the macrosystem level). Research in these areas would offer considerable advancement of understanding of the complexities of proximal processes and development.

Second, methodological concerns are a major limitation within the field, with longitudinal and replication studies sorely needed to expand current understanding. As a major component of ecological theory, processes need to be considered over time to determine whether they remain valid, or if they have been nullified by various societal changes (Bronfenbrenner, 2005). Specifically, given youth are continually growing and changing, researchers should use longitudinal designs to assess their experiences, development, and outcomes through the DMSP's different sport trajectories (Côté et al., 2008; Gould and Carson, 2008). A unique consideration when studying high performing youth is that they have not yet "made it" at a senior level, and there is often little guarantee of continued high performance beyond their youth. As such, the longitudinal study of PYD in high performance youth athletes is critically important to better understand and optimize youths' navigation through potential transition challenges surrounding identity, performance plateaus, injury, motivation, and de-selection. Longitudinal research is also important to continue informing questions surrounding athletes' time investment, and in turn offer insights into issues such as time management, pressure, and depression (Zarrett et al., 2009).

As researchers seek to better understand and address key questions around PYD and high performance youth sport, practitioners in many sports, nations, and across cultures, also appear to be moving forward, and gradually shifting conceptual paradigms to encompass the objectives of PYD and high performance as complementary. For example, in Canada, national training centers provide networks of support and resources for elite youth athletes, often providing key services focused on athletes' well-being. Further, knowledge products to promote PYD have been created to help deliberately deliver optimal sport experiences (see www.projectscore.ca). With growing willingness and eagerness to optimize high performing youth athletes' PYD, the academic community must also rally together and enhance momentum to conduct well-designed empirical research, which will in turn assure athletes' healthy development through sport.

References

Baker, J., Wattie, N., and Schorer, J. (2015). Defining expertise: A taxonomy for researchers in skill acquisition and expertise. In J. Baker and D. Farrow (Eds.), *Handbook of Sport Expertise* (pp. 145–155). London: Routledge.

Benson, P. L. (1997). *All Kids Are Our Kids: What Communities Must Do to Raise Caring and Responsible Children and Adolescents*. San Francisco, CA: Jossey-Bass.

Benson, P. L. (2003). Developmental assets and asset-building community: Conceptual and empirical foundations. In R. Lerner and P. L. Benson (Eds.), *Developmental Assets and Asset-Building Communities: Implications for Research, Policy, and Practice* (pp. 19–43). New York: Kluwer Academic/Plenum Publishers.

Bronfenbrenner, U. (1977). Toward an experimental ecology of human development. *American Psychologist, 32*, 513–531.

Bronfenbrenner, U. (1999). Environments in developmental perspective: Theoretical and operational models. In S. L. Friedman and T. D. Wachs (Eds.), *Measuring Environment Across the Life Span* (pp. 3–28). Washington, DC: American Psychological Association.

Bronfenbrenner, U. (2005). The bioecological theory of human development. In U. Bronfenbrenner (Ed.), *Making Human Beings Human: Bioecological Perspectives on Human Development* (pp. 3–15). Thousand Oaks, CA: Sage.

Bronfenbrenner, U., and Morris, P. A. (1998). The ecology of developmental processes. In W. Damon (Series Ed.), and R. Lerner (Vol. Ed.), *Handbook of Child Psychology: Vol 1. Theoretical Models of Human Development* (5th ed., pp. 993–1028). New York: John Wiley.

Bruner, M., Erikson, K., McFadden, K., and Côté, J. (2009). Tracing the origins of athlete development models in sport: A citation path analysis. *International Review of Sport and Exercise Psychology, 2*, 23–37.

Catalano, R. F., Berglund, M. L., Ryan, J. A., Lonczak, H. S., and Hawkins, J. D. (2002). Positive youth development in the United States: Research findings on evaluation of positive youth development programs. *Prevention and Treatment, 5,* 187–213.

Côté, J. (1999). The influence of the family in the development of talent in sport. *The Sport Psychologist, 13,* 395–417.

Côté, J., and Hay, J. (2002). Children's involvement in sport: A developmental perspective. In J. M. Silva and D. E. Stevens (Eds.), *Psychological Foundations of Sport* (pp. 484–502). Boston, MA: Allyn and Bacon.

Côté, J., and Fraser-Thomas, J. (2015). Youth involvement and positive youth development in sport. In P. R. E. Crocker (Ed.), *Sport and Exercise Psychology: A Canadian Perspective* (3rd ed., pp. 256–287). Toronto: Pearson.

Côté, J., Strachan, L., and Fraser-Thomas, J. (2008). Participation, personal development and performance through youth sport. In N. L. Holt (Ed.), *Positive Youth Development Through Sport* (pp. 34–45). London: Routledge.

Davis, N. W., and Meyer, B. B. (2008). When sibling becomes competitor: A qualitative investigation of same-sex sibling competition in elite sport. *Journal of Applied Sport Psychology, 20,* 220–235.

Durand-Bush, N., and Salmela, J. H. (2002). The development and maintenance of expert athletic performance: Perceptions of world and Olympic champions. *Journal of Applied Sport Psychology, 14,* 154–171.

Ericsson, K. A., Krampe, R. T., and Tesch-Römer, C. (1993). The role of deliberate practice in the acquisition of expert performance. *Psychological Review, 100,* 363–406.

Fraser-Thomas, J., and Côté, J. (2009). Understanding adolescents' positive and negative developmental experiences in sport. *The Sport Psychologist, 23,* 3–23.

Fraser-Thomas, J., Côté, J., and Deakin, J. (2005). Youth sport programs: An avenue to foster positive youth development. *Physical Education and Sport Pedagogy, 10,* 19–40.

Fraser-Thomas, J., Côté, J., and Deakin, J. (2008a). Examining adolescent sport dropout and prolonged engagement from a developmental perspective. *Journal of Applied Sport Psychology, 20,* 318–333.

Fraser-Thomas, J., Côté, J., and Deakin, J. (2008b). Understanding dropout and prolonged engagement in adolescent competitive sport. *Psychology of Sport and Exercise, 9,* 645–662.

Fraser-Thomas, J., Côté, J., and MacDonald, D. J. (2010). Community size in youth sport settings: Examining developmental assets and sport withdrawal. *PHENex Journal, 2*(2), 1–9.

Fraser-Thomas, J., Strachan, L., and Jeffery-Tosoni, S. (2013). Family influence on children's involvement in sport. In J. Côté and R. Lidor (Eds.), *Conditions of Children's Talent Development in Sport* (pp. 179–196). Morgantown, WV: Fitness Information Technology.

Fredricks, J. A., and Eccles, J. S. (2004). Parental influences on youth involvement in sports. In M. R. Weiss (Ed.), *Developmental Sport and Exercise Psychology: A Lifespan Perspective* (pp. 145–164). Morgantown, WV: Fitness Information Technology.

Furman, W., and Buhrmester, D. (1985). Children's perceptions of the qualities of sibling relationships. *Child Development, 56,* 448–461.

Gervis, M., and Dunn, N. (2004). The emotional abuse of elite child athletes by their coaches. *Child Abuse and Neglect, 26,* 697–714.

Gould, D., and Carson, S. (2008). Life skills development through sport: Current status and future directions. *International Review of Sport and Exercise Psychology, 1,* 58–78.

Gould, D., Dieffenbach, K., and Moffatt, A. (2002). Psychological characteristics and their development in Olympic champions. *Journal of Applied Sport Psychology, 14,* 172–204.

Holt, N. L., Tamminen, K. A., Black, D. E., Sehn, Z. L., and Wall, M. P. (2008). Parental involvement in competitive youth sport settings. *Psychology of Sport and Exercise, 9,* 663–685.

Holt, N. L., Tamminen, K. A., Black, D. E., Mandigo, J. L., and Fox, K. R. (2009). Youth sport parenting styles and practices. *Journal of Sport and Exercise Psychology, 31,* 37–59.

Knight, C. J., Neely, K. C., and Holt, N. L. (2011). Parental behaviours in team sports: How do female athletes want parents to behave? *Journal of Applied Sport Psychology, 23,* 76–92.

Lemez, S., Baker, J., Horton, S., Wattie, N., and Weir, P. (2014). Examining the relationship between relative age, competition level, and drop-out rates in male youth ice-hockey players. *Scandinavian Journal of Medicine and Science in Sports, 24,* 935–942.

Lerner, R. M., and Overton, W. F. (2008). Exemplifying the integrations of the relational developmental system: Synthesizing theory, research, and application to promote positive development and social justice. *Journal of Adolescent Research, 23,* 245–255.

Morgan, T. K., and Giacobbi, Jr., P. R. (2006). Toward two grounded theories of the talent development and social support process of highly successful collegiate athletes. *The Sport Psychologist, 20,* 295–313.

Nelson, K. (2015). *Friend, Foe, or Both? A Retrospective Exploration of Sibling Relationships in Elite Youth Sport* (Unpublished master's thesis). Winnipeg, Manitoba: University of Manitoba.

Patrick, H., Ryan, A. M., Alfeld-Liro, C., Fredricks, J. A., Hruda, L. Z., and Eccles, J. S. (1999). Adolescents' commitment to developing talent: The role of peers in continuing motivation for sports and the arts. *Journal of Youth and Adolescence, 28,* 741–763.

Scales, P. C., Benson, P. L., Leffert, N., and Blyth, D. A. (2000). Contribution of developmental assets to the prediction of thriving among adolescents. *Applied Developmental Science, 4,* 27–46.

Scales, P. C., Benson, P. L., Roehlkepartain, E. C., Sesma Jr., A., and van Dulmen, M. (2006). The role of developmental assets in predicting academic achievement: A longitudinal study. *Journal of Adolescence, 29,* 691–708.

Scanlan, T. K., and Lewthwaite, R. (1988). From stress to enjoyment: Parental and coach influences on young participants. In E. W. Brown, and C. F. Branta (Eds.), *Sports for Children* (pp. 41–48). Champaign, IL: Human Kinetics.

Shields, D. L., LaVoi, N. M., Bredemeier, B. L., and Power, C. F. (2007). Predictors of poor sportspersonship in youth sports: An examination of personal attitudes and social influences. *Journal of Sport and Exercise Psychology, 29,* 747–762.

Simpkins, S. D., Ripke, M., Huston, A. C., and Eccles, J. S. (2005). Predicting participation and outcomes in out-of-school activities: Similarities and differences across social ecologies. *New Directions for Youth Development, 105,* 51–69.

Stirling, A. E., and Kerr, G. A. (2007). Elite female athletes' experiences of emotional abuse across time. *Journal of Emotional Abuse, 7,* 89–113.

Strachan, L., and Davies, K. (2015). Click! Using photo elicitation to explore youth experiences and positive youth development in sport. *Qualitative Research in Sport, Exercise, and Health, 7*(2), 170–191.

Strachan, L., Côté, J., and Deakin, J. (2009a). An evaluation of personal and contextual factors in competitive youth sport. *Journal of Applied Sport Psychology, 21,* 340–355.

Strachan, L., Côté, J., and Deakin, J. (2009b). "Specializers" versus "samplers" in youth sport: Comparing experiences and outcomes. *The Sport Psychologist, 23,* 77–92.

Strachan, L., Côté, J., and Deakin, J. (2011). A new view: Exploring positive youth development in elite sport contexts. *Qualitative Research in Sport, Exercise, and Health, 3,* 9–32.

Sulloway, F. J. (1996). *Born to Rebel: Birth Order, Family Dynamics, and Creative Lives.* New York: Pantheon Books.

Turnnidge, J., Hancock, D. J., and Côté, J. (2014). The influence of birth date and place of development on youth sport participation. *Scandinavian Journal of Medicine and Science in Sports, 24,* 461–468.

Weiss, M. R., Smith, A. L., and Theeboom, M. (1996). "That's what friends are for": Children's and teenagers' perceptions of peer relationships in the sport domain. *Journal of Sport and Exercise Psychology, 18,* 347–379.

Zarrett, N., Lerner, R. M., Carrano, J., Fay, K., Peltz, J. S., and Yibing, L. (2008). Variations in adolescent engagement in sports and its influence on positive youth development. In N. L. Holt (Ed.), *Positive Youth Development through Sport* (pp. 9–23). London: Routledge.

Zarrett, N., Fay, K., Yibing, L., Carrano, J., Phelps, E., and Lerner, R. (2009). More than child's play: Variable and pattern centered approaches for examining effects of sports participation on youth development. *Developmental Psychology, 45*(2), 368–382.

PART 2

Measurement and assessment

6

YOUTH THRIVING IN THE CONTEXT OF SPORT PARTICIPATION

Idiographic, differential, and nomothetic dimensions

Andrea Vest Ettekal, Richard M. Lerner, Jennifer P. Agans, Kaitlyn A. Ferris, and Brian M. Burkhard

Out-of-school-time (OST) activities are key ecological assets promoting positive development among diverse youth (Vandell et al., 2015). Within the United States, sports constitute the OST activity most often engaged in by youth (Sabo and Veliz, 2008). Youth participation in sports is not invariantly associated with positive development (e.g. Zarrett et al., 2009). However, under most ecological conditions in at least the United States, sport participation is linked to indicators of positive youth development (PYD), thriving, or well-being (Zarrett and Lerner, 2008). This link is especially the case when sport participation is part of a set of OST activities that includes youth development (YD) programs marked by the "Big Three" components of program design (Zarrett et al., 2009). Within safe spaces for youth, these three components of YD programs are positive and sustained relations with an engaged, competent, and continuously available adult (e.g. coach), youth life skill development opportunities, and opportunities to enact these skills in valued family, school, or community settings, including sport programs (Lerner, 2004).

This link between PYD and engagement with a supportive context may be conceptualized in many ways (e.g. Lerner et al., 2015). Within contemporary developmental science, cutting-edge theoretical models are derived from relational developmental systems (RDS) metatheory (Overton, 2015). RDS ideas have been used to frame what has been termed a PYD perspective about the mutually beneficial relations between developing youth and their contexts (represented as individual ⟷ context relations) that are involved in youth thriving. The purpose of this chapter is to provide conceptual and methodological ideas about conducting research on PYD through sport. At the outset, we briefly review the RDS metamodel and its contributions to the PYD perspective, using one operationalization of PYD, namely the Five Cs model (Lerner et al., 2015), to discuss the link between sport participation and PYD. We devote the remainder of the chapter to a discussion of the methodological issues involved in conducting research on PYD through sports from an RDS lens.

The RDS metamodel and the PYD perspective

Developmental science is a multidisciplinary scholarly domain that seeks to integrate variables from biological through cultural and historical levels of organization across the life span into a synthetic, coactional system. Rejecting earlier notions about human development which were dominated by split, reductionist approaches, the contemporary emphasis on developmental science views variables from each of the multiple levels of organization in the ecology of human development as acting in an integrated system, influencing and being influenced by variables from the other levels in the system (e.g. Elder et al., 2015).

The relational developmental systems (RDS) metatheory that frames this approach to the study of development is derived from a process-relational paradigm (Overton, 2015), in which the organism is seen as inherently active, self-creating (autopoietic), self-organizing, self-regulating (agentic), nonlinear/complex, and adaptive. Accordingly, the conceptual emphasis in RDS-based theories is placed on mutually influential relations between individuals and contexts, on the above-noted individual ←→ context relations (wherein ←→ refers to coaction).

When derived from RDS-based ideas, the PYD perspective emphasizes the potential for these mutually influential individual ←→ context relations to be mutually beneficial, and hence adaptive. Furthermore, RDS metatheory (and thus the PYD perspective) points to the potential for plasticity as a fundamental strength of human development. Plasticity refers to the capacity for systematic change and is always a relative phenomenon within the relational developmental system because the temporal events in the life or lives of an individual or a group, respectively, may also constrain change as well as provide affordances for it (Lerner, 1984). A system that promotes change can also function to diminish it. Nevertheless, relative plasticity, as a strength, affords a basis for changing—for enhancing—human life, for promoting thriving or positive development.

An RDS program of research, such as a study of PYD through sport, might seek to understand the nature of relations between individuals and their contexts, including the dynamics of those relations across the life course. For instance, RDS-based researchers might ask how specific features of the individual and specific features of the sport context coalesce over time to influence the substantive course of individual ←→ context relations. Empirically, however, assessments of positive and/or healthy functioning must be conducted with the recognition that contexts are complex (e.g. they exist at multiple levels of organization as, for instance, denoted by Bronfenbrenner's (2005) notions of the micro-, meso-, exo-, and macro-systems within the ecology of human development). Individuals cannot necessarily act in ways that benefit all levels and all components of the context at all times and places (Elder et al., 2015). Thus, one may need to treat PYD not as a categorical concept (as something that either exists or not) but, instead, as a multivariate concept composed of ordinal or interval dimensions. As such, researchers studying PYD would address issues such as how beneficial the individual ←→ context relation is for specific people or specific social institutions of the context, at specific times and in specific places (e.g. see Bornstein, 2002).

Addressing such complex issues, scientists may do more than just describe and explain development. As well, they may seek to understand the conditions under which they can optimize the course of development (Lerner, 2002). For example, what combinations of activities may best promote PYD among specific groups of athletes at specific times in their development (Zarrett et al., 2009)? Promoting such adaptive individual ←→ context relations is the essence of enhancing PYD. Indeed, all models of the PYD process, and all approaches to PYD program design or instances of youth programs associated with PYD (Lerner et al., 2015) seek to enhance PYD through promoting adaptive exchanges between youth and the resources needed for thriving that may exist within the key settings of their lives (e.g. families, schools, or community-based, youth development programs).

The PYD perspective: the Five Cs model as a sample case

The model of the PYD process devised by Lerner and colleagues explicitly has drawn on the individual ←→ context RDS conception as its foundation (Lerner et al., 2015). This model has been elaborated in the context of Lerner and colleagues' longitudinal study, the 4-H study of PYD (see Lerner et al., 2015). The 4-H program, representing heart, hands, head, and health, is the largest youth development program in the U.S., and is sponsored by both the U.S. Department of Agriculture and the public, land-grant universities within the U.S. The 4-H study sought to identify the individual and ecological relations that may promote thriving and, as well, that may have a preventive effect in regard to risk/problem behaviors. Within this study, thriving was understood as the growth of attributes that mark a flourishing, healthy young person.

In the Lerner and Lerner model, these positive characteristics have been operationalized as the "Five Cs" of PYD—competence, confidence, character, connection, and caring (Lerner et al., 2015). The Lerner and Lerner model specifies that when youth develop high levels of the Five Cs, a high level of a "sixth C," of youth contribution (to self, family, school, community and, ultimately, civil society; Lerner et al., 2015) will emerge (see Figure 6.1). Accordingly, measures of each of the Five Cs are used to index the construct of PYD which, in turn, is then used to predict scores on indices of Contribution (Geldhof et al., 2013).

Several reports from the 4-H study demonstrated that participation in OST activities (e.g. youth development programs) promoted PYD (e.g. Mueller et al., 2011), but only two studies have used these data to examine sport activities specifically. Agans and Geldhof (2012) found that frequent participation in sports (compared to minimal participation) consistently predicted PYD across Grades 7–12 (approximately ages twelve to eighteen years). Zarrett and colleagues (2009) found that patterns of participation were important for PYD; specifically,

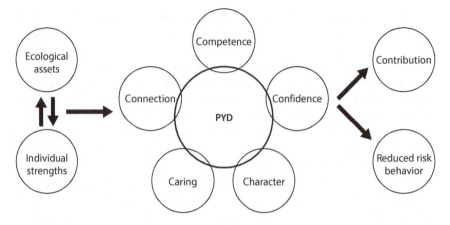

FIGURE 6.1 The Lerner and colleagues' (Lerner et al., 2015) Five Cs model of PYD. Reproduced under the STM Permissions Guidelines.

participating in sports in combination with a youth development program predicted PYD (above and beyond frequency of participation in other OST activities). Taken together, these studies suggest that sports are an important context to promote the growth of positive attributes in young people, as operationalized by the Five Cs.

A fundamental point in understanding the intent of this operationalization of PYD is *not* that there are only five Cs that may describe a thriving youth. Indeed, important work contributing to the understanding of the RDS-based approach to PYD has focused on either more Cs (e.g. the seven Cs studied by Ginsburg, 2011) or fewer Cs (e.g. the four Cs and two Cs studied within sports by Côté et al., 2010, and by Jones et al., 2011, respectively). Moreover, other RDS-based models of PYD have focused on constructs ranging in number from one (e.g. purpose, as studied by Damon, 2008, or resilience, as studied by Masten, 2014) through twenty or more attributes believed to operationalize PYD (e.g. Benson et al., 2011). Therefore, the Five Cs studied by Lerner and Lerner are not used in a hegemonic fashion to preclude other RDS-based models from being tested. Rather, the Five Cs model is used *only* to illustrate the ways in which a relational strength-based approach to positive development may be fruitfully empirically studied through the use of contemporary models of the relational developmental process.

Moreover, the core theory of change tested in this approach to the developmental process of PYD does not rest on any particular operationalization of the PYD construct. That is, the Lerner and Lerner model suggests that if (1) the strengths of youth (e.g. possession of intentional self-regulation skills) can (2) be aligned with the resources for positive growth found in, for instance OST YD programs, ones marked by the "Big Three," then (3) young people's healthy development will be optimized (Lerner et al., 2015).

Testing of RDS-based models of PYD through sport program participation

Whatever the operationalization of PYD, conducting research that derives from RDS metatheory requires that theoretical ideas about development be actualized through methodological approaches involving change-sensitive research designs, measurements, and data analysis methods. This obligation is an essential feature of "good science—selecting features of one's methodology based on the nature of the (theoretically predicated) questions asked" (Lerner and Overton, 2008, p. 250). However, in testing RDS-based ideas about development, researchers must make methodological decisions that acknowledge that the developmental system is embodied. That is, embodiment means that the way individuals behave, experience, and live in the world involves their being active agents with particular kinds of bodies (Agans et al., 2013). According to Overton (2015), the body is integratively understood as form (a biological referent), as lived experience (a psychological referent), and as an entity in active engagement with the world (a sociocultural referent). As such, embodied individuals actively participate in the production of their own ontogenetic development (Lerner, 2002). Thus, RDS-based research must entail a focus on the individual and on the specific course of his or her changes in PYD. This person-centered requirement has profound implications for the future study of the development of PYD within sports.

Molenaar (2014) explained that the standard approach to statistical analysis in the social and behavioral sciences is not focused on change but is, instead, derived from mathematical assumptions regarding the constancy of phenomena across people and, critically, time. He noted that these assumptions are based on the ergodic theorems. These theorems indicate that: (1) all individuals within a sample may be treated as the same (this is the assumption of homogeneity); and (2) all individuals remain the same across time, that is, all time points yield the same results (this is the assumption of stationarity). The postulation of ergodicity leads, then, to statistical analyses placing prime interest on the population level. Interindividual variation, rather than intraindividual change, is the source of this population information (Molenaar, 2014).

Accordingly, if the concept of ergodicity is applied to the study of PYD, then within-individual variation in PYD across time would either be ignored or treated as error variance. In addition, any sample (group) differences in PYD would be constrained to be invariant across time and place.

Within a sport context, applying the assumptions of ergodicity would mean that, for example, all athletes on a team should be exactly the same and remain the same across time—an assumption that is manifestly incorrect. Within the process-relational paradigm (Overton, 2015), development is nonlinear and characterized by autopoietic (self-constructing) and, hence, idiographic intraindividual change, features of human functioning that violate the principles of ergodicity. As such, interindividual differences in trajectories of PYD (i.e. the course of intraindividual changes in thriving) are important foci for research and, as well, for program and policy applications aimed at enhancing PYD among youth within and across time and place, for example, within a given OST sport and/or across a young person's trajectory of engagement in sports.

As a consequence, in order to obtain valid information about the developmental processes involved in PYD through sport (and other contexts), it is necessary to study intraindividual variation with change-sensitive methods. Such assessment of change involves decisions about research designs, including the specification of samples; measurements selected for use within these designs and appropriate for the participants sampled; and data-analytic techniques appropriate for understanding the systematic intraindividual (i.e. within person) changes that define development and, as well, the between-person differences in intraindividual change that may exist across participants in any given study. We delineate these three facets of research designs to assess change and provide recommendations for the study of PYD through sports.

Change-sensitive research designs

In regard to designs, multiple times of observation must be used; only longitudinal designs (e.g. single cohort/panel designs, sequential designs, or time series or P-technique intensive individual assessment designs; Baltes et al., 1977; Nesselroade and Baltes, 1979; Nesselroade and Molenaar, 2010) provide the multiple observation points necessary to index change. One-shot assessments or cross-sectional designs can only appraise interindividual differences at one point in time, and these differences may not reflect differences attributable to intraindividual change (e.g. Nesselroade and Molenaar, 2010). Moreover, change across two points in time does not accurately capture change because of the problem of regression toward the mean (i.e. extreme scores at one point in time will tend to be closer to the average at another point in time; Nesselroade et al., 1980); at least three points in time are necessary to account for this phenomenon. Simply, change can only be detected using longitudinal research designs with at least three measurement points.

In addition, a key but often ignored facet of a longitudinal design is the timing of the repeated observations that one will make (Lerner et al., 2009). That is, researchers must consider the divisions of the x-axis (time) used in a longitudinal design. Typically, these divisions are selected on the basis of convenience or feasibility (Lerner et al., 2009). For instance, in many studies of youth development, annual time points are used (e.g. youth may be sampled at the beginning of Grades 5, 6, and 7); these selections are often made because the budget of a project may not allow more frequent assessments or because the size of a sample will make it difficult to collect data more often. However, the processes of development do not necessarily unfold in ways that correspond to these x-axis divisions. For instance, to assess the development of an individual's sense of mastery of a sport and/or his or her development of commitment to teammates, theory or past research might suggest that x-axis divisions be spaced on the basis of phases of his or her involvement in the sport (e.g. trying out for the team, the beginning of practice sessions, the launch of competitive games or meets, midway through a season, and at the end of a season).

Moreover, in studying the PYD process as it may evolve in the context of sport participation, selections of temporal division should also take into account variables such as the nature of the sport context (e.g. individual sports versus team sports) and any special characteristics of the athletes being sampled (e.g. junior varsity competitors, varsity competitors, elite athletes, or youth competing in special programs, such as the Special Olympics). The point is that theory or inferences from past research and the nature of the youth being studied should dictate the design of timing of observations.

Clearly, issues involved in change-sensitive designs assessing development raise, as well, issues of identifying the appropriate sample. Samples must be selected on the basis of their potential to change during particular portions of development and/or because they are involved in activities (e.g. intervention programs involving participation in sports) wherein it is appropriate to expect systematic change (plasticity) due to their experiences. For instance, if one wanted to study the effect of menarche on the sport participation of female athletes, one would not select a sample of high school seniors to study. Similarly, if one wished to appraise whether one or another type of coaching enhanced youth engagement in sports, one would need to select youth who are at the beginning of their organized sport experiences, as compared to youth who have long and diverse histories of being coached.

Measurement in change-sensitive research designs

The measures used to assess change must be sensitive enough to detect change. This seemingly obvious point is actually deceptively complex, especially when one considers the long history in developmental science and psychology of measuring *traits*. The purported "Big Five" personality traits (conscientiousness, agreeableness, neuroticism, openness to experience, and extraversion) that form what is termed Five Factor Theory (FFT) are a case in point. The Big Five remain the predominant way of measuring personality in the literatures of personality and social psychology (e.g. John and Naumann, 2010). However, these traits are held to be fixed, stable, and biologically set facets of individual functioning. For instance, McCrae et al. (2000, pp. 175–176) believe that personality traits reflect "nature over nurture" and that "personality traits are more or less immune to [the] environment ... significant variations in life experiences have little or no effect on measured personality traits." Given this theoretical orientation (one antithetical to RDS-based conceptions of plasticity, as found in the PYD model; Lerner and Callina, 2014), measures of such characteristics are often developed to eliminate any variation associated with age/time (Nesselroade, 1988). As such, even if one were to use a change-sensitive design and to sample youth for whom change may be expected, employing such change-insensitive measures would constrain, and arguably preclude, the identification of systematic change.

Thus, researchers must evaluate the measures selected for use in their measurement models on the basis of evidence for change-sensitivity. In turn, researchers embarking on investigations of constructs for which no change-sensitive measures exist would be wise to allocate time for the development of change-sensitive measures. Although a discussion of the methodology involved in such work is beyond the scope of this chapter, at this writing there has fortunately been considerable recent work presenting information about the methodological paths that might be pursued by researchers interested in such measurement development (e.g. Molenaar et al., 2014; von Eye et al., 2015).

Techniques for analyzing change-sensitive data

Researchers must analyze scores derived from change-sensitive measures with statistical procedures suitable for identifying intraindividual change. Again, this seemingly obvious task is deceptively complex, given that conventional statistical procedures are based on mathematical theorems that typically regard such change as, at best, error variance. As we have noted, Molenaar (2014) explained that the standard approach to statistical analysis in the social and behavioral sciences is not focused on change but, instead, derived from the mathematical assumptions of the ergodic theorems regarding the constancy of phenomena across people and, critically, time. However, the study of development per se and, as well, the RDS-based PYD model, more specifically, regards individual differences in change (that is, idiographic intraindividual change) as ubiquitous. The presence of such changes violates the ideas of ergodicity. Accordingly, the use of the RDS metamodel as a frame for research requires a rejection of the use of data analytic tools predicated on the ergodic theorems (e.g. Molenaar and Nesselroade, 2015; Nesselroade and Molenaar, 2010).

Simply, developmental processes have time-varying means, variances, and/or time-varying sequential dependencies, and therefore the structure of interindividual variation at the population level is not equivalent to the structure of intraindividual variation at the level of individual (Molenaar, 2014). Developmental processes are therefore non-ergodic. As a consequence, to obtain valid information about developmental processes it is necessary to study intraindividual variation within single individuals. Molenaar and Nesselroade (2015; Nesselroade and Molenaar, 2010) have developed procedures to assess intraindividual variation within single individuals, such as the Idiographic Filter (IF), which involves use of the dynamic factor model at the level of the individual but then generates group-differential or nomothetic latent constructs to enable generalization across participants. Through use of procedures such as the IF, developmental scientists can both capture the non-ergodic nature of intraindividual change and, as well, produce generalities about groups that apply as well to the individuals within them.

To engage in such non-ergodic analyses, measures that capture nomothetic as well as group-differential instances of the Five Cs (or of other operationalizations of PYD) are necessary. There is much empirical support for Lerner and Lerner's original measurement of PYD which captured nomothetic generalities about OST program participants using 78 indicators of the Five Cs (Geldhof et al., 2013). That is, the Five Cs can be conveyed as latent constructs which, in turn, load on a second-order global PYD latent construct (Phelps et al., 2009). Other important research has captured group-differential (i.e. sport-specific) variation in the Five Cs. For example, using measures adapted from Lerner and colleagues (2015) to the sport context, Jones and colleagues (2011) found support for prosocial values and competence/confidence as latent indicators of PYD (see Vierimaa et al., 2012 for a review of sport-specific measures using the Cs framework). These global and context-specific measures of the Five Cs contribute uniquely to our understanding of PYD, reflecting the context-general or context-specific (e.g. sport settings) analysis involved in RDS conceptions of human development.

Conclusions

Given the complex and integrated system of individual ←→ context relations involved in sport participation, and the embodied, self-organizing, and self-creating nature of human development, one might ask, "How, then, should researchers proceed to study PYD in a sport context?" One answer is to use the "specificity principle" forwarded by Bornstein (2006). Recognizing the fundamental idiographic nature of human development but, as do Molenaar and Nesselroade (2015), understanding that individual variance coexists with group and nomothetic variation, the "specificity principle" involves researchers asking multi-part "what" questions when conducting programmatic research exploring the function, structure, and content of development as it may be influenced by sport participation.

Accordingly, to test RDS-based ideas about the ontogenetically changing structure of the individual ←→ sport context relationship that can lead to the development of PYD, the task for scholars is to undertake programs of research to gain insights into the following multi-part "what" question:

1. What individual-context relations in regard to PYD emerge; that are linked to
2. What antecedent and consequent adaptive developmental regulations; at
3. What points in development; for
4. What youth; living in
5. What contexts (e.g. neighborhoods, communities); and engaging in
6. What sport programs; and in
7. What other in-school and OST activities; across
8. What historical periods?

Gaining greater understanding of this complex, multi-part question will enable scientists to understand the content and course of adaptive developmental regulations linked to the development of PYD within and across sport (and other) contexts among and across different groups of youth and, as well, within any member of a sample of youth. In addition, these insights may provide the evidentiary base for applications of PYD research aimed at enhancing individual ←→ sport context relations among diverse individuals across diverse contexts.

Scientists interested in PYD have, in the repertoire of models and methods in their intellectual "tool box," the means to promote more active and positive engagement of youth in sport programs, especially given the fact that these programs constitute the major instance of youth OST activities (Sabo and Veliz, 2008; Vandell et al., 2015). As such, through enhancement of exchanges between the individual young person and the sport context, researchers and practitioners may afford diverse individuals the opportunities needed to maximize their immediate health and create a basis for thriving, in whatever way this construct is operationalized. In order to contribute significantly to promoting such outcomes, scholars need to identify the means with which to alter individual ←→ sport context relations in ways that enhance the probability that all individuals, no matter their individual characteristics or contextual circumstances, have greater opportunities for PYD through sport participation.

Acknowledgment

The preparation of this chapter was supported in part by grants from the John Templeton Foundation.

References

Agans, J. P., and Geldhof, G. J. (2012). Trajectories of participation in athletics and positive youth development: The influence of sport type. *Applied Developmental Science, 16*, 151–165.

Agans, J. P., Säfvenbom, R., Davis, J. L., Bowers, E. P., and Lerner, R. M. (2013). Positive movement experiences: Approaching the study of athletic participation, exercise, and leisure activity through relational developmental systems theory and the concept of embodiment. In R. M. Lerner and J. B. Benson, (Eds.), *Advances in Child Development and Behavior: Embodiment and Epigenesis: Theoretical and methodological issues in understanding the role of biology within the relational developmental system. Part B: Ontogenetic Dimensions.* (pp. 261–286). London: Elsevier.

Baltes, P. B., Reese, H. W., and Nesselroade, J. R. (1977). *Life-Span Developmental Psychology: Introduction to Research Methods.* Montcrey, CA: Brooks/Colc.

Benson, P. L., Scales, P. C., and Syvertsen, A. K. (2011). The contribution of the developmental assets framework to positive youth development theory and practice. *Advances in Child Development and Behavior, 41,* 195–228.

Bornstein, M. H. (2002). Parenting infants. In M. H. Bornstein (Ed.), *Handbook of Parenting: Vol. 1. Children and Parenting* (2nd ed., pp. 3–43). Mahwah, NJ: Erlbaum.

Bornstein, M. H. (2006). Parenting science and practice. In K. A. Renninger and I. E. Sigel (Eds.), *Handbook of Child Psychology, Vol. 4: Child Psychology in Practice* (6th ed., pp. 893–949). Editors-in-Chief: W. Damon, and R. M. Lerner. Hoboken, NJ: Wiley.

Bronfenbrenner, U. (2005). *Making Human Beings Human: Bioecological Perspectives on Human Development.* Thousand Oaks, CA: Sage.

Côté, J., Bruner, M., Erickson, K., Strachan, L., and Fraser-Thomas, J. (2010). Athlete development and coaching. In J. Lyle and C. Cushion (Eds.), *Sport Coaching: Professionalism and Practice* (pp. 63–79). Oxford: Elsevier.

Damon, W. (2008). *The Path to Purpose: Helping Our Children Find their Calling in Life*. New York: Simon and Schuster.

Elder, G. H. Jr., Shanahan, M. J., and Jennings, J. A. (2015). Human development in time and place. In M. H. Bornstein and T. Leventhal (Eds.), *Handbook of Child Psychology and Developmental Science, Volume 4: Ecological Settings and Processes* (7th ed., pp. 6–54). Editor-in-chief: R. M. Lerner. Hoboken, NJ: Wiley.

Geldhof, G. J., Bowers, E. P., Boyd, M. J., Mueller, M. K., Napolitano, C. M., Schmid, K. L., Learner, J. V., and Lerner, R. M. (2013). Creation of short and very short measures of the Five Cs of positive youth development. *Journal of Research on Adolescence, 24,* 163–176.

Ginsburg, K. R. (2011). *Building Resilience in Children and Teens* (2nd ed.). Elk Grove, IL: Academy of Pediatrics.

John, O. P., and Naumann, L. P. (2010). Surviving two critiques by Block? The resilient Big Five have emerged as the paradigm for personality trait psychology. *Psychological Inquiry, 21,* 44–49.

Jones, M. I., Dunn, J. G. H., Holt, N. L., and Sullivan, P. J. (2011). Exploring the '5Cs' of positive youth development in sport. *Journal of Sport Behavior, 34,* 250–267.

Lerner, R. M. (1984). *On the Nature of Human Plasticity*. New York: Cambridge University Press.

Lerner, R. M. (2002). *Concepts and Theories of Human Development* (3rd ed.). Mahwah, NJ: Lawrence Erlbaum Associates.

Lerner, R. M. (2004). *Liberty: Thriving and Civic Engagement among America's Youth*. New York: Sage.

Lerner, R. M., and Overton, W. F. (2008). Exemplifying the integrations of the relational developmental system: Synthesizing theory, research, and application to promote positive development and social justice. *Journal of Adolescent Research, 23,* 245–255.

Lerner, R. M., and Callina, K. S. (2014). The study of character development: Towards tests of a relational developmental systems model. *Human Development, 57,* 322–346.

Lerner, R. M., Schwartz, S. J., and Phelps, E. (2009). Problematics of time and timing in the longitudinal study of human development: Theoretical and methodological issues. *Human Development, 52,* 44–68.

Lerner, R. M., Lerner, J. V., Bowers, E., and Geldhof, G. J. (2015). Positive youth development and relational developmental systems. In W. F. Overton and P. C. Molenaar (Eds.), *Theory and Method. Volume 1 of the Handbook of Child Psychology and Developmental Science* (7th ed., pp. 607–651). Editor-in-chief: R. M. Lerner. Hoboken, NJ: Wiley.

Masten, A. S. (2014). Invited commentary: Resilience and positive youth development frameworks in developmental science. *Journal of Youth and Adolescence, 43,* 1018–1024.

McCrae, R. R., Costa, P. T., Ostendorf, F., Angleitner, A., Hrebickova, M., … Sanchez-Bernardos, M. L. (2000). Nature over nurture: Temperament, personality, and life span development. *Journal of Personality and Social Psychology, 78,* 173–186.

Molenaar, P. C. (2014). Dynamic models of biological pattern formation have surprising implications for understanding the epigenetics of development. *Research in Human Development, 11,* 50–62.

Molenaar, P. C. M., and Nesselroade, J. R. (2015). Systems methods for developmental research. In W. F. Overton and P. C. M. Molenaar (Eds.), *Handbook of Child Psychology and Developmental Science, Volume 1: Theory and Method* (7th ed., pp. 652–682). Editor-in-chief: R. M. Lerner. Hoboken, NJ: Wiley.

Molenaar, P. C. M., Lerner, R. M., and Newell, K. (2014). *Handbook of Developmental Systems Theory and Methodology.* New York: Guilford.

Mueller, M. K., Phelps, E., Bowers, E. P., Agans, J., Urban, J. B., and Lerner, R. M. (2011). Youth development program participation and intentional self-regulation skills: Contextual and individual bases of pathways to positive youth development. *Journal of Adolescence, 34,* 1115–1126.

Nesselroade, J. R. (1988). Some implications of the trait-state distinction for the study of development over the life span: The case of personality. In P. B. Baltes and D. L. Featherman (Eds.), *Life-Span Development and Behavior* (pp. 163–189). Hillsdale, NJ: Erlbaum.

Nesselroade, J. R., and Baltes, P. B. (1979). *Longitudinal Research in the Study of Behavior and Development.* New York: Academic Press.

Nesselroade, J. R., and Molenaar, P. C. M. (2010). Emphasizing intraindividual variability in the study of development over the life span. In W. F. Overton (Ed.), *The Handbook of Life-Span Development. Vol. 1: Cognition, Biology, Methods* (pp. 30–54). Editor-in-chief: R. M. Lerner. Hoboken, NJ: Wiley.

Nesselroade, J. R., Stigler, S. M., and Baltes, S. B. (1980). Regression toward the mean and the study of change. *Psychological Bulletin, 88,* 622–637.

Overton, W. F. (2015). Process and relational developmental systems. In W. F. Overton and P. C. M. Molenaar (Eds.), *Handbook of Child Psychology and Developmental Science, Volume 1: Theory and Method* (7th ed., pp. 9–62). Editor-in-chief: R. M. Lerner. Hoboken, NJ: Wiley.

Phelps, E., Zimmerman, S., Warren, A. E. A., Jelicic, H., von Eye, A., and Lerner, R. M. (2009). The structure and developmental course of positive youth development (PYD) in early adolescence: Implications for theory and practice. *Journal of Applied Developmental Psychology, 30,* 571–584.

Sabo, D., and Veliz, P. (2008). *Go Out and Play: Youth Sports in America.* East Meadow, NY: Women's Sports Foundation.

Vandell, D. L., Larson, R. W., Mahoney, J. L., and Watts, T. W. (2015). Children's organized activities. In M. H. Bornstein and T. Leventhal (Eds.), *Handbook of Child Psychology and Developmental Science, Volume 4: Ecological Settings and Processes* (7th ed., pp. 305–344). Editor-in-chief: R. M. Lerner. Hoboken, NJ: Wiley.

Vierimaa, M., Erickson, K., Côté, J., and Gilbert, W. (2012). Positive youth development: A measurement framework for sport. *International Journal of Sports Science and Coaching, 7,* 601–614.

von Eye, A., Bergman, L. R., and Hsieh, C. (2015). Person-oriented methodological approaches. In W. F. Overton and P. C. M. Molenaar (Eds.), *Handbook of Child Psychology and Developmental Science, Volume 1: Theory and Method* (7th ed., pp. 789–874). Editor-in-chief: R. M. Lerner. Hoboken, NJ: Wiley.

Zarrett, N., and Lerner, R. M. (2008). *Ways to Promote the Positive Development of Children and Youth.* Washington, DC: Child Trends.

Zarrett, N., Fay, K., Li, Y., Carrano, J., Phelps, E., and Lerner, R. M. (2009). More than child's play: Variable- and pattern-centered approaches to examining effects of sports participation on youth development. *Developmental Psychology, 45,* 368–382.

7

QUANTITATIVE ASSESSMENT OF POSITIVE YOUTH DEVELOPMENT IN SPORT

Dany J. MacDonald and Travis McIsaac

Research on the topic of positive youth development (PYD) has grown exponentially in recent years. Throughout its development, the field of PYD has relied on both qualitative and quantitative methods, creating a concept that is investigated from multiple perspectives. The purpose of this chapter is to evaluate the different quantitative measures available within the PYD field and make recommendations on future quantitative research on PYD.

When considering quantitative approaches in research, one of the first issues that need to be addressed is operationalization of the construct. Proper operationalization of the construct is critical to effectively define what is being investigated and can set the stage for enduring research within a given topic (Morling, 2015). However, when we take a close look at the PYD field since its inception in the early 1980s (see also Chapter 3), the construct of PYD has taken on many forms. For example, early work from Weiss and Bredemeier (1983) operationalized development of youth in sport as psychosocial development. Although psychosocial development is a broad concept, it effectively began to narrow the focus of personal development of youth in sport and other structured activities. This initial narrowing of the field led future researchers to define the topic in other ways. For example, PYD has been operationalized as initiative (Larson, 2000), life skills (Danish, 2002; Gould and Carson, 2008), responsibility (Hellison, 2003), developmental assets (Search Institute, 2004), and thriving (Lerner et al., 2003). Although similar in their intent to better understand how youth can positively develop through organized sport participation, these multiple operational definitions fail to create a unified field of research that is anchored upon an agreed definition.

In an attempt to further demonstrate the broad range of topics addressed under the umbrella of PYD, King et al. (2005) reviewed the literature to determine if a set of terms have emerged to capture the essence of PYD. By reviewing thirteen years' worth of published research across nine major journals, King et al. (2005) concluded that there was not a clear group of terms related to the PYD construct. In fact, they found that less than 10 percent of the work published alluded to one or more of the sixteen terms generated by their group of experts on the topic. Given the expansion of interest in the PYD field since the work published by King et al. (2005), it is reasonable to believe that the range of terms currently associated with PYD has continued to diversify over time.

One of the primary issues with using multiple definitions of a construct is that quantitative measures developed to assess the construct will vary based on the definition used. With the recent interest in PYD, a number of different measures aimed at capturing youth development in a quantitative manner have emerged. As can be seen by the various measures outlined in Table 7.1, PYD is measured based on the skills individuals believe should be experienced or gained from participation in organized sports. For example, the Development Assets Profile (Search Institute, 2004) categorizes positive development as 40 assets that youth should develop through participation in structured activities, while the Youth Experience Survey for Sport (YES-S; MacDonald et al., 2012) suggests that development is based on positive experiences in four domains (personal and social skills, initiative, goal setting, and cognitive skills) and a lack of negative experiences in organized sport. These examples demonstrate that the lack of a singular operational definition for PYD has resulted in multiple measures being developed to assess the same construct from different angles. While having multiple measures to capture the same construct may seem beneficial for capturing a wide range of experiences, it does lead to difficulties in explaining the primary focus of the field. This is because different measures will assess the different operational definitions attached to each measure. This can become problematic if some definitions are not directly related to the construct. As mentioned above, and seen in Table 7.1, multiple definitions of PYD have been suggested and there is currently no overarching accepted definition of PYD.

A recent attempt to streamline the process of assessing PYD in sport was proposed by Vierimaa et al. (2012) who proposed a toolkit to assess the construct. Grounded in the Cs of positive development, they suggested a suite of existing measures to assess the Four Cs of positive development: competence, confidence, connection, and character. Suggesting such a toolkit does provide a great alternative to measuring PYD in sport by using existing measures, but is predicated on the assumption that the Cs of PYD represent the conceptualization of the construct. As discussed throughout this chapter, the current conceptualization of PYD is broader than the Cs literature.

TABLE 7.1 Description of quantitative measures currently proposed to measure PYD in sport along with purpose, development and validation, and summary of findings

Measure	Purpose	Development and validation	Summary of findings
Developmental Assets Profile (DAP; Search Institute, 2004) Measures internal and external assets across eight domains:	Measure individual personal development defined as developmental assets	Good reliability estimates (0.59–0.87) for the eight asset categories	Focuses exclusively on assets
	Will provide quantitative scores for each of the asset categories		Cannot be used to determine the presence or absence of each of the 40 assets
● Support			Designed to be sensitive to changes in reported assets over time
● Empowerment			Suited to research and program evaluation
● Boundaries and expectations			
● Constructive use of time			Quick, simple, valid, reliable self-report tool
● Commitment to learning			Documents and quantifies youths' reports of the type of assets working in their lives
● Positive values			
● Social competencies			Useful in schools, mental health and family service practices, youth programs
● Positive identity			
Life Skills Transfer Survey (LSTS; Weiss et al., 2014) Measure of perceived life skills transfer skills transfer over time	Evaluation of *The First Tee* life skills program in teaching life skills transfer over time	Literature review and interviews led to 255 initial items in pool	LSTS moderately correlated with YES 2.0 subscales (0.49–0.62)
Has 50 items across eight life skills:	Evaluate impact of PYD programs in teaching social competencies that can be applied to other life domains	Expert panel feedback cut total items to 90	All eight LSTS subscales have good internal consistency reliability (α = 0.82–0.93)
● Meeting and greeting		Pilot studies—50 items across eleven life skills	
● Managing emotions	Provide a valid and reliable life skills transfer measure		Acceptable invariance for factor patterns, loadings, and variances/covariances across time (one year)
● Goal setting		CFA showed evidence of good model fit with eight domains	
● Resolving conflicts			
● Making healthy choices		Convergent validity of LSTS scores with YES 2.0 scores	
● Appreciating diversity			
● Getting help from others			
● Helping others			

TABLE 7.1 continued

Measure	Purpose	Development and validation	Summary of findings
Prosocial and Antisocial Behavior in Sport Scale (PABSS; Kavussanu and Boardley, 2009; Kavussanu et al., 2013)	Measure a wide range of prosocial and antisocial behaviors in team sport	Preliminary scale development included removal of redundant items, from 68 to 43 items	Antisocial behavior toward teammates positively related to prosocial behavior towards opponents (r = 0.30) and negatively related to prosocial behavior toward teammates (r = -0.18)
Twenty items across four subscales:	Enable research on social behavior in different sports	Scale refinement included examination of items by professionals which resulted in 34 items being retained	Low correlations between the four behavior subscales (r = 0.04–0.46) show discriminant validity between subscales
● Prosocial behavior toward teammates	Examine social–moral conduct occurring in sport setting	Inconsistent loadings across four subscales resulted in removal of items which left a total of twenty items retained	Two antisocial behaviors positively associated with aggression measures of anger, acceptance of cheating and gamesmanship, moral disengagement, and ego orientation which results in good concurrent validity
● Prosocial behavior toward opponents		Four-factor, twenty-item model provides very good fit	Two prosocial behavior subscales positively linked to social affiliation and social recognition, prosocial opponent behavior positively linked to social status
● Antisocial behavior toward teammates		The four subscales show good internal consistency scores (α = 0.74–0.87)	Varying strength of association between prosocial behavior subscales and social affiliation
● Antisocial behavior toward opponents			

Sportsmanship Coaching Behaviors Scale (SCBS; Bolter and Weiss, 2012)			
Assesses five factors	Assess athletes' perception of coaches' behaviors that promote or deter sportsmanlike behaviors	Confirmatory factor analysis with eight initial factors showed acceptable fit, but high correlations between subscales	Coaching behaviors that promote good sportsmanship positively related to prosocial behavior and negatively related to antisocial behavior toward teammates/opponents
Positive subscales:			
● Models good sportsmanship	Assess coaches' influence in promoting athletes' sportsmanship outcomes	Subsequent exploratory factor analysis with six-factor model showed better fit	Coaching behavior that promotes poor sportsmanship positively related to antisocial behavior, negatively related to prosocial behavior
● Reinforces good sportsmanship			
● Teaches good sportsmanship		Confirmatory factor analysis with six-factor model showed good fit, but high correlation between subscales remained	
● Punishes poor sportsmanship			
		One subscale deleted to create a five-factor model which showed good fit	
Negative subscale:			
● Prioritizes winning		Equivalence in factor patterns, loadings, and variances—factorial invariance by gender	

TABLE 7.1 continued

Measure	Purpose	Development and validation	Summary of findings
Sport Friendship Quality Scale (SFQS; Weiss and Smith, 1999) Assesses six friendship dimensions with 22 items: • Self-esteem enhancement and supportiveness • Loyalty and intimacy • Things in common • Companionship and pleasant play • Conflict resolution • Conflict	Examine role of peers in psychosocial development through sport	Friendship Quality Questionnaire (FQQ)—40 items across six dimensions—was refined to the SFQS Six factors composing a higher order factor showed good fit and was retained as final model Acceptable internal consistency reliability for the six subscales ($\alpha = 0.73$–0.92)	Correlations between positive friendship quality dimensions and an existing measure of perceived close friendship
Youth Experience Survey 2.0 (YES 2.0; Hansen and Larson, 2005) Scale is a 70-item self-report survey that explores positive and negative experiences in different organized activities Scale measures the experiences across the seven (six positive, one negative) following domains: • Identity experiences • Initiative experiences • Basic skills • Positive peer relationships • Adult network and social capital • Teamwork and social skills • Negative experiences	Assess youths' experiences across different types of structured activities: • Performance and fine arts • Academic clubs • Community organizations • Sports • Service groups • Faith-based groups	Support for reliability and convergent, congruent validity of the scale Factor structure with 70 items not confirmed Follow-up confirmatory factor analysis was unable to confirm the proposed factor structure	Scale has been used to investigate experiences of youth in different activities and has shown differences across settings Has shown that sport participants have different experiences than individuals in other organized settings The scale is very flexible to measure experiences in multiple domains but may not be ideal for capturing context-specific (i.e. sport only) experiences

Youth Experience Survey for Sport (YES-S; MacDonald et al., 2012) Scale is a 37-item self-report survey that explores positive and negative experiences in different organized activities Scale measures experiences across five (four positive, one negative) domains: • Personal and social skills • Initiative • Cognitive skills • Goal setting • Negative experiences	Measure positive and negative developmental experiences for youth in the sport domain	Initially developed to confirm factor structure of YES 2.0 CFA did not support proposed factor structure which led to an exploratory factor analysis to examine modifications Exploratory analysis retained factors with loadings above 0.32 and removed cross-loadings with values greater than 0.30 Resulted in 33 items being removed due to low factor loadings or high cross-loadings Revised version of YES 2.0, containing 37 items across five factors which was named the YES-S Good reliability coefficients across subscales of the instrument (α = 0.92, 0.94, 0.85, 0.82, 0.82, respectively)	Capable of measuring positive and negative developmental experiences within the youth sport domain Mainly used to predict which sport experiences are associated with positive or negative sport experiences

TABLE 7.1 continued

Measure	Purpose	Development and validation	Summary of findings
Short Form YES-S (Sullivan et al., 2015) Contains 22 items across five factors: • Personal and social skills • Initiative • Cognitive skills • Goal setting • Negative experiences	Measure developmental experiences specific to the sport context	Examined the factor structure of the YES-S utilizing a confirmatory factor analysis on an independent sample of athletes Five-factor model was confirmed by analysis and resulted in good model fit Follow-up analysis investigated modifications to the scale Follow-up model, which has 22 items across the five domains, provided excellent fit Domains also have excellent reliability with Cronbach alpha scores ranging between 0.80 and 0.93	Better model fit than original YES-S Analysis of invariance showed no differences in responses between males and females, which suggest that the scale is acceptable for both sexes Scale has currently not been used in additional studies
Youth Sport Values Questionnaire (YSVQ; Lee et al., 2000) Scale is a twenty-item measure that measures three domains: • Enjoyment • Personal achievement • Winning	Identify the value systems that guide behavior of adolescent athletes in sport Study moral attitudes and behavior in sport Identify value priorities of young athletes	Constructed through a combination of qualitative and quantitative techniques	Results: enjoyment has highest priority for youth, followed by personal achievement, and winning Similar rankings were obtained with different samples from a wider range of age, sports, and level of performance Males had higher mean ratings than females As individuals age, a significant decreasing linear trend is observed across age groups while results produce increasing linear trend across level of performance

Five Cs Measurement of PYD (Bowers et al. 2010; Jones et al., 2011) Scale measures the following five outcomes: • Competence • Confidence • Connection • Character • Caring	Assess youths' possession of five important developmental outcomes These five outcomes are believed to lead to the emergence of the 6th C: Contribution	Initial confirmatory factor analysis provided inadequate fit to the data Model modifications and follow-up confirmatory analysis showed good model fit Evidence of both convergent and discriminant validity, internal consistency of five first-order factors	PYD can be measured across assessment occasions which enables study of development Early work establishes validity of measure across early adolescence Later studies extend validity and utility to older range of adolescents
Four Cs Measurement of PYD (Vierimaa et al., 2012) Scale measures the following four outcomes: • Competence • Confidence • Connection • Character	Assess youths' possession of four important developmental outcomes gained through the sport environment	Measures the four outcomes using previously validated instruments: Sport Competence Inventory (SCI; Causgrove-Dunn et al., 2007) Self-Confidence subscale of revised Competitive State Anxiety Inventory (CSAI-2R; Cox et al., 2003) Coach–Athlete Relationship Questionnaire (CART-Q; Jowett and Ntoumanis, 2004) Peer Connection Inventory (PCI; Coie and Dodge, 1983) Prosocial and Antisocial Behavior in Sport Scale (PABSS; Kavussanu and Boardley, 2009; Kavussanu et al., 2013)	Measurement of 4 Cs proposed as a toolkit to supplement existing measures of PYD

Instruments currently available to measure PYD

Given the increased research attention devoted to the study of PYD, along with the different measures developed to assess the construct, it is useful for researchers and practitioners to be aware of the different tools available. A closer look at Table 7.1 not only shows that definitions vary by measure, but also that the process of personal development is different across the measures. More specifically, existing PYD measures may be operationalized in two broader categories of *experiences* and *outcomes*. Experiences could be explained as situations arising in the sport setting that will *facilitate* positive development while outcomes can be conceived of as skills that *result* from structured sport participation. For example, the YES-S (MacDonald et al., 2012) assesses athletes' sport experience by asking if the participants got to know people in the community as a result of their sport participation. By extension, it is expected that the positive experience of meeting new people in the community will lead to positive development.

Alternatively, the Life Skills Transfer Survey (Weiss et al., 2014) contends that if individuals have a positive experience in sport, they will learn outcomes that are transferable to other aspects of life. The Life Skills Transfer Survey therefore assesses outcomes of sport participation in the following eight domains: meeting and greeting, managing emotions, goal setting, resolving conflict, making healthy choices, appreciating diversity, getting help from others, and helping others. These can be considered outcomes of youth sport if they are explicitly taught in the sport domain and it is reinforced how they can be applied to other life domains (i.e., school). These examples, along with the different measures outlined in Table 7.1, show how the different PYD measures are assessing the construct from different perspectives.

Based on the information discussed above, researchers interested in PYD through sport should take note of the aim or purpose of different measures and whether they assess experiences or outcomes. From the measures described in Table 7.1, we determined that seven of the eleven measures (i.e., Prosocial and Antisocial Behavior in Sport Scale: Kavussanu and Boardley, 2009; Kavussanu et al. 2013; Sportsmanship Coaching Behaviors Scale: Bolter and Weiss, 2012; Sport Friendship Quality Scale: Weiss and Smith, 1999; Youth Experience Survey 2.0: Hansen and Larson, 2005; Youth Experience Survey for Sport: MacDonald et al., 2012; Short Form YES-S: Sullivan et al., 2015; Youth Sport Value Questionnaire: Lee et al., 2000) are currently aimed at measuring experiences, while the remaining four (i.e. Developmental Assets Profile: Search Institute, 2004; Life Skills Transfer Survey: Weiss et al., 2014; Five Cs: Bowers et al., 2010; Jones et al., 2011; Four Cs: Vierimaa et al., 2012) target outcomes. Based on the combination of their research focus (experience versus outcome) and operational definition of the construct, researchers have to select a measure to assess the specific construct they wish to study.

Although the selection process of an instrument is not equivocal and will depend on factors mentioned above, recommendations can be made to assist researchers. For example, Gould and Carson (2008) recommended the use of the Youth Experience Survey (YES) to assess experiences. Given the lack of psychometric support for use of the YES in sport domains outlined in recent research, it would appear that the newly developed YES-S (MacDonald et al., 2012) and Short Form YES-S (Sullivan et al., 2015) may be better suited to study experiences in the sport domain. The toolkit outlined by Vierimaa et al. (2012) provides researchers with validated instruments to assess outcomes. Additionally, the Life Skills Transfer Survey (Weiss et al., 2014) shows promising psychometric properties that render it useful in measuring skills transfer over time into other domains. Although there is no conclusive best measure to measure PYD, a number of instruments appear to have the ability to do so effectively and should be selected depending on the specific aspect of PYD researchers intend to study.

To date, quantitative research on PYD has used a combination of the different measures to understand how youth develop positively through sport. From the experience angle, multiple studies have predicted positive experiences in the sport context. For example, MacDonald et al. (2011), in their study of 637 young athletes aged nine to nineteen, found that aspects of enjoyment and a task-oriented motivational climate were positively associated with positive experiences as measured by the YES-S. Conversely, research related to outcomes of sport participation (i.e. Lerner et al., 2005; Strachan et al., 2009) has pointed to aspects of the sport context being related to increased positive outcomes and decreased negative outcomes. For example, Strachan et al. (2009) sampled 123 athletes aged twelve to sixteen, and used their scores on the DAP (Search Institute, 2004) to predict rates of burnout and enjoyment in sport. Their analyses showed that outcomes of the DAP were useful in reducing occurrences of burnout while increasing athlete enjoyment.

Above and beyond the issues raised above—operationalization, experiences versus outcomes—the majority of existing quantitative studies have examined relationships (or correlations) between organized sport and PYD. One issue that seems to be missing from our current understanding of these relationships is the *process* by which PYD occurs. In order to understand the process, researchers must ask themselves questions such as, "How does PYD happen within the organized sport environment?" This is a very difficult question to answer, but researchers will need to tackle this question to truly understand the process of PYD. This will require researchers to devise novel ways of assessing the sport environment and will likely encompass multiple methods (i.e. quantitative and qualitative). Although this area of research would be a fruitful undertaking, we are not aware of any current measures designed to assess PYD processes. The field would greatly benefit from attention being devoted to understanding the process and would complement the research currently available within the topic of PYD through sport.

Conclusion

The information presented in this chapter reviews and evaluates the different measures utilized in the PYD field and provides thoughts regarding the current state of quantitative research within this field. More specifically, we suggested that the field would benefit from an accepted operational definition for PYD. Based on the information presented, it is clear that quantitative assessments of PYD in sport have flourished and will continue to develop in the future. However, the field must continue to develop novel ways of assessing PYD through sport in order to move beyond summarizing relationships between regular participation in organized youth sport and positive outcomes and experiences. This can be achieved by investigating the *process* by which PYD develops within organized sport.

Almost exclusively, the conclusions drawn from the quantitative findings are correlational in nature and do not permit cause and effect conclusions (Morling, 2015). In order to draw such conclusions, randomized controlled trials would be needed, which would be achieved by manipulating the environment and experiences of sport participants. For example, sport participants from different environments could be randomly selected and assigned to different conditions that actively incorporate PYD into their sport setting. This could follow a design where coaches are asked to follow a coach education program aimed at incorporating PYD into their sport environment (for an example, see www.projectscore.ca) and investigate if youth who participate in environments that promote PYD have better developmental outcomes than athletes who do not. However, the challenge with this design is that it would need to control the influence of other variables (i.e. other setting) and would require that participants are followed longitudinally to understand the long-term impact of a positive environment. Given that part of the goal of PYD is to provide them with skills that transcend sport, it would be necessary to expand the focus over time and outside of the sport setting. Not only does such a study require a great deal of time and resources, but it also raises issues from practical and ethical standpoints. When we consider the realities of youth sport participation and development, we need to question whether it would be possible to provide certain experiences to some athletes but not others who play on the same or different team. Alternatively, is it ethical to deny certain athletes the best possible sport experiences if we know that such experiences can positively shape their development? These questions need to be seriously considered by researchers when devising quantitative methods for studying PYD in sport.

As mentioned, one of the main challenges associated with the quantitative assessment of PYD in sport is the multiple definitions and instruments constructed to investigate the concept. We acknowledge that PYD is broad in nature; however, we believe that the field would benefit from a standard, unified operationalization of PYD. Such a definition would help guide future research and provide direction for new scholars entering the field. Following the development of an accepted PYD definition, the field could move forward and develop a psychometrically valid instrument aimed at assessing the construct.

Another area worthy of future research is in the process by which PYD occurs. There is currently a scarcity of research aimed at uncovering these processes, making this area of research both timely and important. By uncovering the processes through which PYD occurs and combining them with our current understanding of how to promote positive outcomes, the field will be better equipped to positively impact the development of youth sport participants.

References

Bolter, N., and Weiss, M. (2012). Coaching behaviors and adolescent athletes' sportspersonship outcomes: Further validation of the Sportsmanship Coaching Behaviors Scale (SCBS). *Sport, Exercise, and Performance Psychology, 2*, 32–47.

Bowers, E., Li, Y., Kiely, M., Brittian, A., Lerner, J., and Lerner, R. (2010). The Five Cs model of positive youth development: A longitudinal analysis of confirmatory factor structure and measurement invariance. *Journal of Youth and Adolescence, 39*, 720–735.

Causgrove-Dunn, J., Dunn, J., and Bayduza, A. (2007). Perceived athletic competence, sociometric status, and loneliness in elementary school children. *Journal of Sport Behavior, 30*, 249–269.

Coie, J., and Dodge, K. (1983). Continuities and changes in children's social status: A five-year longitudinal study. *Merrill-Palmer Quarterly, 29*, 261–282.

Cox, R., Martens, M., and Russell, W. (2003). Measuring anxiety in athletics: The revised Competitive State Anxiety Inventory-2. *Journal of Sport and Exercise Psychology, 25*, 519–533.

Danish, S. J. (2002). Teaching life skills through sport. In M. Gatz, M. Gessner, and M. Ball-Rokeach (Eds.), *Paradoxes of Youth and Youth Sport* (pp. 49–60). Albany, NY: State University of New York Press.

Gould, D., and Carson, S. (2008). Life skill development through sport: Current status and future directions. *International Review of Sport and Exercise Psychology, 1*, 58–78.

Hansen, D., and Larson, R. (2005). *The Youth Experience Survey 2.0: Instrument Revisions and Validity Testing*. Unpublished manuscript, University of Illinois at Urbana-Campaign.

Hellison, D. (2003). *Teaching Responsibility through Physical Activity*. Champaign, IL: Human Kinetics.

Jones, M. I., Dunn, J. G. H., Holt, N. L., Sullivan, P. J., and Bloom, G. A. (2011). Exploring the '5Cs' of positive youth development in sport. *Journal of Sport Behavior, 34*, 250–267.

Jowett, S., and Ntoumanis, N. (2004). The Coach-Athlete Relationship Questionnaire (CART-Q): Development and initial validation. *Scandinavian Journal of Medicine and Science in Sports, 14*, 245–257.

Kavussanu, M., and Boardley, I. (2009). The prosocial and antisocial behavior in sport scale. *Journal of Sport and Exercise Psychology, 31*, 97–117.

Kavussanu, M., Stanger, N., and Boardley, I. (2013). The prosocial and antisocial behaviour in sport scale: Further evidence for construct validity and reliability. *Journal of Sports Sciences, 31*, 1208–1221.

King, P. E., Schultz, W., Mueller, R. A., Dowling, E. M., Osborne, P., Dickerson, E., and Lerner, R. M. (2005). Positive youth development: Is there a nomological network of concepts used in the adolescent development literature? *Applied Developmental Science, 9*, 216–228.

Larson, R. W. (2000). Toward a psychology of positive youth development. *American Psychologist, 55*, 170–183.

Lee, M., Whitehead, J., and Balchin, N. (2000). The measurement of values in youth sport: Development of the youth sport values questionnaire. *Journal of Sport and Exercise Psychology, 22*, 307–326.

Lerner, R. M., Dowling, E. M., and Anderson, P. M. (2003). Positive youth development: Thriving as a basis of personhood and civil society. *Applied Developmental Science, 7,* 172–180.

Lerner, R., Lerner, J., Almerigi, J., Theokas, C., Phelps, E., Gestdottir, S., and von Eye, A. (2005). Positive youth development, participation in community youth development programs, and community contributions of fifth grade adolescents: Findings from the first wave of the 4-H study of positive youth development. *Journal of Early Adolescence, 25,* 17–71.

MacDonald, D. J., Côté, J., Eys, M., and Deakin, J. (2011). The role of enjoyment and motivational climate in relation to the personal development of team sport athletes. *The Sport Psychologist, 25,* 32–46.

MacDonald, D. J., Côté, J., Eys, M., and Deakin, J. (2012). Psychometric properties of the youth experience survey with young athletes. *Psychology of Sport and Exercise, 13,* 332–340.

Morling, B. (2015). *Research Methods in Psychology* (2nd ed). New York: W.W. Norton and Company Inc.

Search Institute. (2004). *Developmental Assets Profile Preliminary Use Manual.* Minneapolis, MN: Search Institute.

Strachan, L., Côté, J., and Deakin, J. (2009). An evaluation of personal and contextual factors in competitive youth sport. *Journal of Applied Sport Psychology, 21,* 340–355.

Sullivan, P. J., LaForge-MacKenzie, K., and Marini, M. (2015). Confirmatory factor analysis of the Youth Experience Survey for Sport (YES-S). *Open Journal of Statistics, 5,* 421–429.

Vierimaa, M., Erickson, K., Côté, J., and Gilbert, W. (2012). Positive youth development: A measurement framework for sport. *International Journal of Sports Science and Coaching, 7,* 601–614.

Weiss, M. R., and Bredemeier, B. J. (1983). Developmental sport psychology: A theoretical perspective for studying children in sport. *Journal of Sport Psychology, 5,* 216–230.

Weiss, M., and Smith, A. (1999). Quality of youth sport friendships: Measurement development and validation. *Journal of Sport and Exercise Psychology, 21,* 145–166.

Weiss, M., Bolter, N., and Kipp, L. (2014). Assessing impact of physical activity-based youth development programs: Validation of the life skills transfer survey (LSTS). *Research Quarterly for Exercise and Sport, 85,* 263–278.

8

DEFINING AND MEASURING THE 'DEVELOPMENT' IN SPORT-FOR-DEVELOPMENT PROGRAMS

Fred Coalter

Many researchers have commented on the vagueness and lack of theoretical specificity which characterize sport-for-development policy, practice and research (e.g. Black, 2010; Coalter, 2013; Kruse, 2006). With regard to the term 'development', Black (2010) referred to 'the inherently contentious and contested character of this ubiquitous concept' (p. 122). Hartmann and Kwauk (2011) described it as 'deeply complicated and poly-vocal' (p. 286) and Kruse (2006) referred to the term 'development' as intriguingly vague and open for several interpretations.

Coalter (2013) argued that sport for development rhetoric is characterized by major unexamined issues relating to displacement of scope (Wagner, 1964). This refers to the process of wrongly generalizing micro-level effects (e.g. the possible impact on individuals of participation in a sport-for-development program) to the meso or macro levels. Wagner (1964) suggested that the problem of differentiated scope is inherent in the wide range of sociological subject matter itself and this has clear analogies with the sport-for-development field, which has grown without much 'critical and theoretically-informed reflection' (Black, 2010, p. 122). While a degree of studied vagueness might be advantageous for partnership and alliance building – meaning all things to all potential funders – it produces 'inflated promises [with] goals lacking the clarity and intellectual coherence that evaluation criteria should have' (Weiss, 1993, p. 96).

Within this context the multi-national research drawn on for this chapter (Coalter and Taylor, 2010; Coalter, 2013) was commissioned by UK Sport and Comic Relief to explore the hypothesis that sport contributes to the 'personal development and well-being' of disadvantaged children. The data were collected via a series of before and after interviews and self-administered surveys of participants in six *sports plus* programs (i.e. they were sports-based, but had a number of additional activities and workshops which addressed wider issues such as gender equality, drug use and HIV/AIDS). The organizations were:

- *The Kids' League.* An organization working with internally displaced young people in northern Uganda, providing mixed-sex, open-access six- to seven-week football/netball programs for individuals aged twelve years and older.
- *Praajak.* A social development agency based in Kolkata (India) working with 'railway children' – young people who run away from home to work on the railways.
- *Magic Bus.* An organization working in the slums of Mumbai (India), providing a range of age-related sports-based programs.
- *Elimu, Michezo na Mazoezi (EMIMA)* in Dar es Salaam (Tanzania). An organization providing after-school and weekend programs using sport and other activities to develop life skills and raise awareness of HIV and AIDS.
- *Kamwokya Christian Caring Community (KCCC).* A Kampala faith and community-based NGO dealing with issues of HIV and AIDS.

Because of limitations of space I cannot present the findings from all five projects. However, as there were common tendencies I will illustrate the key findings with data from The Kids' League. A much fuller analysis can be found in Coalter (2013) and Coalter and Taylor (2010).

Perceived self-efficacy

Attempts to operationalize 'personal development' led us to the concept of perceived self-efficacy as there are strong arguments for regarding this as a core component of any definition of personal development. For example, Pajares (2002, p.1) argued that:

> Self-efficacy beliefs touch virtually every aspect of people's lives – whether they think productively, self-debilitating, pessimistically or optimistically; how well they motivate themselves and persevere in the face of adversities; their vulnerability to stress and depression, and the life choices they make.

Graham and Weiner (1996) further argued that self-efficacy beliefs have proven to be a more consistent predictor of behavioral outcomes than other motivational constructs. Bandura (1994) placed perceived self-efficacy at the center of social learning theory which, often subconsciously, informs the practice of sport-for-development projects and is a central component of the transtheoretical model of behavior change (Prochaska and Velicer, 1997). Further, while acknowledging the possibility of cultural differences in the relevance or meaning of this construct, Luszczynska et al. (2005) conclude that 'general self-efficacy appears to be a universal construct that yields meaningful relations with other psychological constructs such as self-regulation, goal intentions and outcome expectancies' (p. 439).

Consequently, the issue of perceived self-efficacy is at the center of concerns with (personal) development and is implicit, although rarely precisely defined or measured, in sport-development programs. Further, the development of perceived self-efficacy is central to the hierarchical competence-based model of self-esteem (Sonstroem and Morgan, 1989; Harter, 1999). For example, Shephard (1997) suggests that it is possible that an increased sense of self-efficacy might be developed via increased motor skills and a sense of achievement in physical activity or sport. This, in turn, *might* lead to increased self-esteem, if the achievement is valued in terms of self-definition – an important sufficient condition ignored in generalized rhetoric. Further, in terms of notions of (personal) 'development', the presumption is that this combination of strengthened perceived self-efficacy and improved self-esteem might encourage and enable improved learning – some approaches to HIV and AIDS education view this combination as central to behavior change.

How is perceived self-efficacy developed?

Bandura (1994) states that 'the most effective way of creating a strong sense of self-efficacy is through mastery experiences' (p. 2). In this regard the nature and practice of sport would seem to provide a potentially effective medium for the development of certain self-efficacy beliefs. The emphasis on practice, skill development, mastery and dealing with, and learning from, defeat all seem to be important potential contributors to the development of perceived self-efficacy. However, such a perspective emphasizes the need to understand the context in which this occurs and the processes and experiences involved. It is essential to remember that the nature and extent of any impact on individual participants will depend on a number of contextual factors – the nature of the individuals, the nature of activities, social relationships and the nature of individuals' experience of, and reaction to, programs.

This requires us to abandon simple de-contextualized and un-theorized notions of 'sport' – positive impacts and outcomes are only a *possibility* and a linear relationship between the complex processes of participation and positive impacts cannot be assumed (Svoboda, 1994; Patriksson, 1995). For example, Biddle (2006) emphasizes the importance of the 'social climate' of sport-for-development programs. He argues that the enhancement of perceived self-efficacy is most likely to be achieved in programs that seek to develop intrinsic motivational approaches based on a task-oriented, mastery orientation. In such a context participants' skills are matched with the challenges they face, cooperative learning is encouraged, clear experiences of success are provided and their effort is supported with positive encouragement and affirmation. Conversely, for many young people a social climate based on performance and competition, in which there is constant comparison with others, punishment for mistakes and unequal recognition ('good' and 'bad' players), is unlikely to be inclusive, or to support the development of perceived self-efficacy.

In addition to issues relating to social climate, social cognitive theory proposes that learning occurs via observation and imitation. This is most likely to occur when: (a) there is a lack of social distance and a perceived similarity between the teacher and the learner; (b) there is a self-efficacy expectation on the part of the learner (i.e. she/he is capable of developing the skill/completing the task; this is strengthened by perceived similarities with the teacher – 'if she can do it then so can I' – what Bandura (1994) refers to as 'vicarious experience'); and (c) there is an outcome expectancy that the performance of the activity will have desirable outcomes, which can be affirmed and reinforced by the social climate of the program. Many of these elements are inherent in the community-based, local peer-leader approach adopted by many sport-for-development programs.

Measuring perceived self-efficacy

Perceived self-efficacy is often context- and/or activity-specific and Bandura (1986) states that 'measures of self-precept must be tailored to the domain of psychological functioning being explored' (p. 396). Consequently, the development of sporting self-efficacy, or a sense of efficacy within the supportive environment of a sport-for-development program, may not go 'beyond the touchline' i.e. be transferred to a wider sense of self-efficacy when the individual confronts other tasks or difficulties.

Partly to address this issue we used a generic measure to explore issues of more general self-efficacy beliefs (Coalter, 2013; Coalter and Taylor, 2010). We acknowledge the possible imprecision of such a measure – it is unlikely that respondents will encounter all tasks and situations with the same degree of perceived self-efficacy. However, the use of a sports-specific measure would have raised concerns about its generalizability to wider contexts and would have been a very limited measure of 'development'. Further, because people's motivations and actions are based largely on what they believe, such general self-evaluations can be regarded as being broadly indicative of how they assess their ability to address general issues in their lives. Despite its limitations, we think that this approach has theoretical value because little research in sport-for-development has sought to address such key issues – this is at least a first step, providing a basis for a more theoretically informed debate.

In the research drawn on here (Coalter and Taylor, 2010), perceived self-efficacy was measured using a scale developed by Sherer et al. (1982) and modified by Bosscher and Smit (1998). This is a twelve-item Likert scale based on a series of positive and negative statements, with respondents asked to strongly agree/strongly disagree. The statements were each allocated a score of 0–3 for negative statements and 3–0 for positive statements, with an overall score produced for each respondent in a before and after approach, with participants aged 14 plus (see Appendix).

The first function of the before data was to assess the environmental determinist, deficit model which implicitly underpins sport-for-development programs – deprived communities produce deficient people who can be 'developed' through sport. Such assumptions are required rationales for funding applications, although the evidence suggests that little systematic analysis of prior values, attitudes and behavior is undertaken. The first important finding is that the various groups were not homogeneous and were certainly not uniformly deficient. The distribution of scores formed a broad bell-shaped curve – some had high perceived self-efficacy, some low and most were in the middle. While this should not be surprising, it was contrary to an implicit assumption in universalizing sport-for-development rhetoric and at least one provider expressed surprise at the findings.

Also given the diversity of populations, cultures and contexts it is not surprising that there were slight variations in average scores between the three samples. The Kids' League (the largest sample) had the highest average score (22), followed by the all-female EMIMA (21.6) and then Magic Bus (20). In addition to having lower perceived self-efficacy scores, both Indian projects had lower self-esteem scores than the East African respondents. It is not possible to be definitive about the reasons for these differences. They might indicate the distinct populations from which the India projects recruited – Magic Bus used social workers to gain access to slums and Prajaak recruited runaway children who begged on railways, whereas the East African programs were open access and largely self-selecting. Alternatively, this might reflect cultural differences: less individualistic cultures and a modesty and humility that produce rather self-effacing assessments within the Indian samples.

Overall there was little difference in the distribution of values, with each group containing the same degree of diversity. It could be argued that such data indicate that, in terms of their self-perceptions, these were relatively ordinary young people who live in exceptionally deprived circumstances. Such data raise questions about a 'blame the victim' deficit model which ignores structures and seeks to deal with long-standing broad-gauge problems via a limited focus on behavioral change (Weiss, 1993). There is a paradoxical danger of well-meaning projects being based on negative stereotypes of young people, with the attendant danger of misconceived provision and inappropriate performance indicators.

Program impacts: beyond averages

In most approaches to monitoring and evaluation the increased average scores recorded in two out of three projects might be presented as an indication of the success of the program and affirmation of the simple rhetoric of sports evangelism – sport works. This could even be supported by selective individual testimony to illustrate how participation had increased selected participants' confidence. However, the use of averages disguises a more complex and important set of effects, which illustrate the importance of understanding mechanisms, processes, participant experiences and reactions. Just as the young people could not be regarded as uniformly deficient, the impact of participation in the program was varied and not uni-directional. Adjustments included both increases and *decreases* in self-evaluations – a more complex set of impacts than is assumed in sport-for-development rhetoric.

Figure 8.1 (and the guide to reading the figure) illustrates the nature and degree of changes – each point on the graph represents an individual respondent and the *degree to which their self-evaluation changed* between the two survey points. The data are statistically significant, with only 1 chance in a 1000 that this could have

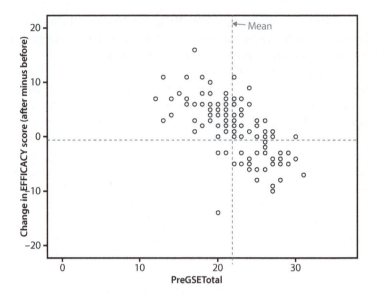

Correlation coefficient $r_s = -.660$, p = .000

Guide to reading Figure 8.1

Before score *below* average and then increased	Before score *above* average and then increased
Before score *below* average and then decreased	Before score *above* average and then decreased

FIGURE 8.1 Kids' League: degree of change in perceived self-efficacy

happened by chance. While all changes are worth noting, the top left and bottom right quadrants could be regarded as the most interesting. The top left quadrant represents a key claim of sport-for-development – that participation in programs increases participants' initially weak perceived self-efficacy.

The overall direction of change was similar in all programs. For example, in the Kids' League (Figure 8.1) although two-thirds (67 per cent) improved their self-evaluation, a quarter (26 per cent) recorded a decline. Among Magic Bus participants the impact of the program was spread more evenly, with half (49 per cent) increasing their perceived self-efficacy score and 44 per cent decreasing. The all-female EMIMA sample exhibited the clearest positive changes, with only 17 per cent decreasing their self-evaluation, while three-quarters (76 per cent) increased. In other words different programs, with different social climates, different participants in different contexts had different effects on different individuals – whence sport-for-development?

Although there were project-specific variations, the overall picture is that many of those with the weakest self-evaluations improved their score. This is in line with previous research which indicates that those with lower perceived self-efficacy have, *in the right circumstances*, the most to gain from participation in appropriate programs (Fox, 1992).

In the Kids' League there was no statistically significant difference in the *degree of change* between males and females – the program did not benefit one sex significantly more than the other. The majority of females (51 per cent) and males (55 per cent) with initially *lower than average* perceived self-efficacy scores increased their scores – with a quarter of females and one-fifth of males with above average scores reducing them. However, females in Magic Bus increased their average score and the male score decreased. Although because of small samples such data must be regarded as indicative, it is thought-provoking. For example, it is not clear if such effects related to the nature of the program and its ethos, or reflected the processes involved in a small, coherent and mutually supportive group of females taking part in activities not usually available to such young women (see also Kay, 2009).

Stating the obvious?

The extent and nature of changes in self-evaluation raise questions about how we assess program impacts. The rhetoric of sport-for-development, which often combines an essentialist view of sport with an implicit universalistic deficit model, implies a rather uni-linear and homogeneous process, in which all participants will *increase* their perceived self-efficacy – all will 'develop'. For whatever reason, this is clearly not the impact recorded in our data. While the overall picture is that many with the weakest self-evaluations improved their scores, others reduced theirs and, for some, participation had little or no impact. There are several possible explanations for this.

First, there may be a methodological testing, re-testing effect in which respondents were more familiar with the scale on the second occasion and gave a more considered, or more self-affirming response (this would be encouraged by the developmental rhetoric of such programs). Second, the social climate and approach to teaching and learning was more appropriate for some participants than others. Third, some who recorded a high initial perceived self-efficacy might have over-estimated their abilities and that a failure to develop certain skills and competence, or recognition that they over-estimated their abilities *in comparison to others*, caused them to readjust. It is clear that we need more information about the variety of mechanisms – context, relationships, rules, experiences and participants' 'reasoning and resources' (Pawson and Tilley, 2000) – which led to such differences, and generalizations about 'sport-for-development' are of little assistance.

It seems to be stating the obvious to say that participation in different programs in different contexts will affect different people in different ways and it would be very surprising if decreases in self-evaluation did *not* occur (Patriksson, 1995; Coakley, 1998; Pawson, 2006; Biddle and Mutrie, 2001). Even in the unusually positive results produced by the all-female EMIMA, about one-fifth of participants reduced their self-evaluations and a number of individuals who started with below average scores *decreased* their evaluations. Clearly perceptions of self-efficacy are tested constantly when participating in new activities or in mixed-ability groups where you discover that you are better or worse than you thought, especially in comparison to others. How this is interpreted depends partly on the social climate of the program, or if individuals have an entity or incremental view of abilities (Dweck, 1999), or if the activity and experiences are deemed to be important to self-definition. Further, it is possible that a reduction in perceived self-efficacy is merely a realistic adjustment based on practical experience. This is not necessarily negative and could be regarded as 'development'. This is a possibility of which program providers should be aware.

Perceived self-efficacy and self-esteem: doing well and feeling good?

Unlike perceived self-efficacy there is a widely accepted 'gold standard' scale for measuring self-esteem (Emler, 2001) – the Rosenberg (1965) self-esteem scale. As with the data on perceived self-efficacy, the first key 'before' finding is that the groups were not homogeneous – they held a variety of self-evaluations and were certainly not uniformly 'deficient'. Although each project had a slightly different profile – the two Indian samples again had lower average scores than two of the three East African samples – in all samples the distribution of self-evaluations conformed broadly to a bell-shaped curve, with the majority within the range regarded as normal (15–25), again raising questions about overly generalized deficit models.

In all but one project the average scores increased, although the strength of the effect was less than for perceived self-efficacy. In only one – the all-female EMIMA group – was the change statistically significant. Further, as with perceived self-efficacy, the average scores disguised a variety of responses to the program – with between 55 per cent and 33 per cent *reducing* their score. Given that several writers have highlighted the possible negative consequences of high self-esteem which is not based firmly in achievement (Hewitt, 1998; Emler, 2001; Baumeister et al., 2003), such downward adjustments could also be regarded as positive personal developments.

However, in terms of 'development' it is the *relationship* between perceived self-efficacy and self-esteem that matters. The implicit assumption of the ideology of sport and sport-for-development is that participation in sport will lead to an increased sense of competence and strengthened perceived self-efficacy, which in turn will lead to increased self-esteem. This combination may lead to desired individual development impacts and outcomes such as improved educational performance (Shephard, 1997) or changed sexual behavior. However, Fox (1992) emphasizes the contingent and mediated nature of this process – improved performance (e.g. football skills) *may* lead to an increase in physical self-efficacy which, if valued, *may* lead to improved perceived self-efficacy which *may* contribute to a strengthened sense of self-esteem, *if* such achievements are deemed to be important and defining of a sense of self. The complexity of such processes and the varied approaches to definition and measurement might explain the varied nature of research findings in this area (Gruber, 1986; Harter, 1988; Ekeland et al., 2005).

Because both measures were taken at the same point in time we could not explore the *direction of cause* – whether perceived self-efficacy impacts on self-esteem or vice versa. However, we examined the broad *relationships between movements* in self-efficacy beliefs and self-esteem for the three projects. To explore the strength of the correlations between the *degree of change* in perceived self-efficacy and self-esteem we used two statistical tests: a *correlation coefficient* (r) to measure the extent to which there is a relationship between both measures and the strength of this relationship; a *significance test* (p) which took into account issues such as sample size and the probability that the measured relationship was a product of chance.

In the Kids' League there were statistically significant increases for both male and female perceived self-efficacy, with males having the larger increase. However, in the case of self-esteem there were marginal and statistically non-significant increases for both sexes. In both cases there was no statistically significant difference in the *degree of change* between males and females – the program did not benefit significantly one sex more than the other. This produced the strongest correlation between changes in perceived self-efficacy and self-esteem – especially for males. For males there was a relatively strong relationship between *changes* in self-efficacy and self-esteem (r_s=.505), with a very strong level of significance (p=.000) – it is unlikely that this relationship occurred by chance. This may reflect the widespread research finding that young men place a relatively high emphasis on sport in terms of their self-definition – although as the correlation coefficient indicates, this relationship varied between individuals.

The correlation coefficient for females was weaker (r_s=.357), but nevertheless there was some relationship between changes in the two evaluations. Also, with a significance level of p=.004, it is unlikely that this relationship is a product of chance. Existing research would suggest that this effect – where there is a close relationship between the two measures for some individuals but not others – might reflect either a positive attitude to body-image and physical self-worth and/or sources of social acceptance and friendship networks. However, the relationship is weaker than for males and certainly indicates a variety of relationships between the two approaches to self-evaluation. In the all-female EMIMA group the increase in the average perceived self-efficacy and self-esteem scores were statistically significant. However, the correlation coefficient for *changes* in perceived self-efficacy and self-esteem was relatively weak (r_s=.229). Further, the level of significance (p=.200) indicates that there is a 20 per cent chance that the relationship was random and subject to a considerable degree of individual randomness. Change in one facet of self-evaluation did not strongly predict change in the other.

The explanation for some of these differences lies in the program processes, relationships, experiences and the individuals' priorities which 'produced' them. We have emphasized that we do not know the direction of cause – whether perceived self-efficacy impacts on self-esteem or vice versa. Some of the programs may, for example, place a strong emphasis on developing perceived self-efficacy and emphasizing its relationship to self-worth – 'your skill as a footballer and your performance in this program indicate that you are a good person'. Further, this may or may not be more effective for females than males. On the other hand it is quite possible that a third factor – a set of experiences which Fox (2000) refers to as the 'attractiveness factors' – leads to a parallel increase in both measures. Both measures are subjective evaluations and known to be influenced by a range of environmental factors and social processes. Some programs may be successful at increasing both sets of beliefs, with no necessarily *causal* relationship between the two.

Conclusions

The data raise important questions about simple deficit models of young people and easy generalizations about 'development needs'. Although all respondents lived in extremely deprived social and economic circumstances they cannot be regarded as uniformly 'deficient' – at least not in terms of their self-perceptions of their self-efficacy and self-esteem. Of course it is possible that some of these evaluations reflect a certain self-protective element, with a degree of denial and suppression necessary for survival (Jenkins, 1997; Hunter, 2001) – we have no way of knowing from our data, although this cannot explain the relatively normal distribution of self-perceptions across a variety of contexts and cultures.

Although there were project-specific variations, the overall picture is that many of those with weaker self-evaluations improved their scores. However, the extent, diversity and direction of changes in self-evaluation raise interesting questions about how we assess program impacts, especially as the uni-linear deficit model would imply that all, or most, will *increase* their self-evaluations. It is inevitable that participation in different programs, in different contexts will affect different people in different ways and it would be very surprising if decreases in self-evaluation did not occur. Self-evaluations are tested constantly and more so when participating in new activities, or in mixed-ability or mixed-sex groups. It is possible that reductions in both perceived self-efficacy and self-esteem are merely realistic adjustments based on practical experience. This is not necessarily a negative impact and from certain perspectives can be viewed as developmental. To ignore this contains obvious ideological and pedagogic dangers. It raises important questions about how 'need' and 'development' are conceptualized and how desired impacts and behavioral outcomes are defined and measured.

Although the data indicate general *tendencies*, the variations between the programs indicate that, not surprisingly, there is no simple and predictable 'sport-for-development effect' – would we expect a universal 'education effect', or a 'crime prevention effect'? As with all forms of social intervention, causation is contingent, reflects the nature of participants, circumstances, relationships and interactions and no impacts are guaranteed. In this regard Pawson et al. (2004) state that 'it is through the workings of entire systems of social relationships that any changes in behaviors … are effected … Rarely if ever is the "same" program equally effective in all circumstances because of the influence of contextual factors' (p. 7).

In the absence of control groups it is difficult to attribute any changes in self-evaluations simply to participation in the programs. Further, the data *cannot* be viewed as providing an indication of the impact of 'sport' in the essentialist sense it is often used in sport-for-development. All programs contained a number of non-sporting elements and provided a wide variety of social relationships and experiences. Perhaps most importantly many young people may live in reasonably homogeneous cultural and/or religious communities which serve to sustain relatively normal levels of perceived self-efficacy and self-esteem beliefs – albeit with individual differences.

While the impact of the programs varied and raised important questions about the nature of 'development', they also leave unanswered the issues relating to displacement of scope. The issues here bring to mind Ungar's (2006) comments about programs that seek to develop resilience (closely related to perceived self-efficacy). He suggests that it might be better to 'change the odds' rather than try to resource individuals to 'beat the odds' in environments that frequently do not support behavior change, or offer opportunities for 'development'. If we extend slightly Wagner's (1964) notion of displacement of scope, our data and theoretical position suggest a series of basic questions related to sport-for-development programs:

- In what ways are the participants in need of 'development'?
- Does participation positively affect the combination of values, attitudes, knowledge and aptitudes contained in a notion of 'development', for all or some?
- How does the program achieve such impacts and for whom?
- Does this result in an intention to change specific behaviors, for all or some?
- Does this lead to an actual change in behavior, for all or some?
- Does the participants' environment enable desired changes in behavior?
- If not, how does this contribute to broader processes of social and economic development?

References

Bandura, A. (1986). *Social Foundations of Thought and Action: A Social Cognitive Theory*. Englewood Cliffs, NJ: Prentice-Hall.

Bandura, A. (1994). Self-efficacy. In V. S. Ramachaudran (Ed.), *Encyclopaedia of Human Behaviour* (Vol. 4, pp. 71–81). New York: Academic Press.

Baumeister, R. F., Cambell, J. D., Krueger, J. I., and Vohs, K. D. (2003). Does high self-esteem cause better performance, interpersonal success, happiness, or heathier lifestyles? *Psychological Science in the Public Interest, 4*, 1–44.

Biddle, S. (2006). Defining and measuring indicators of psycho-social well-being in youth sport and physical activity. In Y. Vanden Auweele, C. Malcolm, and B. Meulders (Eds.), *Sports and Development* (pp. 163–184). Leuven: Lannoo Campus.

Biddle, S., and Mutrie, N. (2001). *Psychology of Physical Activity*. London: Routledge.

Black, D. (2010). The ambiguities of development: Implications for 'development through sport'. *Sport in Society, 13*, 121–129.

Bosscher, R. J., and Smit, J. H. (1998). Confirmatory factor analysis of the General Self-Efficacy Scale. *Behaviour Research and Therapy, 36*, 339–343.

Coakley, J. (1998). *Sport in Society: Issues and Controversies* (6th ed.). Boston, MA: McGraw Hill.

Coalter, F. (2013). *Sport for Development: What Game Are We Playing?* London: Routledge.

Coalter, F., and Taylor, J. (2010). *Sport-for-Development Impact Study*. Available from www.uksport.gov.uk/docLib/MISC/FullReport.pdf

Dweck, C. (1999). *Self-theories: Their Role in Motivation, Personality and Development*. Philadelphia, PA: Taylor and Francis.

Ekeland, E., Heian, F., and Hagen, K. B. (2005). Can exercise improve self-esteem in children and young people? A systematic review of randomised control trials. *British Journal of Sports Medicine, 39*, 792–798.

Emler, N. (2001). *Self-esteem: The Costs and Causes of Low Self-Worth*. York, UK: Joseph Rowntree Foundation.

Fox, K. R. (1992). Physical education and the development of self-esteem in children. In N. Armstrong (Ed.), *New Directions in Physical Education (Vol. 2): Towards a National Curriculum* (pp. 33–54). Leeds, UK: Human Kinetics.

Fox, K. R. (2000). The effects of exercise on self-perceptions and self-esteem. In S. J. H. Biddle, K. K. Fox and S. H. Boutcher (Eds.), *Physical Activity and Psychological Well-being* (pp. 88–117). London: Routledge.

Graham, S., and Weiner, B. (1996). Theories and principles of motivation. In D. C. Berliner and R. C. Calfee (Eds.), *Handbook of Educational Psychology* (pp. 63–84). New York: Simon & Schuster Macmillan.

Gruber, J. (1986). Physical activity and self-esteem development in children: A meta-analysis. *American Academy of Physical Education Papers, 19*, 30–48.

Harter, S. (1988). Developmental processes in the construction of the self. In T. D. Yawkey and J. E. Johnson (Eds.), *Integrative Processes and Socialisation: Early to Middle Childhood* (pp. 45–78). Hillsdale, NJ: Erlbaum.

Harter, S. (1999). *The Construction of the Self: A Developmental Perspective*. New York: Guilford Press.

Hartmann, D., and Kwauk, C. (2011). Sport and development: An overview, critique and reconstruction. *Journal of Sport and Social Issues, 35*, 284–305.

Hewitt, J. (1998). *The Myth of Self-esteem: Finding Happiness and Solving Problems in America*. New York: St Martin's Press.

Hunter, J. (2001). A cross-cultural comparison of resilience in adolescents. *Journal of Pediatric Nursing, 16*, 172–179.

Jenkins, J. (1997). Not without a trace: Resilience and remembering among Bosnian refugees. *Psychiatry, 60*, 40–43.

Kay, T. (2009). Developing through sport: Evidencing sport impacts on young people. *Sport in Society, 12*, 1177–1191.

Kruse, S. E. (2006). *Review of Kicking AIDS Out: Is Sport an Effective Tool in the Fight Against HIV/AIDS?* Unpublished draft report for NORAD.

Luszczynska, A., Scholz, U., and Schwarzer, R. (2005). The general self-efficacy scale: Multicultural validation studies. *The Journal of Psychology, 139*, 439–457.

Pajares, F. (2002). *Self-efficacy Beliefs in Academic Contexts: An Outline*. Available from http://des.emory.edu/mfp/efftalk.html

Patriksson, M. (1995). Scientific review Part 2. In *The Significance of Sport for Society – Health, Socialisation, Economy: A Scientific Review*, prepared for the 8th Conference of European Ministers responsible for Sport, Lisbon, 17–18 May 1995. Strasbourg: Council of Europe Press.

Pawson, R. (2006). *Evidence-based Policy: A Realist Perspective*. London: Sage.

Pawson, R., and Tilley, N. (2000). *Realistic Evaluation*. London: Sage.

Pawson, R., Greenhalgh, T., Harvey, G., and Walshe, K. (2004). *Realist Synthesis: An Introduction*. ESRC Research Methods Programme University of Manchester, RMP Methods Paper 2/2004.

Prochaska, J., and Velicer, W. (1997). The transtheoretical model of health behaviour change. *American Journal of Health Promotion, 12*, 38–48.

Rosenberg, M. (1965). *Society and the Adolescent Self-image*. Princeton, NJ: Princeton University Press.

Shephard, R. J. (1997). Curricular physical activity and academic performance. *Pediatric Exercise Science, 9*, 113–126.

Sherer, M., Maddux, J. E., Mercandante, B., Prentice-Dunn, S., Jacobs, B., and Rogers, R. W. (1982). The self-efficacy scale: Construction and validation. *Psychological Reports, 51*, 663–671.

Sonstroem, R. J., and Morgan, W. P. (1989). Exercise and self-esteem: Rationale and model. *Medicine and Science in Sport and Exercise, 21*, 329–337.

Svoboda, B. (1994). *Sport and Physical Activity as a Socialisation Environment, Scientific Review Part 1*. Strasbourg: Council of Europe, Committee for the Development of Sport (CDDS).

Ungar, M. (2006). Resilience across cultures. *British Journal of Social Work, 38*, 218–235.

Wagner, H. L. (1964). Displacement of scope: A problem of the relationship between small-scale and large-scale sociological theories. *The American Journal of Sociology, 69*, 571–584.

Weiss, C. H. (1993). Where politics and evaluation research meet. *Evaluation Practice, 14*, 93–106.

Appendix

Perceived self-efficacy measure (Bosscher and Smit, 1998)

	Strongly disagree	Disagree	Agree	Strongly agree
If something looks too complicated I will not even bother to try it.				
I avoid trying to learn new things when they look too difficult.				
When trying something new, I soon give up if I am not initially successful.				
When I make plans, I am certain I can make them work.				
If I can't do a job the first time, I keep trying until I can.				
When I have something unpleasant to do, I stick to it.				
When I decide to do something, I go right to work on it.				
Failure just makes me try harder.				
When I set important goals for myself, I rarely achieve them.				
I do not seem to be capable of dealing with most problems that come up in my life.				
When unexpected problems occur, I don't handle them very well.				
I feel insecure about my ability to do things.				

PART 3

PYD across youth sport contexts

9

POSITIVE YOUTH DEVELOPMENT AND TALENT DEVELOPMENT

Is there a best of both worlds?

Chris Harwood and Julie Johnston

Talent identification is the process in which current sports participants are recognized with the potential to excel in a particular sport while talent development involves the process of providing resources to realize this potential (Vaeyens et al., 2008). Collectively, these objectives comprise what is now commonly referred to within national sports organizations as the performance pathway. With an increasing emphasis in elite-level sport on achieving predetermined medal targets at major games, and a focus on national team positions and international medal tables, the identification and development of talent has become big business. Whole industries, replete with leading technological innovations and human resources, now exist to support the development of talent; multi-disciplinary teams comprised of exercise physiologists, bio-mechanists, strength and conditioning specialists, physiotherapists, massage therapists, sport psychologists and even team doctors work together to support athletes in their quest to fulfil their potential.

At the junior levels of sport, performance pathway teams have emerged within sport federations to identify athletes showing the greatest potential, working with them to develop smoother transitions towards an elite level (MacNamara et al., 2010a, 2010b). Although the aims and objectives of creating such pathways appear clear, questions arise surrounding the impact of such a performance-focused approach on young athletes' personal development and their long-term relationship with sport and physical activity. This is particularly relevant given the very large percentage of young athletes who may specialize and invest in a specific sport, yet fall short of making the successful transition to a professional level. Beyond the more commercial focus on talent transition lies a coach's or sport organization's social and moral attention towards maximizing positive developmental experiences and outcomes for all protégés, at the same time as maintaining a balanced focus on qualities most associated with performance improvement (see Johnston et al., 2013). This is precisely where the fields of talent development and positive youth development (PYD) start to collide; the intricacies of which form the focus of the current chapter.

The purpose of this chapter is to examine the similarities and differences between those models or frameworks arising from the talent development literature with those traditionally associated with PYD. The importance and relevance of integrating PYD outcomes in the development of talented athletes will be discussed in tandem with the external roles of parents, coaches and practitioners. Finally, research recommendations will be proposed with respect to how young athletes may gain the best of both worlds regarding pathways towards their personal and athletic development.

Talent development: a historical overview of frameworks and models

Simonton (1999) defined talent as 'any innate capacity that enables an individual to display exceptionally high performance in a domain that requires special skills and training' (p. 436). However, Gagné (1993) proposed a distinction between giftedness and talent; giftedness was the possession of a unique set of innate abilities, whereas talent served as the end product of a development process focused on transforming these gifts into abilities through processes of maturation, learning, training, and practice. It is this developmental process – what informs it, what impacts it and what it looks like – that has led to extensive research over the last twenty-five years. Gagné's model acknowledged the key interaction of both intrapersonal and environmental catalysts to realize an individual's potential. The intrapersonal catalysts included personal traits constituting both physical and mental characteristics in addition to self-management processes such as awareness of others, emotional control and volition. The environmental catalysts included in this model were termed contextual, interpersonal, provisions and events, and he was the first to acknowledge the role of chance. This multidimensional approach reflects the current consensus of talent development (Tranckle and Cushion, 2006). However, not all talent development models since Gagné (1993) have been so inclusive.

Physically focused models

Of the talent development models that have emerged over the past twenty years (e.g. Balyi and Hamilton, 2003; Bloom, 1985; Côté, 1999; Wylleman and Lavallee, 2004), the majority outline a phased or staged approach to development whereby athletes' participation in their chosen sport becomes more intensive and focused. One of the most influential models in sport has been the Long Term Athlete Development (LTAD) model, introduced by Istvan Balyi (Balyi and Hamilton, 2003) which has been adopted and promoted in the UK within the majority of sport governing bodies (Bailey et al., 2010). Grounded in physiological traditions, the central focus of this model is on physiological development, and integrates factors linked to physical outcomes such as peak height velocity, and windows of optimal trainability that are promoted as critical periods of time during which accelerated adaptation can be achieved. Mental-cognitive and emotional development are both referred to within the model but a comparative focus on the intricacies of how to develop these areas is distinctly lacking. In a recent attempt to address perceived weaknesses and concerns with the LTAD model (Ford et al., 2011), Lloyd and Oliver (2012) devised the Youth Physical Development Model. This model promotes a more in-depth and individualized 'physical' approach, yet once again does not specifically consider psychosocial development. Instead, the authors propose that the model's focus on the mastery oriented process of technical and physical gains should lead to enhancements in intrinsic motivation, task orientation, perceived competence, and indices of psychological well-being (Lloyd and Oliver, 2012).

Psychosocially focused models

Whereas the LTAD and Youth Physical Development Models are both grounded in the physical domain, other popular talent development models are more firmly rooted in the social-psychological domain. Côté (1999) introduced the Developmental Model of Sport Participation, identifying three progressive phases of sport participation in line with Bloom's (1985) three stages of learning. Each phase was distinguished by age and labelled the sampling years, the specializing years and the investment years. His model was later refined to allow for individual differences in both motives of participation in sport and in sport choice itself, resulting in three possible outcomes of continued participation in sport. These three pathways, labelled 'trajectories' result in either recreational participation through sampling, elite performance through sampling or elite performance through early specialization. In addition to these three core trajectories, the refined model also allows for horizontal transition between the stages – for example, the opportunity to move from investment to recreational, as is likely to occur upon retirement from elite sport (Côté and Fraser-Thomas, 2007).

Côté et al. (2010) have recently proposed how coach interactions with their athletes should be influenced by both the developmental stage of the athletes being coached (e.g. sampling, specializing, investment), and their developmental trajectory. Such interactions are aimed at developing a number of psychosocial outcomes within their athletes defined by the authors as the 4Cs. Selection of these 4Cs – competence, confidence, connection, and character/caring – signify a more holistic approach to athlete development and reinforce how Côté and colleagues (2010) were influenced by Lerner et al.'s (2000) work on the 5Cs of PYD.

Within the UK, Abbott and Collins (2004) proposed Psychological Characteristics of Developing Excellence (PCDEs) as facilitators to development, and cited such skills as goal setting, imagery, planning and organization, and effective evaluation. Further sport-based refinements by MacNamara and colleagues (McNamara et al., 2010a, 2010b) revised this PCDE taxonomy with the addition of such assets as commitment, self-belief, vision, the ability to cope with pressure, and focus effectively. Such psychological characteristics are posited to assist with development by providing athletes with the resources to successfully engage with and manage their environment and significant others, thereby allowing them to successfully negotiate periods of transition and change (Schlossberg, 1981).

Indeed, a number of additional models focused on athlete career development have concentrated in greater detail on these transitionary periods, and the holistic components required by athletes for successful navigation. Such models (e.g. Stambulova, 2000; Taylor and Ogilvie, 1994) emphasize coping strategies and the factors influencing them as central to an athlete's ability to successfully negotiate a transition. Importantly therefore, it is not only the internal resources of the athlete (such as the PDCEs) that will impact upon the utility of the strategies at the athlete's disposal, but external factors such as social support, which will influence the athlete's transitional experience. Wylleman and Lavallee's (2004) developmental lifespan model provides a framework for understanding how multidimensional forces can impact an athlete's talent development journey. These authors adopt the staged approach of Bloom (1985) and Côté (1999) but expand this work by acknowledging the athlete as a person operating in a complex and developing world with additional commitments and goals. Derived from research with elite and former elite athletes, they propose how athletes concurrently face developments in psychological/cognitive, psychosocial, academic and/or vocational domains. As such, challenges exist in multiple domains of development that need to be recognized by coaches, parents, practitioners, and organizations (e.g. a seventeen-year-old athlete who is transitioning from a 'development' to 'mastery' stage may also be coping with the academic/vocational demands of schoolwork and examinations). This model also explicitly integrates significant others (coaches, parents, peers, siblings, partners), and attempts to specify those who are the most salient influences at each stage of an individual's personal development.

In sum, these latter models emphasize how a multidimensional and evolving social support network is crucial for athletes to learn and develop effective physical and psychosocial skills. Such skills and network support are believed to enhance coping, provide relief from distress and adversity, and encourage athletes to learn how to develop healthy relationships (Morgan and Giacobbi, 2006).

Talent development versus positive youth development

It is noticeable that as talent development models have evolved over recent years, researchers have increasingly noted the importance of social support networks, significant others and the development of internal psychosocial assets as crucial factors in providing athletes with the resources to realize their talent. Although these models may never have intended to be representative of PYD, the introduction of such themes in talent development research has started to lead to a blurring of the two genres. The underlying premise and models of PYD have previously been well established within this text. However, in order to emphasize the similarities between the two approaches, a brief synopsis is necessary.

Positive youth development can be conceptualized as a holistic approach which looks to encourage thriving and development in young people by providing them with appropriate support and developmental opportunities (Scales et al., 2000). These experiences then assist in the development of positive qualities and characteristics, known collectively as internal assets. Such assets are used as resources which play an enhancement role to encourage thriving within young people, displayed by outcomes such as being successful at school, displaying leadership and taking time to help others (Scales et al., 2000). This process resonates with how theorists in talent development have promoted the importance of psychosocial development and social support to assist in the transition of athletes from junior to elite-level sport (Morgan and Giacobbi, 2006; Wylleman and Lavallee, 2004).

A number of influential models initiated the PYD era (Benson et al., 1998; Hansen and Larson, 2002; Lerner et al., 2000), with each suggesting specific internal assets to focus on and, in the case of both Benson and colleagues, and Hansen and Larson, specific external assets that should be employed to aid their development. Benson's work targeted the role of social support, empowerment, boundaries and expectations, and constructive use of time, while Hansen and Larson conceptualized external factors such as positive relationships, teamwork and social skills, adult networks, and social capital. Whereas PYD interventions have commonly focused on youth and community settings, recent research has considered the advantages and possibilities that sport can offer for PYD (e.g. Côté et al., 2010; Johnston et al., 2013). It is this transfer of ideas and concepts from developmental psychology into sport psychology that muddies the water (so to speak) when positioned alongside concepts from developing theories of sport talent development. However, even though there does appear to be a large degree of similarity, the overall aims and objectives of both are distinguishable.

Talent development approaches look to develop the athlete to fulfil their potential in a specific achievement domain (i.e. competitive sport); whereas PYD scholars focus on protection, enhancement and resiliency objectives, using sport as a vehicle through which to 'develop better people' (Fraser-Thomas et al., 2005, p. 20; Harwood, 2008), and to prevent young people from participating in deviant and anti-social behaviours such as drug taking, alcohol use and crime. Positive youth development approaches do note the importance of the context within which the activity occurs, with the National Research Council and Institute of Medicine (NRCIM, 2004) noting eight developmental and necessary features. These include a physically and psychologically safe environment that has appropriate structure and supportive relationships, integrating school, family and the community where possible. There also needs to be opportunities to belong and feel valued in order to develop confidence in addition to the presence of positive social norms to adhere to and follow. Opportunities to build and develop new skills within an intrinsically motivating activity that happens over time must also be present (Fraser-Thomas et al., 2005; NRCIM, 2004; Petitpas et al., 2005).

An inspection of the talent development literature does provide a somewhat similar outline of environmental features that are considered conducive to a positive talent development environment. For example, the Talent Development Environment Questionnaire (Martindale et al., 2010) assesses seven characteristics of effective talent development environments, and many features, including the presence of a challenging and supportive environment, integration with other areas of the athlete's life such as school, and access to a strong support network resonate with those pertinent to PYD settings. Martindale and colleagues also indicated the importance of long-term strategy and planning, coherent communication, individualized training programmes and an emphasis on long-term development and progress in lieu of a focus on early results as additional key features. Echoes of these findings can be seen in subsequent holistic, ecological work in sport by Henriksen et al. (2010) and MacNamara and Collins (2011). The element of support seems to be the most enduring throughout all of these models, whether talent development or PYD focused (see Table 9.1 for a comparative summary of the two approaches).

TABLE 9.1 Similarities and differences between talent development and positive youth development

	Talent development	*Positive youth development*
Aim	Systematic learning, training and practice with the aim of realizing an athlete's full athletic potential	The acquisition of psychological, social, and emotional characteristics through interactions and experiences with significant others in achievement domains to provide individuals with the resources to participate in less deviant behaviours
Features of the environment	Staged and progressive approach Long-term strategy and planning Coherent communication Individualized approach Strong social support networks Emphasis on long-term development and progress in lieu of a focus on early results as additional key features	Physically and psychologically safe Appropriate structure Supportive relationships Opportunities to belong and feel valued in order to develop confidence Presence of positive social norms Opportunities for skill building within intrinsically motivating activities that happen over time Integration of wider social networks
Features of development	Focus on physical, technical, and tactical skill development Psychological characteristics viewed as facilitators to development	Psychological, social, and emotional characteristics

Although similarities in these approaches are clearly noticeable, there are some contextual differences that may emerge more prominently given the differing overall objectives of the two approaches. Most significantly, there are features of PYD environments that resonate with greater safety, caring and broader community belonging through the process of helping young people develop psychosocial assets. Talent development models purport to create environments that facilitate sport-specific psychological characteristics; however, the degree of psychological care which existing talent development environments afford to the person behind those characteristics may be non-existent, or at best, an afterthought.

High-performance youth sport environments – ones more likely to espouse a talent development focus – may not be the most psychologically safe environment (Edmondson, 1999). They may be highly competitive, with fierce competition for places and selection, leading to settings that do not always foster cooperation. Professional coaches employed within talent development pathways are most likely to behave differently than coaches, teachers or mentors who originate from a PYD perspective. Athletes within this system may not have the same type of support or involvement from parents, family or community as posited in PYD models, or as espoused by Côté et al. (2010). They may also be 'challenged to belong' solely with sport peers and have limited relationships and interactions with non-sport peers, even if there is some attention to ensuring that education is supported in some way. In sum, even though talent development models may promote psychological characteristics as key for long-term potential, the motivational or psychological climate that can exist in real-world settings (to get the job done) is potentially different to what one might expect from a PYD setting. It is perhaps these considerations that have led a number of scholars recently towards an integration of PYD in sport, and a focus on blending PYD objectives into performance environments that have been more talent development focused in nature (e.g. Harwood, 2008; Johnston et al., 2013).

A positive youth development approach to talent development

Alongside the many positive benefits of sports participation, evidence also points to poor psychosocial experiences and high attrition rates within youth sport, with as many as 70 per cent of participants of organized sports within the United States dropping out by adolescence (Visek et al., 2015). With only 0.001 per cent of young people involved in sport likely to excel and reach the highest level in their chosen sport (Bailey, 2007), do we have a duty of care to young athletes to provide them with an environment that will: (a) facilitate the development of skills necessary for potential professional transitions; and (b) nurture those skills required for them to successfully thrive and transition into other domains of life (e.g. academic, social, personal, family, work)? How much should sports be responsible for providing youth athletes with the best of both worlds?

A number of scholars believe that better efforts should be made in this direction. Côté and Hancock (2014) present an inclusive sport structure for children under the age of thirteen designed to target the areas of performance, participation and personal development (coined the 3Ps). With a list of ten specific recommendations, covering areas not dissimilar to Visek and colleagues' (2015) notion of FUN MAPS, they posit that sport structures and the governing bodies in charge of such structures do not have to sacrifice one 'P' at the expense of the others. Beyond Côté and colleagues' (2010) aforementioned 4Cs approach, additional frameworks have also championed specific psychosocial assets for coaches to promote that are relevant to personal and performance development. Harwood (2008) employed an alternative 5Cs framework (targeting commitment, communication, concentration, control, and confidence) to help build coaching efficacy in integrating these psychosocial characteristics in soccer training sessions. Beyond coach-reported improvements in delivery, players were reported to have improved in their demonstration of the 5Cs, validated further by parental comments on their children's communication skills in other settings (i.e. school). A recent single case design study with U13 players in soccer reported similar behavioural effects as a result of coach education with further triangulation of data by parents and coach (see Harwood et al., 2015).

A qualitative investigation by Johnston et al. (2013) explored the psychosocial assets that were perceived to be relevant to personal and talent development in the context of youth swimming. Seventeen different assets emerged through expert validation in swimming, grouped within five higher order categories of self-perceptions, behavioural skills, social skills, approach characteristics and emotional competence (see Table 9.2 for the full list of assets). In follow-up quantitative research (Johnston, 2014), even though a substantial sample of swimming coaches and parents reported that they valued these seventeen assets in their athletes/ children, interesting between-asset differences emerged. Results revealed that coaches and parents both placed greater value on the more intrapersonal assets that were contained within the self-perceptions, approach characteristics and behavioural skills groups, while the interpersonal assets contained within the social skills and emotional competence groups appeared to receive lesser value. Furthermore, parents placed significantly greater value than coaches on the majority of the assets, although the assets that were more clearly linked to achievement in swimming were valued to the same degree by both parties (i.e. self-appraisal, communication, positive attitude, perceived sport competence, discipline and motivation). Interestingly, self-reported levels of attention paid to developing these assets were significantly lower than the cognitive value placed on them. These findings demonstrated that although key stakeholders in youth sport may appear to place value in assets associated with PYD outcomes, when it comes to matters of priority attention in sport, some assets may be compromised.

Turning towards recommendations for interventions in sport, coach and parent education and awareness of PYD principles continues to be necessary. Workshops based on Côté et al.'s (2010) proposed strategies for coaches of different developmental groups with the aim of developing the 4Cs may be an appropriate starting point for such interventions. The development of similar workshops based

TABLE 9.2 Psychosocial assets in youth swimming (adapted from Johnston et al., 2013)

Asset group name	Individual assets
Self perceptions	Perceived sport competence Self-esteem Clear and positive identity
Behavioural skills	Organization Discipline Self-appraisal
Social skills	Communication Conflict resolution Cooperation Leadership
Approach characteristics	Character Positive attitude Motivation Resilience
Emotional competence	Empathy Emotional self-regulation Connection

on additional assets (Johnston et al., 2013) may be considered important to develop over time. Work by Gould et al. (2007) has also highlighted both direct and indirect strategies for asset development, many of which do not require extra time to implement. Examples include developing meaningful relationships with the athletes, providing a good role model through awareness of the coach's own behaviours, having clear and consistent rules and boundaries, providing leadership opportunities, engaging in team-building efforts and promoting positive social norms (Camiré et al., 2011; Gould et al., 2007; Gould et al., 2013). Furthermore, coaches could intentionally plan to develop particular assets within predetermined sessions, and integrate teachable moments into session plans, an approach successfully modeled by Harwood (2008) and suggested by both Camiré et al. (2011), and Gould et al. (2013).

It is clear that role of social support permeates across both talent development and PYD and it is critical that coaches and parents are on the same page with respect to creating an environment in which athletes have both the internal and external resources to succeed. While coaches should focus on developing a task-involving climate in which effort, persistence and skill development are emphasized and rewarded in training and competition settings (Harwood et al., 2015), parents should be the main provider of unconditional emotional support, working to provide a home environment that feels safe, secure and distinct from the pressures of the sporting environment (Lauer et al., 2010). Parents are also often best placed to provide esteem support focused on developing an athlete's overall global self-worth and self-esteem, by drawing on achievements from other areas of the athlete's life that they may lack knowledge about.

Conclusion

In this chapter, a gradual proximity has been demonstrated with respect to the processes and objectives of more recent, inclusive talent development models and the principles that underpin PYD. However, a cohesive, cross-disciplinary model of talent development that more skilfully embraces PYD principles is still lacking. This may be a limiting factor in terms of recent research impacting on practice in national governing bodies of sport. The current models of talent development that are being applied in many national sport organizations (e.g. LTAD; Youth Physical Development Model) remain focused on the physical and technical development of youth as opposed to psychosocial elements. There is only anecdotal evidence at best that national governing bodies understand the importance of PYD principles. As a result, frontline staff (e.g. coaches and volunteers) may not fully appreciate the value of a more inclusive approach nor possess the mandate or 'know how' to implement a coaching or support style that caters for performance, participation and personal development (3Ps) outcomes within the single environment (Côté and Hancock, 2014).

In terms of future research, in order to supplement the staged approach of existing talent development models, it would be useful to consider which particular psychosocial assets are most relevant and require the most attention from parents and coaches at particular developmental stages. Longitudinal research that appropriately tracks athletes, their parents and their coaches may help to ascertain which assets are most important 'when' and to establish the developmental periods where significant others may most effectively contribute to the growth of each asset. In addition, by extending intervention programmes such as the 5Cs (Harwood, 2008; Harwood and Anderson, 2015; Harwood et al., 2015) beyond coaches to parents and teachers, significant others may provide more congruent support that reinforces the development of positive psychosocial qualities through settings that are concurrently allied to sport (e.g. education).

In conclusion, with greater evidence-based outcomes in this area, youth sport organizations may take the holistic development of the athlete as a person more seriously, and target psychosocial attributes that enable them to thrive in any future career. In this respect, while striving for excellence in sport, young athletes can expect to benefit from 'the best of both worlds' in environments that prepare them for the demands of society and with the skills to cope with any subsequent life transitions.

References

Abbott, A., and Collins, D. (2004). Eliminating the dichotomy between theory and practice in talent identification and development: Considering the role of psychology. *Journal of Sports Sciences*, 22, 395–408.

Bailey, R. (2007). Talent development and the luck problem. *Sport, Ethics, and Philosophy*, 1, 367–377.

Bailey, R., Collins, D., Ford, P., MacNamara, A., Toms, M., and Pearce, G. (2010). *Participant Development in Sport: An Academic Review*. London: Sportscoach UK.

Balyi, I., and Hamilton, A. (2003). Long-term athlete development update: Trainability in childhood and adolescence. *Faster, Higher, Stronger, 20,* 6–8.

Benson, P. L., Leffert, N., Scales, P. C., and Blyth, D. A. (1998). Beyond the 'village' rhetoric: Creating healthy communities for children and adolescents. *Applied Developmental Science, 2,* 138–159.

Bloom, B. S. (1985). *Developing Talent in Young People*. New York: Ballantine.

Camiré, M., Forneris, T., Trudel, P., and Bernard, D. (2011). Strategies for helping coaches facilitate positive youth development through sport. *Journal of Sport Psychology in Action, 2,* 92–99.

Côté, J. (1999). The influence of the family in the development of talent in sport. *The Sport Psychologist, 13,* 395–417.

Côté, J., and Fraser-Thomas, J. (2007). Youth involvement in sport. In P. R. E. Crocker (Ed.), *Sport Psychology: A Canadian Perspective* (pp. 266–294). Toronto: Pearson Prentice Hall.

Côté, J., and Hancock, D. J. (2014). Evidence-based policies for youth sport programmes. *International Journal of Sport Policy and Politics, 7,* 1–15.

Côté, J., Bruner, M., Erickson, K., Strachan, L., and Fraser-Thomas, J. (2010). Athlete development and coaching. In J. Lyle and C. Cushion (Eds.), *Sport Coaching: Professionalism and Practice* (pp. 63–83). Oxford: Elsevier.

Edmondson, A. (1999). Psychological safety and learning behavior in work teams. *Administrative Science Quarterly, 44,* 350–383.

Ford, P., De Ste Croix, M., Lloyd, R., Meyers, R., Moosavi, M., Oliver, J., Till, K., and Williams, C. (2011). The long-term athlete development model: Physiological evidence and application. *Journal of Sports Sciences, 29,* 389–402.

Fraser-Thomas, J., Côté, J., and Deakin, J. (2005). Youth sport programs: An avenue to foster positive youth development. *Physical Education and Sport Pedagogy, 10,* 19–40.

Gagné, F. (1993). Constructs and models pertaining to exceptional human abilities. In K. A. Heller, F. J. Mönks, and A. H. Passow (Eds.), *International Handbook of Research and Development of Giftedness and Talent* (pp. 63–85). Oxford: Pergamon Press.

Gould, D., Carson, S., and Blanton, J. (2013). Coaching life skills. In P. Protrac, W. Gilbert and Denison, J. (Eds.), *Routledge Handbook of Sports Coaching* (pp. 259–270). London: Routledge.

Gould, D., Collins, K., Lauer, L., and Chung, Y. (2007). Coaching life skills through football: A study of award winning high school coaches. *Journal of Applied Sport Psychology, 19,* 16–37.

Hansen, D. M., and Larson, R. W. (2002). *The Youth Experience Survey 1.0: Instrument Development and Testing*. Unpublished manuscript, University of Illinois at Urbana-Champaign.

Harwood, C. (2008). Developmental consulting in a professional football academy: The 5Cs coaching efficacy program. *The Sport Psychologist, 22,* 109–133.

Harwood, C. G., and Anderson, R. (2015). *Coaching Psychological Skills in Youth Football: Developing the 5Cs*. London: Bennion-Kearney.

Harwood, C. G., Keegan, R. J., Smith, J. M. J., and Raine, A. S. (2015). A systematic review of the intrapersonal correlates of motivational climate perceptions in sport and physical activity. *Psychology of Sport and Exercise, 18,* 9–25.

Harwood, C. G., Barker, J. B. and Anderson, R. (2015). Psychosocial development in youth soccer players: Assessing the effectiveness of the 5Cs intervention program. *The Sport Psychologist, 29*, 319–334.

Henriksen, K., Stambulova, N., and Roessler, K. K. (2010). Holistic approach to athletic talent development environments: A sailing milieu. *Psychology of Sport and Exercise, 11*, 212–222.

Johnston, J. (2014). *Positive Youth Development in Swimming: The Roles of Coaches and Parents.* Unpublished manuscript. School of Sport, Exercise and Health Sciences, Loughborough University, Loughborough, UK.

Johnston, J., Harwood, C., and Minniti, A. M. (2013). Positive youth development in swimming: Clarification and consensus of key psychosocial assets. *Journal of Applied Sport Psychology, 25*, 392–411.

Lauer, L., Gould, D., Roman, N., and Pierce, M. (2010). Parental behaviors that affect junior tennis player development. *Psychology of Sport and Exercise, 11*, 487–496.

Lerner, R. M., Fisher, C. B., and Weinberg, R. A. (2000). Toward a science for and of the people: Promoting civil society through the application of developmental science. *Child Development, 71*, 11–20.

Lloyd, R. S., and Oliver, J. L. (2012). The youth physical development model: A new approach to long-term athlete development. *Strength and Conditioning Journal, 34*, 61–72.

MacNamara, Á., and Collins, D. (2011). Development and initial validation of the psychological characteristics of developing excellence questionnaire. *Journal of Sports Sciences, 29*, 1273–1286.

MacNamara, Á., Button, A., and Collins, D. (2010a). The role of psychological characteristics in facilitating the pathway to elite performance. Part 1: Identifying mental skills and behaviours. *The Sport Psychologist, 24*, 52–73.

MacNamara, Á., Button, A. and Collins, D. (2010b). The role of psychological characteristics in facilitating the pathway to elite performance. Part 2: Examining environmental and stage related differences in skills and behaviours. *The Sport Psychologist, 24*, 74–96.

Martindale, R. J. J., Collins, D., Wang, J. C. K., McNeill, M., Lee, K. S., Sproule, J., and Westbury, T. (2010). Development of the talent development environment questionnaire for sport. *Journal of Sports Sciences, 28*, 1209–1221.

Morgan, T. K., and Giacobbi, P. R. (2006). Toward two grounded theories of the talent development and social support process of highly successful collegiate athletes. *The Sport Psychologist, 20*, 295–313.

National Research Council and Institute of Medicine. (2004). *Community Programs to Promote Youth Development* (Report Brief). Washington, DC: National Academy Press.

Petitpas, A. J., Cornelius, A. E., Van Raalte, J. L., and Jones, T. (2005). A framework for planning youth sport programs that foster psychosocial development. *The Sport Psychologist, 19*, 63–80.

Scales, P. C., Benson, P. L., Leffert, N., and Blyth, D. A. (2000). Contribution of developmental assets to the prediction of thriving among adolescents. *Applied Developmental Science, 4*, 27–46.

Schlossberg, N. K. (1981). A model for analyzing human adaptation to transition. *The Counseling Psychologist, 9*, 2–18.

Simonton, D. K. (1999). Talent and its development: An emergent and epigenetic model. *Psychological Review, 106*, 435–457.

Stambulova, N. B. (2000). Athlete's crises: A developmental perspective. *International Journal of Sport Psychology, 31*, 584–601.

Taylor, J., and Ogilvie, B. C. (1994). A conceptual model of adaptation to retirement among athletes. *Journal of Applied Sport Psychology, 6*, 1–20.

Tranckle, P., and Cushion, C. J. (2006). Rethinking giftedness and talent in sport. *Quest, 58*, 265–282.

Vaeyens, R., Lenoir, M., Williams, A. M., and Philippaerts, R. M. (2008). Talent identification development programmes in sport. *Sports Medicine, 38*, 703–714.

Visek, A. J., Achrati, S. M., Manning, H., McDonnell, K., Harris, B. S., and DiPietro, L. (2015). The fun integration theory: Towards sustaining children and adolescents sport participation. *Journal of Physical Activity and Health, 12*, 424–433.

Wylleman, P., and Lavallee, D. (2004). A developmental perspective on transitions faced by athletes. In M. R. Weiss (Ed.), *Developmental Sport and Exercise Psychology: A Lifespan Perspective* (pp. 507–527). Morgantown, WV: Fitness Information Technology.

10

COACHING FOR POSITIVE YOUTH DEVELOPMENT IN HIGH SCHOOL SPORT

Martin Camiré and Kelsey Kendellen

Sport is one of the most popular activities for youth, and school represents a particularly attractive setting in which to practice sport given that it is where youth spend the greater part of their day (Danish et al., 2005). High school sport participation is deemed a meaningful activity for youth because of the prevailing belief that it enhances physical activity, increases connection to school, and develops athletic talents (Gould and Carson, 2008). In addition to these outcomes, there has been increased attention paid to the notion of high school sport being a context facilitating positive youth development (PYD). For instance, the mission statement of School Sport Canada, the governing body for high school sport in Canada, is to "promote and advocate for positive sportsmanship, citizenship and the total development of student athletes through interscholastic sport" (School Sport Canada, 2013). High school sport is seen as an educational setting where youth development should be approached comprehensively.

We use the term high school sport to refer to school-sponsored sports practiced outside regular class hours in which students compete in organized interscholastic leagues that lead to end-of-season championships. The organized, competitive, and interscholastic nature of high school sport is what differentiates it from other school-based physical activities (e.g. physical education classes or intramural sport). High school sport is classified as a developmental-level context, defined by a strong commitment from students and coaches, team selections based on skills tryouts, and specialized sport-specific training (Trudel and Gilbert, 2006).

High school sport provides opportunities for male and female students, usually between the ages of fourteen and eighteen, to voluntarily engage in a wide variety of team and individual sports. The amount and types of sports available to students can vary based on a school's resources, geographic location, and population. Typically, high school sport teams are overseen by teachers from within the school but community coaches are occasionally recruited to fill vacant positions (Camiré,

2014). The high school sport context is most prevalent in North America, whereas competitive youth sport is often delivered through clubs in other regions (Camiré, 2014; Pot and van Hilvoorde, 2013). Although this chapter is primarily based on North American research, some of the implications for structuring and delivering youth sport may serve as a model for club sport in other regions.

The purpose of this chapter is to investigate optimal ways to structure and deliver high school sport to promote PYD. A brief overview of the developmental outcomes reported in the literature is presented, followed by an examination of the role of coaches in facilitating the developmental process. The chapter concludes with suggestions to enhance the high school sport experience and recommendations for future research.

Developmental outcomes associated with high school sport participation

As Camiré (2014) discussed in a review of the literature, findings from research on the developmental outcomes associated with high school sport participation must be interpreted prudently given that much of the recent empirical work has used cross-sectional and self-report designs. Nevertheless, the current body of research has yielded some important insights that are worthy of closer examination. Cross-sectional quantitative studies conducted within high school sport have indicated how participation contributes to students' development in two distinct ways. First, findings have suggested that participation leads to reductions in the adoption of negative attitudes and behaviours. When comparing participants to non-participants, studies have demonstrated how participation in high school sport is associated with fewer dietary problems, declines in mental health issues, less suicidal thoughts, and lower levels of emotional distress (Harrison and Narayan, 2003; Steiner et al., 2000). Second, findings have indicated that participation leads to increases in the adoption of prosocial attitudes and behaviours. In several studies, high school sport participants have been shown to experience increases in physical activity levels, academic attainment, time-management skills, emotional regulation, self-esteem, and positive self-image (Bruner et al., 2014; Fox et al., 2010; Harrison and Narayan, 2003; Marsh and Kleitman, 2003; Wilkes and Côté, 2010).

Some qualitative studies have examined students' perspective on how participation in high school sport has influenced their personal development. Findings indicated how students believed high school sport afforded them opportunities to develop diverse life skills and values, including time management, self-efficacy, responsibility, communication, leadership, and perseverance (Camiré and Trudel, 2010, 2013; Camiré et al., 2009; Voelker et al., 2011). Additionally, students believed the life skills and values they developed in high school sport were transferable to multiple life domains such as school, work, and community (Camiré and Trudel, 2013; Camiré et al., 2012; Hayden et al., 2015). Although some initial work has examined the transfer of life skills from high school sport to other areas of life, to date, the notion of transfer remains generally under explored.

Although a range of positive outcomes has been associated with participation in high school sport, it is important to note that negative outcomes have also been reported (Camiré, 2014). For example, high school students have reported resorting to the use of gamesmanship tactics to gain advantages over opponents (Camiré and Trudel, 2010) and being repeatedly exposed to discrimination, racism, and overly competitive environments (Buford-May, 2001). Dworkin and Larson (2006) revealed how negative experiences were often predicated on poor quality interactions with coaches (e.g. favouritism, demeaning behaviour), parents (e.g. inappropriate performance pressures), and peers (e.g. formation of cliques).

Combined, current research demonstrates that high school sport exposes youth to a range of experiences that can positively and negatively influence many facets of their development. Although a complex interplay of variables must be considered to explain developmental trajectories, the quality of youth's interactions with their coaches is often upheld as one of the variables exerting the most extensive influence on development (Petitpas et al., 2005). In fact, from a PYD perspective, high school coaches probably play the most crucial roles as they are responsible for creating the climates that greatly influence the nature of youth's developmental experiences (Bergeron et al., 2015; Gould and Carson, 2008).

Role of the coach

Studies have investigated the types of developmental outcomes coaches expect youth to gain from high school sport, with findings indicating that coaches have high expectations of themselves to foster youth's physical, psychological, and social development (Forneris et al., 2012; Gould et al., 2006). Yet, in terms of how coaches actually go about facilitating PYD in high school sport, the literature is mixed.

On one hand, studies have revealed how some high school coaches have deliberate and intentional approaches to PYD. Gould and colleagues conducted several studies with high school coaches in the US and findings demonstrated how these coaches used strategies deliberately aimed at development, such as building meaningful relationships, helping youth set goals, providing individualized feedback, and conducting leadership seminars (Collins et al., 2009; Gould et al., 2007; Gould et al., 2013). Similarly, Camiré and colleagues conducted a series of studies with Canadian high school coaches who reported using several developmental strategies, such as modelling appropriate behaviours, teaching leadership principles, helping youth persevere academically, and providing youth with opportunities to display their skills in non-sport settings (Camiré and Trudel, 2013; Camiré et al., 2012). The coaches with deliberate approaches reported how they acquired the pedagogical tools necessary to facilitate PYD by identifying themselves as lifelong learners and constantly seeking out opportunities to improve their craft (Camiré et al., 2014).

On the other hand, studies have indicated how some high school coaches rarely implemented strategies to directly promote PYD (Hayden et al., 2015; Holt et al.,

2008; Lacroix et al., 2008; Trottier and Robitaille, 2014). Camiré (2014) took a closer look at the demographic profiles of high school coaches and revealed how those who promoted development in a deliberate manner were typically more experienced and better trained than their peers who reported few or no developmental strategies. However, it is essential to note that the absence of deliberate strategies for PYD on the part of coaches does not necessarily equate to the absence of PYD outcomes for youth. In studies where little direct teaching was observed (e.g. Holt et al., 2008; Lacroix et al., 2008), positive developmental outcomes were nonetheless reported as high school sport was deemed a context conducive to the learning of life skills such as stress management, perseverance, initiative, and teamwork. Such findings suggest that the inherent features (e.g. competition) and social dimensions (e.g. peer group interactions) of high school sport, if experienced in a positive manner, implicitly foster some desired outcomes, irrespective of what coaches are doing. Thus, sport's inherent features and social dimensions appear to allow some students, to varying extents, to be the producers of their own developmental experiences and to find ways to benefit from sport within the contexts established by their coaches. In recent years, there have been calls for coaches to be more deliberate in their approach to PYD. However, moving forward, the exact role that "intentionality" plays in the developmental process must be examined more closely to determine how explicit high school coaches should be in order to optimally foster life skills development and transfer (Turnnidge et al., 2014).

A key element to consider in the context of high school sport, particularly in Canada, is that coaching positions are assumed primarily on a voluntary basis by teachers who offer their services to coach sport teams at their school. Thus, high school teachers are not professionally obliged to coach but generally undertake coaching roles because they have a passion for sport and feel a moral obligation to contribute to the enhancement of school life. Camiré (2015a, 2015b) examined the working conditions of individuals undertaking the dual role of high school teacher–coach. Findings indicated that the greatest benefit to holding both teaching and coaching positions was how it facilitated the development of meaningful relationships with students through increased opportunities for interaction. Meaningful relationships built on trust and respect were deemed essential in nurturing the developmental process because they created a greater openness from students to partake in the initiatives implemented by teacher–coaches to promote PYD (Camiré, 2015a). However, the increased responsibilities associated with coaching led to instances of role overload and role conflict, which ultimately impacted the teacher–coaches' ability to navigate their obligations in sport, at school, and at home (Camiré, 2015b). Thus, it appears that the dual role of high school teacher–coach offers working conditions that can be strategically used to optimize student development. However, having a dual role leads to increased duties and teacher–coaches need further resources to maintain a healthy work/family balance and to continue to offer students quality educational experiences.

Suggestions to enhance the high school sport experience

High school sport is associated with many positive and negative experiences. Coaches have been shown to play a critical role in determining the nature of students' experiences in high school sport, but they themselves face many challenges that hinder their ability to navigate their multiple obligations. Therefore, there is a need for evidence-informed practical strategies to help coaches promote PYD within the constraints they face. The following suggestions, informed by existing evidence, represent concrete initiatives requiring few resources that, if implemented properly, can genuinely impact efforts to promote PYD in high school sport.

Healthy competition

Video-sharing websites provide a vast array of examples portraying altercations and even brawls that have occurred within the confines of high school sport. Although rivalries, racism, and other forms of discrimination are often blamed for the occurrence of such deplorable events, the manner by which competition is framed in many Western countries is also a major underlying factor at play. Participation in sport, including high school sport, is often perceived as a form of preparation for life in competitive societies (Rudd, 2005). Thus, ego-oriented climates (e.g. teammates competing for playing time) are often promoted and youth participants are pushed to enhance their position at the expense of others. There have been calls for reducing or outright eliminating competition in youth sport, but some researchers (e.g. Shields and Bredemeier, 2009) have discussed how competition should simply be reconceptualized closer to its original meaning, which is rooted in togetherness, collaboration, and enjoyment.

To promote healthy competition, Côté and Hancock (2014) provided recommendations for children's sport which can be adapted to high school sport. First, high school sport seasons are generally short in duration, a structure that allows students, if they choose so, to experience multiple sports during the school year. Such a system is inherently conducive to the sampling of sports (Côté, 1999), which has been shown to promote skill building and help students develop the physical literacy needed to be active throughout adulthood. Second, success in high school sport must be viewed in relation to developmental processes rather than performance outcomes. Given that high school sport is framed as an extension of the classroom (Holt et al., 2008), coaches must strive to achieve an intricate balance between challenging their students to perform while enabling them to experience success through mastery orientation and the development of personal assets (Bergeron et al., 2015). Redefining students' appreciation of success in such a manner requires a shift from the dominant "sport as business" culture (Danish et al., 2004), a shift that must be instigated by all stakeholders involved. In concrete terms, it warrants that administrators revise their policies, parents amend their expectations, coaches adapt their approach, and students modify their goals.

Healthy relationships

Positive developmental outcomes in sport have been shown to emerge in large part from the quality of the relationships formed between youth and adult leaders (Petitpas et al., 2008; Petitpas et al., 2005). Therefore, it is essential for high school coaches to dedicate time and energy to foster meaningful relationships with their students which are built on mutual trust and respect. There are several strategies that high school coaches can integrate in their day-to-day coaching practices to help foster strong coach–student relationships. First, while taking into account restrictions on their time, coaches should make efforts to create opportunities for one-on-one time to get to know their students on a personal level. For students, such opportunities represent a safe haven where they can seek advice and confide in a private setting, if they ever feel a need to do so. Second, high school coaches should offer their students constructive feedback on a consistent basis. The feedback should be framed in the form of precise autonomy-supportive instructions that promote psychological well-being while also allowing students to improve their physical skills and sport performance (Cronin and Allen, 2015). Coaches who demonstrate that they genuinely care and take the steps necessary to develop quality relationships are those who can most effectively foster their students' relatedness, which is an especially important need to support within an adolescent population.

Peer interactions in sport play a significant role in influencing the nature of youth's developmental experiences (Fraser-Thomas and Côté, 2009) and as such, deliberate efforts from coaches are needed to help foster positive relationships between teammates. In concrete terms, coaches should try to minimize the formation of cliques (Dworkin and Larson, 2006) on their teams by creating environments that promote cooperation and inclusiveness. Further, given that conflict is inherently part of peer interactions with high-school-aged students, coaches must also dedicate efforts to teaching conflict resolution skills (Holt et al., 2012). As Camiré et al. (2013) have discussed, another effective strategy for relationship-building consists of having students take part in team volunteer activities (e.g. giving sport clinics to young children) that necessitate collaborative work.

Parents represent vital sources of support for youth in the context of sport (Petitpas et al., 2005). Although parents are sometimes viewed as a nuisance, coaches are encouraged to see them as important assets with whom healthy relationships must be formed in order to maximize the potential of high school sport as a vehicle for development. One example of a coach–parent relationship-building strategy consists of ensuring open communication lines. This can be achieved by, for example, scheduling coach–parent–student meetings during the season that allow for shared goals to be established and revisited (Camiré et al., 2013). When coaching strategies and parenting styles are consistent, higher levels of synergy can be achieved between the lessons taught in sport and at home (Blom et al., 2013; Knight and Holt, 2014). For instance, perseverance is a value often promoted by coaches in sport that can be further developed if comparable perseverance messages are reinforced by parents at home. By working as a unified front, coaches and parents can promote PYD in a significant manner.

Development and transfer of life skills

In recent years, researchers have paid closer attention to understanding how the context of sport can be optimized to promote PYD through the acquisition of life skills. For instance, Turnnidge et al. (2014) have stipulated that life skills can be fostered through adult-driven as well as youth-driven approaches. Adult-driven approaches involve coaches taking more of an explicit stance on development by intentionally teaching life skills to their students. The adult-driven approach has been associated with opportunities for youth to learn particular life skills such as goal setting and responsibility (Camiré et al., 2013; Walsh et al., 2010). Youth-driven approaches take on more of an implicit stance as the learning of life skills is influenced primarily by the higher level of autonomy provided to youth as well as sport's inherent competitive and social demands. Research has indicated how youth-driven approaches are conducive to the learning of particular life skills such as taking initiative, problem-solving, and creativity (Camiré et al., 2009; Holt et al., 2008). Moving forward, coaches must aim to find a balance between both approaches to maximize the range of life skills youth can acquire through high school sport.

High school coaches should also ensure that they work to promote life skills transfer, beyond simply discussing the notion of transfer with students. To genuinely promote transfer, coaches must create networks with parents and teachers to provide students with tangible opportunities to apply their life skills outside of sport. Allen et al. (2015) demonstrated how transfer is unlikely to occur if no opportunities exist to apply skills, even if students are aware of their existing life skills and the importance of using them beyond sport. In practical terms, high school coaches should join forces with teachers to plan how the life skills learned in sport can be applied in the classroom. Closer partnerships between sport and teaching staff in the high school setting can foster situations where, for example, coaches teach teamwork in sport and this skill is concurrently reinforced by teachers in class by emphasizing the importance of collaborative work in group projects. Another strategy for coaches seeking to foster the transfer of life skills consists of promoting peer debriefing. As researchers have discussed, debriefing is a powerful reflective exercise that can help stimulate the internalization of the life skills learned in sport (Allen et al., 2015). Coaches should dedicate time at the end of practices or during team bus rides to get students to share and critically reflect on the successes and failures they have experienced with transfer attempts. By learning from the experiences of their peers, students can potentially increase their motivation and confidence in using their life skills in situations outside of sport through a better understanding of how certain skills are best applied at school, at home, and in the community.

Conclusion

The empirical evidence suggests that high school sport is an appropriate setting in which to promote PYD, but it is essential to bear in mind that it is just one of many contexts in which students engage. Moving forward, the developmental outcomes associated with high school sport should not be considered in isolation, but rather research is needed to more closely examine the rightful contribution of high school sport within the bigger picture of all activities students partake in. Moreover, few studies (e.g. Camiré and Trudel, 2013) have addressed the notion of skill transfer and as such, greater research attention must be paid to understanding the mechanisms of how the life skills learned in high school sport can generalize and be applied in settings beyond sport. Coaches have consistently been identified as important stakeholders within sport and can significantly influence the behaviours and attitudes of athletes (Bergeron et al., 2015). However, within high school sport, more research is needed to better understand the unique features of this setting to determine how coaches can facilitate PYD in an optimal manner. The recent work of Camiré (2015a, 2015b) suggests that individuals serving as teacher–coaches may be in ideal positions to promote PYD, due to their prolonged and consistent interactions with students, but that they also face many challenges in maintaining both roles. As it stands, more research is needed in this area to explore the working conditions of teacher–coaches more comprehensively.

In sum, high school sport will continue to be an activity practiced by millions of students who, hopefully, will all have opportunities to form lasting friendships and acquire a wide range of life skills. Although there appears to be evidence that the inherent demands of high school sport implicitly foster positive developmental outcomes, it is highly recommended that high school coaches be deliberate in their approach and design strategies to facilitate the development and transfer of life skills. Transfer can be greatly facilitated if coaches work with parents and teachers to provide students with opportunities to apply their life skills in concrete manners.

References

Allen, G., Rhind, D., and Koshy, G. (2015). Enablers and barriers for male students transferring life skills from the sports hall into the classroom. *Qualitative Research in Sport, Exercise and Health, 7*, 53–67.

Bergeron, M. F., Mountjoy, M., Armstrong, N., Chia, M., Côté, J., Emery, C. A., Faigenbaum, A., Hall Jr, G., Kriemler, S. Léglise, M., Malina, R. M., Pensgaard, A. M., Sanchez, A., Soligard, T., Sundgot-Burgen, J., van Mechelen, W., Weissensteiner, J. R., and Engebretsen, L. (2015). International Olympic Committee consensus statement on youth athletic development. *British Journal of Sports Medicine, 49*, 843–851.

Blom, L. C., Visek, A. J., and Harris, B. S. (2013). Triangulation in youth sport: Healthy partnerships among parents, coaches, and practitioners. *Journal of Sport Psychology in Action, 4*, 86–96.

Bruner, M. W., Boardley, I. D., and Côté, J. (2014). Social identity and prosocial and antisocial behavior in youth sport. *Psychology of Sport and Exercise, 15*, 56–64.

Buford-May, R. A. (2001). The sticky situation of sportsmanship: Contexts and contradictions in sportsmanship among high school boys basketball players. *Journal of Sport and Social Issues, 25,* 372–389.

Camiré, M. (2014). Youth development in North American high school sport: Review and recommendations. *Quest, 66,* 495–511.

Camiré, M. (2015a). Examining high school teacher-coaches' perspective on relationship building with student-athletes. *International Sport Coaching Journal, 2,* 125–136.

Camiré, M. (2015b). Being a teacher-coach in Ontario high schools: Challenges and recommendations. *Revue phénEPS/PHEnex Journal, 7,* 1–15.

Camiré, M., and Trudel, P. (2010). High school athletes' perspectives on character development through sport participation. *Physical Education and Sport Pedagogy, 15,* 193–207.

Camiré, M., and Trudel, P. (2013). Using high school football to promote life skills and student engagement: Perspectives from Canadian coaches and students. *World Journal of Education, 3*(3), 40–51.

Camiré, M., Trudel, P., and Forneris, T. (2009). High school athletes' perspectives on support, communication, negotiation and life skill development. *Qualitative Research in Sport and Exercise, 1,* 72–88.

Camiré, M., Trudel, P., and Forneris, T. (2012). Coaching and transferring life skills: Philosophies and strategies used by model high school coaches. *The Sport Psychologist, 26,* 243–260.

Camiré, M., Trudel, P., and Bernard, D. (2013). A case study of a high school sport program designed to teach athletes life skills and values. *The Sport Psychologist, 27,* 188–200.

Camiré, M., Trudel, P., and Forneris, T. (2014). Examining how model youth sport coaches learn to facilitate positive youth development. *Physical Education and Sport Pedagogy, 19,* 1–17.

Collins, K., Gould, D., Lauer, L., and Chung, Y. (2009). Coaching life skills through football: Philosophical beliefs of outstanding high school football coaches. *International Journal of Coaching Science, 3,* 29–54.

Côté, J. (1999). The influence of the family in the development of talent in sport. *The Sport Psychologist, 13,* 395–417.

Côté, J., and Hancock, D. J. (2014). Evidence-based policies for youth sport programmes. *International Journal of Sport Policy and Politics.* Advance online publication. http://www.tandfonline.com/doi/abs/10.1080/19406940.2014.919338

Cronin, L. D., and Allen, J. B. (2015). Developmental experiences and well-being in sport: The importance of the coaching climate. *The Sport Psychologist, 29,* 62–71.

Danish, S. J., Forneris, T., Hodge, K., and Heke, I. (2004). Enhancing youth development through sport. *World Leisure, 46,* 38–49.

Danish, S. J., Forneris, T., and Wallace, I. (2005). Sport-based life skills programming in the schools. *Journal of Applied School Psychology, 21,* 41–62.

Dworkin, J., and Larson, R. (2006). Adolescents' negative experiences in organized youth activities. *Journal of Youth Development, 1*(3), 1–19.

Forneris, T., Camiré, M., and Trudel, P. (2012). The development of life skills and values in high school sport: Is there a gap between stakeholder's expectations and perceived experiences? *International Journal of Sport and Exercise Psychology, 10,* 9–23.

Fox, C. K., Barr-Anderson, D., Neumark-Sztainer, D., and Wall, M. (2010). Physical activity and sports team participation: Associations with academic outcomes in middle school and high school students. *Journal of School Health, 80,* 31–37.

Fraser-Thomas, J., and Côté, J. (2009). Understanding adolescents' positive and negative developmental experiences in sport. *The Sport Psychologist, 23*, 3–23.

Gould, D., and Carson, S. (2008). Life skills development through sport: Current status and future directions. *International Review of Sport and Exercise Psychology, 1*, 58–78.

Gould, D., Chung, Y., Smith, P., and White, J. (2006). Future directions in coaching life skills: Understanding high school coaches' views and needs. *Athletic Insight, 8*(3), 28–38.

Gould, D., Collins, K., Lauer, L., and Chung, Y. (2007). Coaching life skills through football: A study of award winning high school coaches. *Journal of Applied Sport Psychology, 19*, 16–37.

Gould, D., Voelker, D. K., and Griffes, K. (2013). Best coaching practices for developing team captains. *The Sport Psychologist, 27*, 13–26.

Harrison, P. A., and Narayan, G. (2003). Differences in behavior, psychological factors, and environmental factors associated with participation in school sports and other activities in adolescence. *Journal of School Health, 73*, 113–120.

Hayden, L. A., Whitley, M. A., Cook, A. L., Dumais, A., Silva, M., and Scherer, A. (2015). An exploration of life skill development through sport in three international high schools. *Qualitative Research in Sport, Exercise and Health, 7*, 759–775.

Holt, N. L., Tink, L. N., Mandigo, J. L., and Fox, K. R. (2008). Do youth learn life skills through thier invovlement in high school sport? A case study. *Canadian Journal of Education, 31*, 281–304.

Holt, N. L., Knight, C. J., and Zukiwski, P. (2012). Female athletes' perceptions of teammate conflict in sport: Implications for sport psychology consultants. *The Sport Psychologist, 26*, 135–154.

Knight, C. J., and Holt, N. L. (2014). Parenting in youth tennis: Understanding and enhancing children's experiences. *Psychology of Sport and Exercise, 15*, 155–164.

Lacroix, C., Camiré, M., and Trudel, P. (2008). High school coaches' characteristics and their perspectives on the purpose of school sport participation. *International Journal of Coaching Science, 2*(2), 23–42.

Marsh, H. W., and Kleitman, S. (2003). School athletic participation: Mostly gain with little pain. *Journal of Sport and Exercise Psychology, 25*, 205–228.

Petitpas, A. J., Cornelius, A. E., Van Raalte, J. L., and Jones, T. (2005). A framework for planning youth sport programs that foster psychosocial development. *The Sport Psychologist, 19*, 63–80.

Petitpas, A. J., Cornelius, A., and Van Raalte, J. (2008). Youth development through sport: It's all about relationships. In N. L. Holt (Ed.), *Positive Youth Development through Sport* (pp. 61–70). London: Routledge.

Pot, N., and van Hilvoorde, I. (2013). Generalizing the effects of school sports: Comparing the cultural contexts of school sports in the Netherlands and the USA. *Sport in Society, 16*, 1164–1175.

Rudd, A. (2005). Which "character" should sport develop? *Physical Educator, 62*, 205–211.

School Sport Canada (2013). *About SSC*. Available from http://www.schoolsport.ca

Shields, D. L., and Bredemeier, B. L. (2009). *True Competition: A Guide to Pursuing Excellence in Sport and Society*. Champaign, IL: Human Kinetics.

Steiner, H., McQuivey, R. W., Pavelski, R., Pitts, T., and Kraemer, H. (2000). Adolescents and sports: Risk or benefit? *Clinical Pediatrics, 39*, 161–166.

Trottier, C., and Robitaille, S. (2014). Fostering life skills development in high school and community sport: A comparative analysis of the coach's role. *The Sport Psychologist, 28*, 10–21.

Trudel, P., and Gilbert, W. D. (2006). Coaching and coach education. In D. Kirk, M. O'Sullivan and D. McDonald (Eds.), *Handbook of Physical Education* (pp. 516–539). London: Sage.

Turnnidge, J., Côté, J., and Hancock, D. J. (2014). Positive youth development from sport to life: Explicit or implicit transfer? *Quest, 66,* 203–217.

Voelker, D. K., Gould, D., and Crawford, M. J. (2011). Understanding the experience of high school sport captains. *The Sport Psychologist, 25,* 47–66.

Walsh, D. S., Ozaeta, J., and Wright, P. M. (2010). Transference of responsibility model goals to the school environment: Exploring the impact of a coaching club program. *Physical Education and Sport Pedagogy, 15,* 15–28.

Wilkes, S., and Côté, J. (2010). The developmental experiences of adolescent females in structured basketball programs. *Revue phénEPS/PHEnex Journal, 2,* 1–21.

11

COACHING FOR POSITIVE YOUTH DEVELOPMENT

Jennifer Turnnidge, Blair Evans, Matthew Vierimaa, Veronica Allan, and Jean Côté

From a child's first time throwing a ball, to involvement in elite or recreational sport as a young adult, personal relationships form the foundation of development through sport. As a demonstration of this, Fraser-Thomas et al. (2005) reviewed literature revealing that positive and negative experiences in sport are closely bound to the quality of interpersonal relationships that young athletes develop with parents, peers, and coaches. Broadly, researchers have explored how adults shape the sport activities in which athletes engage during early stages of development (Côté, 1999) and how athletes may decide to pursue a given sport based on whether they have positive relationships with teammates (Evans et al., 2013). Given that the need for belonging is a core social motive (Baumeister and Leary, 1995), it is not surprising that relationships shape sport involvement.

A growing body of literature highlights the integral role that quality interpersonal relationships play in facilitating positive youth development (PYD) in sport (Petitpas et al., 2008). Specifically, relationships feature prominently in numerous frameworks describing athlete development and are often conceptualized as necessary for positive experiences in sport (Fraser-Thomas et al., 2005). This conceptual view is also reflected in the practical nature of athlete development, as sport programs that successfully develop athletes from childhood through to elite competition often prioritize positive personal relationships, whereby coach–athlete relationships, group cohesion, and a sense of community form key ingredients in athlete development (Henriksen et al., 2010). As such, it is crucial for researchers and youth sport organizations to develop strategies that enable young athletes to develop and maintain high quality relationships within sport.

The purpose of this chapter is to demonstrate the potential utility of Transformational Leadership (TFL; Bass and Riggio, 2006) theory for understanding and facilitating high-quality coach–athlete relationships, and ultimately, for fostering PYD in sport. This chapter begins with an overview of a framework that outlines the elements necessary for PYD in sport, and positions quality relationships within this framework. The remainder of this chapter focuses specifically on coach–athlete relationships and presents TFL as a valuable framework for PYD research. In particular, this chapter will illustrate how TFL theory may be useful for both understanding the associations between coaching behaviors and PYD and supporting the development of interpersonally focused coach education. To highlight the utility of TFL, this chapter will outline its practical application to sport coaching, and will lay out an agenda for conducting interventions and research that may advance our understanding of the influence of coach–athlete relationships on PYD in sport.

Quality relationships as the foundation of PYD in sport

Over the past ten years, the number of studies on PYD in sport has steadily proliferated (Holt and Neely, 2011). Drawing upon theoretical and empirical research from developmental and positive psychology, researchers have identified sport as a fertile context in which to cultivate PYD (Fraser-Thomas et al., 2005). Recently, the Personal Assets Framework has been proposed as a conceptual framework that accounts for the mechanisms and outcomes that constitute PYD in sport (Côté et al., in press). Central to this framework is the presumption that youth sport experiences are influenced by three dynamic elements: (a) the types of sport activities that young athletes engage in (i.e. personal engagement in activities); (b) the nature of relationships that athletes form (i.e. quality relationships); and (c) the broader physical and social environments surrounding sport (i.e. appropriate settings). This framework thus outlines the *what*, *who*, and *where* elements that shape youth sport experiences. When designed in a developmentally appropriate manner, the interaction of these three elements provide an immediate positive sport experience that, when repeated over time, will generate changes in an athlete's personal assets.

It is important to note that the Personal Assets Framework conceptualizes athlete development using the 4Cs model (Côté et al., 2010), rather than the 5Cs model (Lerner et al., 2005) of PYD. Although the 5Cs model represents one of the most dominant conceptualizations of PYD within the developmental psychology literature, it has been suggested that the 5Cs may not be entirely appropriate in the sport context. In reviewing the sport literature, Côté and colleagues (2010) found that the constructs of caring, compassion, and character were not well differentiated. As such, Côté et al. (2010) proposed that the constructs of caring and compassion could be integrated into the character domain, resulting in the 4Cs model. This model therefore represents a sport-specific adaptation of the 5Cs, rather than a separate model entirely. This collapsed 4Cs model also marks a return to Little's (1993) original conceptualization, which was later expanded to 5Cs through a similar review process (Lerner et al., 2005).

Research suggests that sport programs and coaching approaches that prioritize the 4Cs (Côté and Gilbert, 2009) are more likely to help young athletes reap the long-term benefits of sport (i.e. the 3Ps): higher levels of performance (i.e. sport expertise), participation (i.e. lifelong participation in sport and physical activity), and personal development (i.e. psychosocial outcomes, such as initiative). Sport programs that focus on developing personal assets might, as an example, provide opportunities for social interactions with peers and adults (e.g. friendships, mentorship), empower athletes to develop skills and to be confident in their abilities (e.g. learning skills through play), and put athletes in situations that promote character development (e.g. establishing moral guidelines). Although this framework highlights that development in sport is a dynamic process that involves several working elements, this particular chapter will focus on the role of *quality relationships* in facilitating PYD through sport.

Quality coach–athlete relationships

While it is clear that youths' development through sport hinges upon adaptive social relationships with many actors in the sport environment, coaches represent one of the most powerful sources of influence. Coaches wield the potential to elicit both positive and negative effects on youth's development. Indeed, a fundamental competency for coaching effectiveness involves coaches' knowledge about how to form interpersonal relationships that promote the 4Cs (Côté and Gilbert, 2009). Evidence suggests that effective coaches meaningfully influence these personal assets (Côté et al., 2010), in addition to the long-term objectives of the 3Ps (Vella et al., 2011).

Although a range of theories highlight the value of coaches' behaviors in relation to youths' development (Smith and Smoll, 2007), TFL theory provides a particularly valuable standpoint to explore how youths' sport experiences are influenced by their coach–athlete relationships. As such, the remainder of this chapter will explore how TFL theory may enhance our understanding of the influence of coaches on PYD in sport.

Transformational Leadership (TFL) theory

Taking the perspective of a current or former athlete, consider how you would respond to the following request: *What characteristics distinguish the coach who had the most positive influence on your sport career?* This type of question was at the heart of the foundational research on TFL where followers were asked to describe influential leaders (Bass et al., 1987). Bass and colleagues' approach for identifying characteristics of effective leaders differed from more traditional approaches in an important way. It centered on employees' reflections and, as such, represents a *follower-centered* conceptualization of leadership.

Over decades of research, TFL has emerged as a formal concept which includes characteristics such as being authentic, promoting cooperation, establishing ethical standards, mentoring employees, and promoting the common good. There are important distinctions between TFL and more transactional forms of leadership. Notably, transactional leadership is considered a necessary foundation for effective leadership, and involves behaviors that involve reward or punishment contingencies or feedback (Avolio, 1999). Transformational leaders build upon this foundation by developing person-centered relationships that empower, inspire, and challenge followers (Bass and Riggio, 2006).

TFL theory may hold significant potential for studying coach–athlete relationships in youth sport because researchers can benefit from the extensive body of literature that has examined TFL in other domains. Studies from a wide range of contexts (e.g. education, healthcare, and organizational settings) have consistently linked TFL with follower outcomes that parallel the 4Cs, such as enhanced performance, self-efficacy, trust, and helping behaviors (see Table 11.1 for a list of outcomes associated with TFL; Barling, 2014).

Although TFL involves a constellation of behaviors, continued research has formed a definition that involves four higher-order themes (Bass and Riggio, 2006):

1. *Idealized influence*, whereby leaders gain trust by modeling prosocial behaviors, treating group members fairly, and following a consistent set of values.
2. *Inspirational motivation*, which is when leaders spur on goal pursuit by holding high expectations and forming a clear vision of the future.
3. *Intellectual stimulation*, which is when leaders provide opportunities for followers to feel autonomous and to contribute creative ideas.
4. *Individualized consideration*, whereby followers have opportunities to form individual relationships with their leader that demonstrate unique expectations and concerns.

TABLE 11.1 Outcomes associated with TFL

PYD outcome	Outcomes associated with TFL
Performance	Performance (organizational, military, sports)
	Effort
	Effectiveness
Participation	Commitment
	Motivation
	Reduced turnover intentions
	Reduced burnout
Personal development:	Self-efficacy
Competence	Empowerment
Confidence	Identification (leader, group, organization)
Connection	Trust
Character	Cohesion
	Creativity/innovation
	Well-being
	Helping behaviors
	Reduced aggressive behaviors

Note: See Barling, 2014; Bass and Riggio, 2006 for more detailed reviews.

With a focus on followers' development, it is not surprising that TFL has gained recognition as a valuable framework for sport research. Particularly in regards to coaching athletes as they develop through childhood and adolescence, TFL parallels the goals of promoting PYD through sport (see Table 11.2 for a comparison of the components of TFL and PYD research). Recently, researchers have explored the utility of TFL theory in sport with promising results. Studies suggest that transformational coaching is associated with positive individual and group-level outcomes, such as athlete satisfaction, effort, performance, and group cohesion (Arthur et al., 2011; Charbonneau et al., 2001; Rowold, 2006; Stenling and Tafvelin, 2014). Of particular interest to PYD researchers, Vella et al. (2013a) demonstrated that transformational coaching behaviors were linked with youths' personal development in sport, including the development of personal and social skills, cognitive skills, goal-setting skills, and initiative. The effectiveness of TFL within sport thus appears to mirror its positive influence in other contexts.

Contrasting TFL with comparable coaching styles in sport

Transformational coaching is also well-matched for sport research because it complements existing coaching theories in many ways. Specifically, it parallels the uptake of contemporary relationship-centered models of coach leadership. Jowett's model (e.g. Jowett and Cockerill, 2003) is a notable example, revealing the power of coach–athlete relationships that feature closeness, commitment, and complementarity. Other sport research more directly addresses coach leadership, for example, Chelladurai's (1990) model of sport leadership places athletes' expectations for coaches as a component influencing leadership.

TFL also aligns with existing models that describe how coaches may shape athlete experiences by adopting *styles* that prioritize components such as autonomy support or mastery-oriented goals. Notably, Smith, Smoll, and colleagues published numerous studies that support the positive outcomes that result when coaches use a mastery-oriented approach—focusing on personal development and demonstrating high levels of supportive and instructional coach behaviors (see Smith and Smoll, 2007 for a review). Similarly, coaches can adopt an autonomy-supportive coaching style by using behaviors that provide athletes with choices, acknowledge feelings, and avoid controlling behaviors (Mageau and Vallerand, 2003). This coaching approach has proven to be efficacious among youth sport coaches, where autonomy-supportive coach behaviors have been associated with athletes' need satisfaction and psychosocial outcomes such as self-esteem and initiative (Coatsworth and Conroy, 2009).

Although each of these coaching models and styles reflect certain elements of TFL, transformational coaching is nevertheless a novel approach within the sport realm because it *integrates* these elements within a single leadership style. Furthermore, it is uniquely relevant for PYD because it involves components that are not addressed in existing sport coaching models (e.g. moral and ethical components featured within the idealized influence dimension of TFL). As such, transformational coaching may be an ideal model to understand how coaches can influence PYD.

TABLE 11.2 Parallels between TFL theory, PYD research, and practical strategies

TFL component	Parallels to PYD research	Practical strategies for implementing TFL in sport
Idealized influence	Effective coaches develop a strong understanding of their coaching values and make an effort to demonstrate these values in their interactions with their athletes (Becker, 2013). Coaches who are firm and confident in their values are more likely to behave in a consistent manner, which can help athletes focus on their own development (Becker, 2009).	Discuss personal values (e.g. treating others respectfully, good sportspersonship, honesty, integrity, humility) with athletes. Model personal values during athlete interactions. Recognize athletes who exhibit pro-social behaviors. Display humility (e.g. apologize for one's mistakes).
Inspirational motivation	Coaches enhance athletes' confidence and motivation by believing in them as athletes and by holding high expectations for their athletes (Fraser-Thomas and Côté, 2009).	Encourage athletes to set challenging goals. Communicate an optimistic team vision. Communicate clear expectations. Provide genuine feedback.
Intellectual stimulation	Coaching styles that offer athletes choices, provide initiative-building opportunities, and encourage athlete input foster a myriad of positive athlete outcomes, such as well-being and engagement (Mageau and Vallerand, 2003).	Seek athletes' input on aspects such as leadership choices, coaching preferences, and the content and organization of sport activities. Provide athletes with opportunities to take on decision-making roles (e.g. leading practices).
Individualized consideration	Effective coaches individualize their coaching behaviors (Becker, 2013), which can positively contribute to PYD (Erickson et al., 2011). Coaches' communication with their athletes about outside-sport topics is linked with higher levels of sport enjoyment and commitment (Stuntz and Spearance, 2010).	Show interest in youth, not just as athletes, but as well-rounded individuals. Discuss athletes' lives outside of sport. Find ways to support their athletes' interests, goals, and development both inside and outside of sport. Adapt practice activities to suit athletes' needs and abilities.

How TFL works

While a great deal of attention has been paid to the potential positive *outcomes* that are associated with TFL (Barling, 2014; Bass and Riggio, 2006), the *processes* through which TFL affects followers' outcomes are not as well understood. This is a significant limitation to acknowledge since TFL primarily exerts indirect effects on outcomes (Barling, 2014). Indeed, there are several intervening variables (i.e. mediators) through which the effects of TFL may ultimately influence PYD. As such, it is crucial for researchers to not only explore *if* TFL works, but also *how* and *why* it works (Turnnidge and Côté, 2014).

Intrapersonal mediators

With regards to the intrapersonal mediators, transformational leaders help their followers develop more adaptive perceptions of their tasks and themselves. Previous research highlights that transformational leaders may indirectly influence developmental outcomes by encouraging their followers to discover meaning and value in their activities (Arnold et al., 2007). Transformational leaders may also enhance their followers' enthusiasm for their tasks and self-determined forms of motivation (Charbonneau et al., 2001). Additionally, transformational leaders may indirectly influence developmental outcomes by enhancing followers' perceptions of their own abilities (Nielsen and Munir, 2009) and emotions (Rowold and Rohmann, 2009).

Interpersonal mediators

Transformational leaders can also shape followers' development by improving the quality of relationships with their leader and group. For instance, transformational leaders can foster followers' personal identification and trust in their leader (Barling, 2014). More specifically, a TFL style may contribute to PYD because followers perceive that: (a) their leaders' values should be respected and adopted; (b) their leaders' intentions and behaviors can be trusted; and (c) their leaders care and support them (Barling, 2014). Similarly, TFL may exert its influence by enhancing the quality of relationships with one's peers. Transformational leaders influence processes such as team norms, group identification, and cohesion to enhance their followers' connection to their team (Pillai and Williams, 2004). Moreover, by emphasizing shared goals and a collective mission, transformational leaders enable members to believe in their group's potential and to build stronger relationships with their teammates.

Environmental mediators

Additionally, transformational leaders can indirectly influence followers' developmental outcomes by creating environments that encourage autonomy and initiative, state clear goals and expectations, involve followers in decision-making processes, recognize followers' achievements, and facilitate fair, trusting, and respectful relationships (Nemanich and Keller, 2007). Given that the majority of research examining mediating mechanisms has been conducted outside of sport, it may be worthwhile to explore which variables may be particularly salient for fostering PYD in sport.

Facilitating TFL in youth sport

It is important to consider what transformational coaching may look like in practice (see Table 11.2 for a list of practical strategies). For instance, idealized influence could be embodied by coaches who both discuss their personal values with their athletes and act in accordance with these values. Transformational coaches *practice what they preach* and thus, coaches who stress the importance of pro-social behaviors among teammates or opponents (e.g. helping others) should employ such behaviors in their interactions with athletes and other coaches. Second, inspirational motivation can be enhanced when coaches convey enthusiasm and optimism in their athletes' abilities. By holding high expectations and encouraging athletes to set challenging goals, transformational coaches communicate that they believe in their athletes' potential. Third, coaches can facilitate intellectual stimulation by challenging their athletes to critically approach their sport activities. For instance, coaches may seek athletes' perspectives by asking questions such as, "Why do you think this game strategy didn't work?" or "What drill do you think we should do in order to improve this skill?" By encouraging athletes to solve problems and contribute new ideas, coaches can provide invaluable opportunities for development. Lastly, individually considerate coaches can make a concerted effort to understand their athletes. This may involve discussing both sport- and non-sport-related matters, as well as adapting sport activities to an individual athlete's needs or abilities. For instance, coaches may recognize when an athlete is having a tough day and adjust their practice plan accordingly.

Training transformational coaches: looking back

The importance of a TFL style and its potential for positively influencing athletes lends credit to a very important area for future development: training youth sport coaches to be transformational leaders. Research from a variety of contexts, including military, organizations, and physical education, demonstrates that TFL behaviors can be improved through training, and can ultimately improve follower outcomes (Kelloway and Barling, 2000). As such, the following section will provide a brief overview of TFL-based interventions, followed by practical suggestions for the design, implementation, and evaluation of future transformational coaching interventions.

The first evidence to suggest that TFL behaviors are not only trainable, but can also produce positive outcomes for followers, involved Popper et al.'s (1992) training program for infantry cadets in the Israeli army. This work provided an initial foundation for TFL training interventions, and experimental follow-up studies with bank branch managers (Barling et al., 1996) and district managers of large healthcare corporations (Kelloway et al., 2000) solidified a base of evidence for the success of TFL training programs.

More recent experimental research has reaffirmed the causal propositions of TFL theory. Particularly relevant for PYD research, investigations of TFL training among physical educators (Beauchamp et al., 2011) and youth sport coaches (Vella et al., 2013b) have also demonstrated success in developing transformational behaviors. In the physical education context, Beauchamp et al. (2011) revealed that students in the intervention condition rated their teachers as displaying significantly higher levels of transformational teaching and reported significantly higher levels of self-determined motivation, self-efficacy, and intentions to be physically active. Applying TFL training in the youth sport environment, Vella et al. (2013b) found that their intervention was associated with higher rates of perceived transformational coaching, in addition to more positive developmental experiences among athletes. Given this evidence, it appears that transformational coaching interventions might help to foster PYD.

Training transformational coaches: looking forward

Kelloway and Barling (2000) recommend that effective TFL interventions should: (a) present TFL principles; (b) demonstrate what TFL behaviors look like; (c) create opportunities to practice TFL behaviors; and (d) offer feedback on the performance of TFL behaviors. Further, transformational coaching interventions should help coaches become aware of how their leadership behaviors can influence PYD. By raising coaches' awareness of their ability to make a difference in the quality of athletes' sport experiences, such interventions may also enhance coaching efficacy and encourage greater effort and persistence in adopting a transformational coaching style.

A transformational coaching workshop may include activities such as reviewing the components of TFL theory and discussing how they relate to effective coaching, providing examples of behaviors that are representative of transformational coaching (e.g. case studies, videos), role-playing exercises to practice transformational coaching behaviors, the development of personalized leadership development plans, and identifying potential barriers to adopting a transformational coaching style in practice, as well as discussing strategies to overcome these barriers (Beauchamp et al., 2011; Vella et al., 2013b).

In an effort to support coaches' continued use of transformational coaching behaviors, researchers and practitioners should ensure that interventions incorporate behavior change techniques into their design. This is particularly important given that existing coach education programs have often overlooked behavior change theories in their design or evaluation (Langan et al., 2013). Behavior change techniques may involve action planning, goal setting, modelling, self-monitoring, and providing feedback (Michie et al., 2013). By integrating these techniques, it is hoped that such interventions may better support coaches' sustained use of transformational coaching behaviors once the interventions have ended.

Outside of formal transformational coaching interventions, previous research indicates that the primary source of knowledge for most coaches is experience and observation of other coaches (Cushion et al., 2003). Thus, it is also important to acknowledge and incorporate alternative sources of coach learning to complement transformational coaching workshops. Informal networks or information-sharing platforms of colleagues and peers may provide additional support for the adoption and maintenance of desirable coach behaviors. As such, coach educators may consider the inclusion of learning communities or communities of practice as a valuable component of transformational coaching initiatives (Culver and Trudel, 2008). Overall, the development of transformational coaching interventions represents a particularly exciting avenue for future research, as PYD researchers may explore not only whether such interventions work, but how and why transformational coaching interventions may contribute to PYD in sport.

Conclusion

Considering the fundamental role that relationships play in facilitating PYD through sport, it is not surprising that researchers and sport organizations have spent decades understanding how to promote positive coach–athlete relationships. Indeed, an entire field of youth sport research has emerged, resulting in: (a) numerous frameworks that conceptualize potential coaching approaches to promote athlete development; and (b) several interventions that correspondingly strive to promote these coaching approaches. TFL nevertheless integrates and adds to this emerging body of knowledge, as a person-centered leadership approach that features athlete development as a priority in coach–athlete relationships—which is fostered when coaches demonstrate idealized influence, inspirational motivation, intellectual stimulation, and individualized consideration.

The majority of TFL research in sport to date has focused on examining the types of outcomes associated with transformational coaching. Moving forward, it is imperative for researchers to examine the *black box* of TFL to explore how and why transformational coaching contributes to PYD in sport. For instance, future research could investigate how variables such as motivation, meaningful tasks, team dynamics, and motivational climate serve as mediators between transformational coaching and PYD. Since the TFL literature has been dominated by questionnaire-based, correlational designs, there is also a need to embrace a diversity of research designs and methodologies to shed new light on the inner workings of TFL. For instance, longitudinal studies may help to both strengthen the evidence in relation to the causality of process-based mechanisms and illustrate the dynamic nature of coach–athlete relationships over time. Qualitative studies may serve to provide an in-depth and contextualized picture of coaches', athletes', and other stakeholders' perceptions of the processes that influence athlete development. Further, observational methods may help to uncover the behavioral processes underpinning the association between transformational coaching and PYD. The findings of such studies may enable researchers and practitioners to: (a) educate coaches on the importance of transformational coaching; (b) offer insight into how to integrate this coaching style into practice and competition; and (c) design, implement, and evaluate interventions that will help coaches develop their TFL behaviors. In doing so, this research may provide considerable insight into how high-quality coach–athlete relationships can foster PYD, and ultimately facilitate the long-term outcomes of performance, participation, and personal development.

Acknowledgment

The writing of this chapter was supported by a standard research grant from the Social Sciences and Humanities Research Council of Canada (SSHRC Grant # 435-2014-0038).

References

Arnold, K. A., Turner, N., Barling, J., Kelloway, E. K., and McKee, M. C. (2007). Transformational leadership and psychological well-being: The mediating role of meaningful work. *Journal of Occupational Health Psychology, 12*, 193–203.

Arthur, C. A., Woodman, T., Ong, C. W., Hardy, L., and Ntoumanis, N. (2011). The role of athlete narcissism in moderating the relationship between coaches' transformational leader behaviors and athlete motivation. *Journal of Sport and Exercise Psychology, 33*, 3–19.

Avolio, B. J. (1999). *Full Leadership Development: Building the Vital Forces in Organizations.* Thousand Oaks, CA: Sage.

Barling, J. (2014). *The Science of Leadership: Lessons from Research for Organizational Leaders.* New York: Oxford University Press.

Barling, J., Weber, T., and Kelloway, E. K. (1996). Effects of transformational leadership training on attitudinal and financial outcomes: A field experiment. *Journal of Applied Psychology, 81*, 827–832.

Bass, B. M., and Riggio, R. E. (2006). *Transformational Leadership* (2nd ed.). New York: Psychology Press.

Bass, B. M., Avolio, B. J., and Goodheim, L. (1987). Quantitative description of world-class industrial, political, and military leaders. *Journal of Management, 13*, 7–19.

Baumeister, R. F., and Leary, M. R. (1995). The need to belong: Desire for interpersonal attachments as a fundamental human motivation. *Psychological Bulletin, 117*, 497–529.

Beauchamp, M. R., Barling, J., and Morton, K. L. (2011). Transformational teaching and adolescent self-determined motivation, self-efficacy, and intentions to engage in leisure time physical activity: A randomised controlled pilot trial. *Applied Psychology: Health and Well-Being, 3*, 127–150.

Becker, A. (2009). It's not what they do, it's how they do it: Athlete experiences of great coaching. *International Journal of Sport Science and Coaching, 4*, 93–119.

Becker, A. (2013). Quality coaching behaviors. In P. Potrac, W. Gilbert, and J. Denision (Eds.), *Routledge Handbook of Sports Coaching* (pp. 184–195). New York: Routledge.

Charbonneau, D., Barling, J., and Kelloway, E. K. (2001). Transformational leadership and sports performance: The mediating role of intrinsic motivation. *Journal of Applied Social Psychology, 31*, 1521–1534.

Chelladurai, P. (1990). Leadership in sports: A review. *International Journal of Sport Psychology, 21*, 328–354.

Coatsworth, J. D., and Conroy, D. E. (2009). The effects of autonomy-supportive coaching, need satisfaction, and self-perceptions on initiative and identity in youth swimmers. *Developmental Psychology, 45*, 320–328.

Côté, J. (1999). The influence of the family in the development of talent in sport. *The Sport Psychologist, 13*, 395–417.

Côté, J., and Gilbert, W. (2009). An integrative definition of coaching effectiveness and expertise. *International Journal of Sport Science and Coaching, 4*, 307–323.

Côté, J., Bruner, M. W., Erickson, K., Strachan, L., and Fraser-Thomas, J. (2010). Athlete development and coaching. In J. Lyle and C. Cushion (Eds.), *Sport Coaching: Professionalism and Practice* (pp. 3–83). Oxford: Elsevier.

Côté, J., Turnnidge, J., and Vierimaa, M. (in press). A personal assets approach to youth sport. In A. Smith and K. Green (Eds.), *Handbook of Youth Sport*. London, UK: Routledge.

Culver, D., and Trudel, P. (2008). Clarifying the concept of communities of practice in sport. *International Journal of Sports Science and Coaching, 3*, 1–10.

Cushion, C. J., Armour, K. M., and Jones, R. L. (2003). Coach education and continuing professional development: Experience and learning to coach. *Quest, 55*, 215–230.

Erickson, K., Côté, J., Hollenstein, T., and Deakin, J. (2011). Examining coach–athlete interactions using state space grids: An observation analysis in competitive youth sport. *Psychology of Sport and Exercise, 12*, 645–654.

Evans, M. B., Eys, M. A., and Wolf, S. A. (2013). Exploring the nature of interpersonal influence in elite individual sport teams. *Journal of Applied Sport Psychology, 25*, 448–462.

Fraser-Thomas, J., and Côté, J. (2009). Understanding adolescents' positive and negative developmental experiences in sport. *The Sport Psychologist, 23*, 3–23.

Fraser-Thomas, J., Côté, J., and Deakin, J. (2005). Youth sport programs: An avenue to foster positive youth development. *Physical Education and Sport Pedagogy, 10*, 19–40.

Henriksen, K., Stambulova, N., and Roessler, K. K. (2010). Successful talent development in track and field: Considering the role of environment. *Scandinavian Journal of Medicine and Science in Sports, 20*, 122–132.

Holt, N. L., and Neely, K. C. (2011). Positive youth development through sport: A review. *Revista de Iberoamericana de Psicología del Ejercicio y el Deporte, 6*, 299–316.

Jowett, S., and Cockerill, I. M. (2003). Olympic medallists' perspective of the athlete–coach relationship. *Psychology of Sport and Exercise, 4*, 313–331.

Kelloway, E. K., and Barling, J. (2000). What have we learned about developing transformational leaders? *Leadership and Organizational Development Journal, 21*, 355–362.

Kelloway, E. K., Barling, J., and Helleur, J. (2000). Enhancing transformational leadership: The roles of training and feedback. *Leadership and Organizational Development Journal, 21*, 145–149.

Langan, E., Blake, C., and Lonsdale, C. (2013). Systematic review of the effectiveness of interpersonal coach education interventions on athlete outcomes. *Psychology of Sport and Exercise, 14*, 37–49.

Lerner, R. M., Lerner, J. V., Almerigi, J., Theokas, C., Naudeau, S., Gestsdottir, S., … et al. (2005). Positive youth development, participation in community youth development programs, and community contributions of fifth grade adolescents: Findings from the first wave of the 4-H Study of positive youth development. *Journal of Early Adolescence, 25*, 17–71.

Little, R. R. (1993). *What's Working for Today's Youth: The Issues, the Programs, and the Learnings.* Paper presented at the Institute for Children, Youth, and Families Fellows' Colloquium, Michigan State University, East Lansing, MI.

Mageau, G. A., and Vallerand, R. J. (2003). The coach-athlete relationship: A motivational model. *Journal of Sports Science, 21*, 883–904.

Michie, S., Richardson, M., Johnston, M., Abraham, C., Francis, J., Hardeman, W., … and Wood, C. E. (2013). The behavior change technique taxonomy (v1) of 93 hierarchically clustered techniques: Building an international consensus for the reporting of behavior change interventions. *Annals of Behavioral Medicine, 46*, 81–95.

Nemanich, L. A., and Keller, R. T. (2007). Transformational leadership in an acquisition: A field study of employees. *The Leadership Quarterly, 18*, 49–68.

Nielsen, K., and Munir, F. (2009). How do transformational leaders influence followers' affective well-being? Exploring the mediating role of self-efficacy. *Work and Stress, 23*, 313–329.

Petitpas, A. J., Cornelius, A., and Van Raalte, J. (2008). Youth development in sport: It's all about relationships. In N. L. Holt (Ed.) *Positive Youth Development through Sport* (pp. 61–70). London, UK: Routledge.

Pillai, R., and Williams, E. A. (2004). Transformational leadership, self-efficacy, group cohesiveness, commitment, and performance. *Journal of Organizational Change Management, 17*, 144–159.

Popper, M., Landau, O., and Gluskinos, U. M. (1992). The Israeli defence forces: An example of transformational leadership. *Leadership and Organization Development Journal, 13*, 3–8.

Rowold, J. (2006). Transformational and transactional leadership in martial arts. *Journal of Applied Sport Psychology, 18*, 312–325.

Rowold, J., and Rohmann, A. (2009). Transformational and transactional leadership styles, followers' positive and negative emotions, and performance in German nonprofit orchestras. *Nonprofit Management and Leadership, 20*, 41–59.

Smith, R. E., and Smoll, F. L. (2007). Social-cognitive approach to coaching behaviors. In S. Jowett, and D. Lavallee (Eds), *Social Psychology in Sport* (pp. 75–90). Champaign, IL: Human Kinetics.

Stenling, A., and Tafvelin, S. (2014). Transformational leadership and well-being in sports: The mediating role of need satisfaction. *Journal of Applied Sport Psychology, 26*, 182–196.

Stuntz, C. P., and Spearance, A. L. (2010). Cross-domain relationships in two sport populations: Measurement validation including prediction of motivation-related variables. *Psychology of Sport and Exercise, 11*, 267–274.

Turnnidge, J., and Côté, J. (2014, October). *How Leadership Works: A Systematic Review of the Processes by which Transformational Leadership Influences Follower Development.* Poster presented at the meeting of the Canadian Society for Psychomotor Learning and Sport Psychology (SCAPPS), London, Canada.

Vella, S., Oades, L., and Crowe, T. (2011). The role of the coach in facilitating positive youth development: Moving from theory to practice. *Journal of Applied Sport Psychology*, *23*, 33–48.

Vella, S., Oades, L., and Crowe, T. (2013a). The relationship between coach leadership, the coach–athlete relationship, team success, and the positive developmental experiences of adolescent soccer players. *Physical Education and Sport Pedagogy, 18*, 549–561.

Vella, S., Oades, L., and Crowe, T. (2013b). A pilot test of transformational leadership training for sports coaches: Impact on the developmental experiences of adolescent athletes. *International Journal of Sports Science and Coaching, 8*, 513–530.

12

LEADERSHIP AS A LIFE SKILL IN YOUTH SPORTS

Daniel R. Gould

Global warming, water shortages, hunger, and a complex and ever changing world are some of the major challenges today's youth will face in their adult lives. It is not surprising, then, that adults are often concerned with ways they can help prepare young people to deal with these challenges. Teaching or instilling leadership skills in young people is thought to be one of the most important ways for accomplishing this goal. In a survey study of high school coaches, for example, Gould et al. (2006) found that coaches believed leadership was one of the most important life skills that young athletes must acquire and develop.

Sport participation is often thought to be a powerful vehicle for developing leadership and other important life skills in young people. Martinek and Hellison (2009) argue that these contexts provide numerous opportunities for young people to gain leadership experience (e.g. working with teammates to pursue common goals) and also have the benefit of being highly interactive. Furthermore, they suggest that sport and physical activity provide an opportunity for youth to learn leadership in an enjoyable, motivating, and meaningful environment.

Given the above, it is not surprising that over the last several decades there has been increased interest in understanding how involvement in sport and physical-activity-based programs can contribute to the development of youth leadership. Are leadership skills learned through sport participation or is this mere rhetoric from those involved in sport and sport-related activities? How do youth learn leadership? What factors influence youth leadership effectiveness? These are just some of the key questions that need to be answered. This chapter reviews the research that focuses on leadership as a life skill and the relationship between youth sports and physical activity involvement and leadership development in young people. Specifically, leadership and youth leadership will be defined and types of leaders will be discussed, the research on youth leadership in general and youth leadership in sport will be summarized, and implications for understanding and developing youth leadership through sport and physical activity participation examined.

Leadership and types of leaders

There is no one universal definition of either leadership in general or youth leadership in particular. Instead, leadership has been defined in many different ways. For example, youth leadership has been operationalized in the literature in the form of personal characteristics, demonstrated actions, or the process of leading itself and has been viewed as anything from self-esteem to peer approval (Libby et al., 2006). However, this does not mean that we do not have any good working definitions of leadership. After reviewing the literature and examining many of the major theoretical models, Northouse (2010), for example, identified a number of common characteristics of most definitions and conceptualizations of leadership. These characteristics include the notion that leadership is a process, occurs in groups, involves influence, and involves the pursuit of common goals. Thus, Northouse (2010, p. 3) defined leadership as "a process whereby an individual influences a group of individuals to achieve a common goal." For the purposes of this chapter, we will adopt the definition of Gould et al. (2012, p. 164), who extended and slightly modified Northouse's view where youth leadership is seen as "a complex process that involves the effort of an individual (i.e., a leader) to help groups identify and achieve personal and group goals."

Scholars have also identified types of leaders. For example, distinctions are made between formal or assigned and emergent leaders (Northouse, 2010). Formal leaders occupy a specific position in a group or on a team (e.g. a sport captain) while emergent leaders do not occupy official positions but often are perceived as leaders by other group members (e.g. a peer leader on a sport team). Reference is also often made to transactional versus transformational leaders (Bass, 1998). Transactional leaders focus on exchanges between a leader and those who follow him or her. They focus on accomplishing group tasks by providing direction and feedback. They tell people what to do and reward them for doing it. In contrast, a transformational leader engages with followers in ways that create connections that raise those followers' levels of motivation and help them see and reach their full potential. Transformational leaders also help followers to view challenges and tasks from new perspectives and achieve long-term visions of success. Finally, while distinctions can be made between transactional versus transformational leaders, in reality they are not mutually distinctive. Transformational leaders, for example, may need to employ many of the skills emphasized in transactional leaders like giving directions and providing feedback. However, they go beyond these transactional skills in that they create close connections and inspire and motivate their followers often to do more than even the followers think they are capable of achieving.

Theories of leadership

General psychology theories

Thousands of leadership studies have been conducted, so it is not surprising that a number of theories of leadership have been developed over the years. These include trait theories that emphasize the importance of leader characteristics, style approaches that make distinctions between task- and relationship-oriented approaches to leadership, situational models that focus on leadership in particular situations, contingency theories that consider leader styles and the situations they lead in, path-goal theories that focus on how leaders work with and motivate followers to complete specific goals, leader member exchange models that center on interactions between leaders and followers, transformational leadership which focuses attention on the charismatic and emotional aspects of leadership, and authentic leadership that, as the name implies, focuses on the authenticity of leaders (Northouse, 2010). In general, these theories have moved from a focus on individual traits and situational influences to more interactional views that consider how leader characteristics interact with situational determinants to determine leadership effectiveness. Contemporary approaches also place greater emphasis on how leaders influence followers via their authenticity, charisma, and motivational and affective processes.

Sport-based theories of leadership

Sport-based theories and views of leadership have paralleled developments in general psychology and other fields, although the number of researchers working in these areas are far fewer and the total body of work is much less (Chelladurai, 2007; Schonfeld, 2008; Weinberg and Gould, 2015). Most of the research has examined coaching leadership and two theories have emerged: Chelladurai's multidimensional model of leadership (Chelladurai, 2007; Chelladurai and Saleh, 1978) and Smoll and Smith's (1989) cognitive-mediational leadership model. Other initial work has also applied transactional–transformational leadership models to sport (Rowold, 2006; Charbonneau et al., 2001).

Chelladurai's multidimensional model of leadership contends that the effectiveness of a leader depends on the characteristics of the athletes and the constraints of the sport situation. According to this theory, the satisfaction and performance of athletes depends on three types of leader/coach behavior: required, preferred, and actual. When these three types of behaviors are aligned, the model predicts that athlete satisfaction and performance will be maximized.

The cognitive-mediational model developed by Smoll and Smith (1989) contends that the leadership behaviors of a coach are influenced by characteristics of the coach, the athletes, and the situation. Based on these factors coaches emit certain behaviors, their athletes' perceive these behaviors, and based on those perceptions the athletes react and respond. The Coach Behavior Assessment System

(CBAS) was developed (Smith et al., 1977) to test this model. Results have shown that coach behaviors have been related to athletes' perceptions of those behaviors, as well as to the attitudes, motivation, and behaviors of the athletes (Smoll and Smith, 2010).

Both the multidimensional and cognitive-mediational models of leadership have garnered support in the literature. However, neither theory is seen as the single dominant explanation for understanding coaching leadership. However, both have provided a strong foundation for studying and understanding coaching leadership. They have also demonstrated that complex sets of factors, athlete perceptions, and interactional models are needed to understand coaching leadership. While these models have not been applied to youth leadership, it is likely that similar complex relationships linking leader behaviors, situational parameters, and follower perceptions would explain youth leadership.

Youth leadership models

Several models of youth leadership have been discussed in the literature with one focusing on leadership development in youth generally (van Linden and Fertman, 1998) and the second focusing on leadership development in physical activity contexts (Martinek and Hellison, 2009). In their book *Youth Leadership* van Linden and Fertman (1998) forwarded a model explaining how youth leaders develop, regardless of the setting. This model holds that all youth can learn to lead and that youth leadership is a continuous process that involves three stages: awareness, interaction, and mastery (see Table 12.1). In the awareness stage a young person must realize that he or she has leadership capabilities and can lead. This is an important task as many young people never think of themselves as leaders or have a very simplified understanding of leadership (e.g. leadership is bossing people around). It is during the interaction stage that the young person develops a more sophisticated knowledge of leadership and begins to view him or herself as a leader. He or she begins to work on key leadership skills like learning how to listen and fundamental communication skills like speaking in front of a group. Finally, in the mastery stage the young person has a much better understanding of what leadership involves and his or her leadership capabilities, and he or she further refines his or her leadership skills.

Van Linden and Fertman (1998) also contend that young people must learn a number of cognitive, emotional, and behavioral skills if they are to learn to lead. These skills improve across the three stages of leader development and are organized into five dimensions (see Table 12.1). These dimensions include: *leadership information* or what young people need to know about leaders and leadership; *leadership attitudes* comprised of the dispositions, thoughts, and feelings youth have about themselves as leaders; *communication skills*; *decision-making skills*; and *stress management skills*. Finally, the model suggests that to effectively lead others, youth must develop both transactional skills like learning to speak to groups or how to provide feedback to others, as well as transformational skills that allow them to connect with and motivate others.

TABLE 12.1 Van Linden and Fertman's (1998) stages of youth leadership model

	Stage 1: Awareness ★	*Stage 2: Interaction* ★	*Stage 3: Mastery* ★
Leadership Information			
Transformational	Group expectations and dynamics	Internalizing group expectations and dynamics	Internalizing group expectations and dynamics
Transactional	What and why of leadership development	Learning to assess needs of self and others	Focusing attention and allocating resources
Leadership Attitude			
Transformational	Awareness of personal leadership	Validating attitudes, being ethical	Vision, competence
Transactional	Shared group leadership, assertiveness	Acting ethically and sensitively	Requesting feedback, working toward goals
Communication Skills			
Transformational	Distinctions made among aggressiveness, assertiveness, and passivity	Listening	Processing thoughts and feelings effectively
Transactional	Verbal and non-verbal messages	Practicing assertiveness	Expressing thoughts successfully
Decision-Making Skills			
Transformational	Awareness of decision-making as a leadership quality	Beginning to see alternatives and consequences	Higher levels of decision-making
Transactional	Active awareness of decision-making process	Practicing using a decision-making model	Regularly evaluating decisions made
Stress-Management Skills			
Transformational	Identifying personal stress	Managing the environment and self	Monitoring need to increase or decrease stress
Transactional	Stress management	Keeping a schedule, trying out new ways to cope.	Routinely practicing methods of managing stress

★ Note. Examples only. Please see van Linden and Fertman (1998, p. 73, p. 93, and p. 110) for more details.

Unfortunately, there are few, if any, empirical tests of van Linden and Fertman's model of youth leadership development. However, it does provide a useful heuristic framework to understand youth leadership as a developmental process that takes time and involves the development of a number of cognitive, behavioral, and emotional skills. Based on their work with underserved youth taking part in sport and physical activity clubs, Martinek and Hellison (2009) developed a model of stages of youth leadership. This model is based upon Hellison's (1995) five-stage personal and social responsibility model of youth development. The stages of youth leader development include:

* taking responsibility;
* leadership awareness;
* cross-age leadership; and
* self-actualized leadership.

In this model Hellison and Martinek contend that before youth can learn to lead they must first learn how to take responsibility for themselves and their own actions. Once they are responsible for themselves, young people can begin to become aware of their own leadership potential. Cross-age leadership opportunities, then, allow young people to learn to care for others and begin to become compassionate leaders. Lastly, in the self-actualization stage youth leaders begin to transfer or extend their leadership skills to other life domains. Like the van Linden and Fertman model, few empirical tests of this model have been carried out. However, the model grew out of Hellison and Martinek's fieldwork with youth in sport and physical activity settings.

In summary, both these models suggest that leadership is a developmental process that unfolds over time. Since it is a developmental process scholars suggest that young people learn to lead by progressing through sequential stages and learn skills that progressively build upon one another. Lastly, learning to be a leader not only involves learning a variety of transactional and transformational skills but also involves the young person better understanding leadership and forming impressions of him or herself as a leader.

Research on youth leadership and youth leadership in sport

Unfortunately, there is only scant research on youth leadership in sport. This parallels general psychology where youth leadership is understudied. However, over the last two decades some studies have been conducted, fewer with youth under the age of eighteen years and more with college-aged athletes. The research that has been carried out can be examined within four general categories: antecedents of youth leadership; roles youth leaders play as sport captains; consequences of youth leadership; and sport- and physical-activity-based leadership development programs and interventions. The research in each of these areas will be discussed below.

Antecedents and characteristics of youth leadership

Research in general psychology has shown that youth leaders tend to be older (Dhuey and Lipscomb, 2008) and have higher emotional intelligence and ability than their peers (Charbonneau and Adelheid, 2002). Peer leaders are viewed as having higher social support, status, an effective personality, and motivational attributes that make them leaders (Schneider et al., 2002; Ward and Ellis, 2008). Finally, emerging research shows that early youth experiences are related to both later life leadership patterns and leadership styles used. Child-rearing and parenting practices have been associated with becoming a leader. For example, authoritative parenting and modest rule breaking in childhood was correlated to adult leadership roles (Avolio et al., 2009) while a relationship has been shown between parents who demonstrate transformational leadership and transformational leadership use in children (Zacharatos et al., 2000).

Sport psychologists have also examined characteristics and antecedents of youth leaders. Athlete leaders have been shown to have an internal locus of control (Yukelson et al., 1983) and demonstrate responsibility (Klonsky, 1991). They also demonstrate high levels of competitiveness, high aspirations, emotional expressiveness, and acceptance as perceived by coaches (Klonsky, 1991). Pease and Zhang (2002) found a significant and positive relationship between self-esteem and coach and player perceptions of leadership roles in male athletes, aged nine to twelve. In a study of male university team captains, Dupuis et al. (2006) found that athlete leaders were perceived as being trustworthy, respectful, and optimistic. They also had the ability to effectively communicate and regulate their emotions.

Other investigators have examined athletes', teammates', and coaches' views regarding athlete leaders. Glenn and Horn (1993) examined predictors of self-perceived leadership in scholastic female soccer players. It was found that high self-esteem, perceived sport competence, a mixture of masculine or instrumental and feminine or expressive characteristics, and low competitive trait anxiety were viewed as important peer leader characteristics. Coach and peer ratings of athlete leadership tendencies, however, were more strongly related to player skill level than other psychological variables. Moran and Weiss (2006), studying leadership in male and female high school soccer players, found similar results. These studies suggest that athletic ability is an important factor in selecting youth leaders in sport.

In summary, this research suggests that youth leaders have high ability, higher self-esteem, positive motivational attributes and personality characteristics, and status and are seen as trustworthy and respected. They also have high perceived competence, demonstrate competitiveness, tend to have low competitive trait anxiety, and have effective communication skills as well as good emotional regulation skills. Outside of high ability, the skills that are seen as important in youth leaders in sport are most likely dependent on whether coaches, peers, or peer leaders are making these ratings.

Roles youth leaders play

Several researchers have examined the roles youth leaders play. Todd and Kent (2004), for instance, surveyed high school athletes to determine which characteristics of an ideal peer leader were judged to be most important. Findings revealed that instrumental items such as "works hard in practices and games," "shows respect of others on your team," and "expects high levels of performance from self and teammates" were judged to be most important. Some gender differences emerged with males rating instrumental items like those previously mentioned more important than females, who placed equal importance on both instrumental and expressive items (e.g. "warm and friendly towards teammates").

Gould and his colleagues conducted a series of studies that have focused on the high school sport captain experience. In their first study qualitative interviews were conducted with thirteen college freshmen who had served as high school sport captains the year before beginning college (Voelker et al., 2011). Results revealed that the vast majority of the participants viewed their captaincy experience as positive. However, they identified key challenges they faced, such as dealing with their captaincy responsibilities and being held accountable for them, meeting expectations and being scrutinized, and maintaining neutrality in peer conflict situations. The captains also reported that their coaches seldom provided formal leadership training on how to be a captain. Instead, the youth reported that they used their previous life experiences (e.g. observing others) and their own trial and error experiences to learn to lead. The captains also noted that coaches did not clearly define roles. Based on these results it was recommended that coaches make greater efforts to provide formal leadership training to their captains.

A follow-up qualitative study was conducted to determine what exemplary high school coaches do to best work with and develop leadership skills in their captains (Gould et al., 2013). Ten high school coaches known for developing leadership in their captains took part in qualitative interviews. Findings revealed that these coaches were very proactive in developing captains, doing things like holding coach–captain meetings, communicating with their captains on an ongoing basis, providing their captains with feedback and reinforcement about their leadership, conducting or encouraging formal leadership training, and teaching their captains concepts relevant to their leadership role. It was concluded that these outstanding coaches were very consistent and intentional in their efforts to develop leadership skills in their captains.

Finally, in the most recent study in the series (Blanton et al., 2012) a national survey of high school coaches was conducted to determine their views, attitudes, and practices regarding leadership training and the overall development of team captains. Results indicated that on average coaches have two captains on their teams. They also indicated that the top three characteristics they wanted for their captains included working hard in practices and games (rated very important by 81.0 percent), exhibiting high levels of performance from self and teammates (62.8 percent), and showing respect for others on the team (48.9 percent). Relative to the most important roles the coaches expected their captains to fulfill, the ability to mediate conflict with teammates, confront teammates when they violate rules, take risks such as confronting tough issues, taking care of things in the coaches' absence, and providing constructive criticism to coaches were rated as most important.

Coaches were also asked to cite the biggest mistakes they committed when working with their captains. These included failing to educate their captains on leadership, making assumptions about what their captains knew and understood, and not giving captains enough responsibility. The coaches' perceptions of the most common mistakes captains made were not understanding what it means to be a leader and thinking captainship is about recognition instead of previous hard work. A large number of challenges for captains were cited, but most were seen by coaches as moderately challenging. These challenges included coping with pressure from teammates, balancing multiple roles, and staying neutral in conflict situations with teammates. Finally, coaches varied greatly on the type of training they gave their captains and the challenges that they believed coaches faced in the captain experience. The most frequently cited ways to train captains were by setting a good example, providing captains with support, communicating specific expectations, and talking about leadership with captains. On a positive note, coaches were unlikely to specify that they trained their captains by intimidation or limiting their opportunities to lead. However, coaches also scored below the midpoint on items that assessed whether they trained captains formally, engaged them in the practice planning process, and provided resources on leadership.

In summary, this research on high school sport captains reveals that most receive little formal training but are expected to handle some complex leadership roles like mediating conflict between teammates and confronting difficult team issues. Most coaches are not providing captains with formal leadership training. Yet, exemplary coaches, known for developing captains as leaders, are very proactive and intentional in their efforts to train captains.

Consequences of youth leadership

Several researchers have identified the consequences of youth leadership. In the business community, for example, it is often assumed that being an athlete teaches competition which later transfer to business success. However, it has been found that athletic status was not related to adult business life success. Being a school leader or sport captain did (Extejt and Smith, 2009; Kuhn and Weinberger, 2005). It is also important to note that not all the consequences of being a youth leader are positive. Bullying is seen as a destructive form of youth leadership (Ferris et al., 2007). Given concerns of bullying in sport (Waldron, 2012), this topic would be particularly important to pursue in future research.

Sport-based leadership development programs and interventions

There have been several efforts to develop youth leadership training programs. For example, Hammond-Diedrich and Walsh (2006) evaluated the utility of a responsibility-based program designed to promote leadership in eleven- to fifteen-year-old underserved boys. These boys taught physical activities to fourth grade youth, and lesson observations as well as field notes and interviews were used to measure the boys' leadership development. The program was found to be successful in that the boys' leadership skills improved, and they demonstrated enhanced confidence. Consistency was problematic, however, in some of the youth leaders.

Martinek et al. (2006) described a program to develop compassionate and caring adolescent apprentice teacher leaders. These youth leaders participated in after-school physical activity programs teaching sport and life skills to underserved youth. Four case studies were conducted and revealed that the program was successful in helping youth develop their leadership skills, although the participants differed in the stages of youth leadership development achieved. One participant, for instance, showed difficulty demonstrating higher order leadership skills outside of the program while another advanced a leadership stage but was unsuccessful advancing to the next level of leader development and left the program. The authors concluded that youth advance to higher stages but at times can regress as well.

In a professional practice article, Gould and Voelker (2010) discussed their efforts to develop a statewide captains leadership training program for high school athletes. This program involved a one-day interactive workshop where several hundred youth learned what leadership involves. They also received a captain's leadership guide that reinforced and expanded upon the points covered in the workshop. Topics discussed in the program included what leadership and being a captain involves, effective communication, team motivation, team building and communication, handling difficult situations, and interacting with coaches. While a formal evaluation of the program has not taken place, post clinic feedback from the participants was positive. Moreover, the authors indicated that over time they have moved from a lecture presentation format to one that involved more experiential and active learning and increased their emphasis on convincing the young people that leadership skills can be learned. Challenges were also identified and included stimulating discussions on the part of student athletes, identifying the right students (those genuinely interested in improving their leadership skills) to be involved, determining the capacity of participants to develop transformational leadership skills, and finding ways to have coaches and administrators do follow-up work after the workshop to reinforce and further discuss with the student athletes their leadership development as they served as captains of their high school teams.

A final program developed by Blanton et al. (2014) involved the reporting of their experience facilitating a youth leadership club (primarily composed of athletes) that was designed to facilitate the development of leadership in high school athletes by empowering them to create meaningful projects that allowed them to learn and refine their leadership skills. In this report the student athletes developed a middle school leadership program that was implemented by the club members and designed to help middle school youth learn leadership skills and transition to high school. This involved the club members developing meaningful and varying roles and learning leadership by doing as they developed and executed the program. Most interesting were the authors' reflections on what they had learned about facilitating such a program with the high school athletes. Specifically, they discussed the importance of empowering the youth by allowing them to make decisions and giving them responsibility while resisting the urge to step in and direct them. They also mentioned that program facilitators must be consistent across time with the leadership skills they are teaching and developing while at the same time being flexible in both their planning and implementation.

In summary, while more empirical tests are needed to evaluate the effectiveness of youth leadership development efforts in sport and physical activity contexts, initial studies and program reports are encouraging. Youth not only learn what leadership involves but are able to develop their own self-perceptions regarding leadership. They also learn by doing and can develop a number of important leadership skills. At the same time the research shows that numerous challenges arise in developing and implementing these programs, and results can be variable.

Developing youth leadership as a life skill

Based on the existing research and theory, including several literature reviews (Gould and Voelker, 2012; Gould et al., 2012; Martinek and Hellison, 2009), a number of implications for developing youth leadership through sport and physical activity settings can be derived. These are outlined below.

Recognize that sport and physical activity settings are excellent contexts for developing youth leaders

Sport and physical activity settings can be powerful contexts for youth to develop leadership skills. These contexts are highly popular youth settings in which young people want to take part. They also involve interactions with others that give rise to numerous teachable moments and often entail achievement striving that requires focused efforts to improve. Finally, they are settings where youth have agency and their actions count for something that they believe is important (Larson, 2000).

All youth can learn to lead

There has been some debate in the literature on whether youth leadership development should focus on young people who show an inclination and ability to lead or whether leadership is a skill set that all young people need to develop. I take a centralist stand on this issue. Recent research reveals that up to 47 percent of athletes on a team were identified as informal leaders while up to 15 percent were identified as formal leaders (Loughead et al., 2006). This certainly suggests that captains are not the only leaders on teams. It makes sense, then, that all young people need to learn how to lead and follow and could benefit from learning how to be positive role models and good teammates, how to more effectively communicate, and how to develop and pursue team goals. At the same time, research reveals that not all young people are ready to or desire to assume formal leadership roles (Holt et al., 2008). Youth who emerge and are thrust into, and/or are appointed to, formal leadership roles need training to effectively fulfill those roles and to gain the most from such experiences for leadership to truly become a life skill. In that way those with an aptitude for and desire to lead can maximize their leadership potential. What they learn can not only help them in sport, but if done under the right conditions, can be transferred to other endeavors in their adult lives.

Youth leadership is a complex developmental process

Leadership is a complex process that unfolds over time and involves the interaction of leader characteristics and behaviors, follower characteristics and behaviors, and situational influences. Young people, then, must understand that leadership involves much more than the personal characteristics of the leader. Leaders must strive to understand their followers, develop contextual intelligence so that they can understand how situational influences affect both their followers and themselves, learn how to make good decisions, and communicate in transparent fashions. We also know that learning to lead is a development process with young people progressing through stages of leadership understanding and leader development. A large number of transactional and transformational skills must be developed.

Adult leaders must be intentional in their efforts to develop youth leadership

While young people can certainly develop their leadership capabilities on their own by experiencing leadership opportunities, they will profit much more if coaches and other adult leaders intentionally foster leadership skills. Adult leaders must be "purposeful" in choosing, implementing, and assessing specific leadership development strategies. It is critical to recognize, however, that part of being intentional is purposefully giving up some control, empowering youth, and allowing them to make meaningful choices. Giving them meaningful responsibilities and holding them accountable for their actions is an important way to facilitate leadership development.

Youth need to learn both transactional and transformational leadership skills

Youth leadership development involves the acquisition and development of both intrapersonal and interpersonal skills. First and foremost, young athletes must understand what leadership involves. It is much more than directing people and giving orders. They must also become aware of their own leadership potential and capabilities. A number of skills must be developed. These involve basic transactional leadership skills like being able to speak to groups, making eye contact when communicating, listening, and focusing on positive reinforcement, as well as more advanced transformational skills such as understanding the complexity of leader–

follower dynamics, learning how to inspire others, and learning how to develop and share a team vision. Lastly, an important aspect of leadership is learning how to regulate oneself. Van Linden and Fertman (1998) suggest that decision-making and stress management skills are especially important in this regard.

Model and reinforce leadership and leadership skills, especially transformational leadership

Transformational leadership involves inspiring and empowering others, often helping them realize that they can accomplish things they did not think were possible. It involves leaders understanding and connecting with followers, helping followers define their values and goals, and then motivating them to achieve those goals (Northouse, 2010). It is a difficult task for adults, much less young people, to implement. Helping youth become transformational leaders involves helping them learn to care for others, demonstrate optimism even in the face of adversity, and inspiring those around them. At the same time they must promote group problem-solving, foster acceptance of group goals, encourage teamwork, and hold their peers accountable. It is absolutely essential that adult leaders not only help young people understand that this is what good leadership involves, but work to provide feedback and reinforce youth leaders' efforts to exhibit these characteristics.

Experiential learning is essential for teaching youth leadership

Youth learn to lead by doing; that is, engaging in actual youth leadership experiences. Too often, however, adults are hesitant to give young people a voice or meaningful responsibilities and decision-making opportunities. Instead they think that merely lecturing youth about leadership will develop needed leadership characteristics. This is especially true in competitive sport settings where coaches are afraid that giving up control will lead to performance failure. Ironically, the latest coaching motivation research shows that coaches who allow youth choices and give meaningful responsibilities have more motivated athletes, so by doing so not only helps develop leadership skills but enhances performance (Gillet et al., 2010). If coaches and other adults are serious about fostering leadership in young people in sport and physical activity context, it is especially important for them to give young people real responsibilities and allow them to make their own choices.

Teaching for leadership transfer is critical

Recent research reveals that life skills, like youth leadership, can be learned through sport and physical activity participation (Gould and Westfall, 2014). Life skills also have the potential to transfer beyond sport to other life settings. However, this transfer is not automatic. It is more likely to occur when coaches talk about how life skills, like leadership, can be transferred to contexts outside of sport and reinforce young people's efforts to make such transfer.

Use a variety of educational techniques

Learning to lead is a complex multidimensional process. Youth learn to lead through modeling, mentorship, experiential learning, and formal education. Therefore, it is critical that adult leaders discuss with young people what good leadership involves and looks like, provide numerous examples of good leadership, provide opportunities for them to practice leadership skills (e.g. have players help run a practice), provide feedback on their leadership behaviors, and allow young athletes to learn from their own leadership mistakes. An important but difficult leadership development task is to find the balance between direct instruction and constructing environments that allows for leadership development to emerge. Similarly, effective instructors find ways to balance their support of youth leadership development with challenging young people to move out of their leadership comfort zones. Lastly, effective instructors also take advantage of formal educational opportunities (e.g. workshops, conferences, books) and encourage young people to use these.

Be patient and hold realistic expectations

Young people who are learning to lead will certainly make mistakes along their leadership development journeys. Some will struggle with assuming responsibility, others with following through on their commitments, and still others in learning how to effectively interact with others. For this reason, coaches and other adults working with young people to develop leadership in sport and physical activity contexts will need to demonstrate patience, expect some setbacks, and be on guard not to overreact when problems arise. As Gould et al. (2012, p. 176) suggest:

> The key is to recognize that making mistakes, acknowledging them, and devising plans for improvement is an integral part of the leadership learning process, especially in young people. At the same time, the art of developing youth leadership is providing enough guidance and intervention to ensure that the overall experience is positive and that errors are treated as learning opportunities.

Additional youth leadership guidelines

Based on their extensive experience helping underserved youth develop leadership in sport and physical activity contexts, Martinek and Hellison (2009) and Hammond-Diedrich and Walsh (2006) have derived a number of guidelines for teaching youth leadership. For example, they suggest that it is essential for adult leaders to identify and acknowledge examples of good leadership in young people, that cross-age teaching and mentoring-type experiences are excellent ways for helping young people learn to lead, that providing opportunities for young people to self-evaluate and reflect on their leadership experiences is essential, that focusing on youth leader strengths versus weaknesses is important, and that providing frequent opportunities for youth to discuss their leadership efforts is important.

Conclusion

Developing youth leadership, like most worthwhile things in life, takes considerable effort on the parts of caring adults. As legendary football coach Vince Lombardi said, "Leaders aren't born, they are made. And they are made just like anything else, through hard work." This chapter summarizes the theory, research, and best practice literature on youth leadership through sport and physical activity involvement in the hopes of helping researchers and practitioners to better understand and develop leadership as a life skill in sport and physical activity contexts. They are urged to do so as sport and physical activity contexts can and should be used to prepare young people to lead both on and off the field of play.

References

Avolio, B. J., Rotundo, M., and Walumbwa, F. O. (2009). Early life experiences as determinants of leadership role occupancy: The importance of parental influence and rule-breaking behavior. *The Leadership Quarterly, 20,* 329–342.

Bass, B. M. (1998). *Transformational Leadership: Industrial, Military, and Educational Impact.* Mahway, NJ: Lawrence Erlbaum Associates.

Blanton, J., Voelker, D. K., and Gould, D. (2012, October). *High school coaches' views of the use, training and development of team captains.* Presentation made at the Association for the Advancement of Applied Sport Psychology Conference, Atlanta, GA.

Blanton, J. E., Sturges, A. J., and Gould, D. (2014). Lessons learned from a leadership development club for high school athletes. *Journal of Sport Psychology in Action, 5,* 1–13.

Charbonneau, D., and Adelheid, A. M. (2002). Emotional intelligence and leadership in adolescents. *Personality and Individual Differences, 33,* 1101–1113.

Charbonneau, D., Barling, J., and Kelloway, E. K. (2001). Transformational leadership and sports performance: The mediating effect of intrinsic motivation. *Journal of Applied Social Psychology, 31,* 1521–1534.

Chelladurai, P. (2007). Leadership in sports. In G. Tenenbaum, and R. C. Eklund (Eds.), *Handbook of Sport Psychology* (3rd ed., pp. 113–135). Hoboken, NJ: Wiley.

Chelladurai, P., and Saleh, S. D. (1978). Preferred leadership in sports. *Canadian Journal of Applied Sport Sciences, 3,* 85–92.

Dhuey, E., and Lipscomb, S. (2008). What makes a leader? Relative age and high school leadership. *Economics of Education Review, 27,* 173–183.

Dupuis, M., Bloom, G. A., and Loughead, T. M. (2006). Team captain's perceptions of athlete leadership. *Journal of Sport Behavior, 29,* 60–78.

Extejt, M. M., and Smith, J. E. (2009). Leadership development through sports participation. *Journal of Leadership Education, 8,* 224–237.

Ferris, G. R., Zinko, R., Brouer, R. L., Buckley, M. R., and Harvey, M. G. (2007). Strategic bullying as a supplementary, balanced perspective on destructive leadership. *The Leadership Quarterly, 18,* 195–206.

Gillet, N., Vallerand, R. J., Amoura, S., and Baldes, B. (2010). Influence of coaches' autonomy support on athletes' motivation and sport performance: A test of the hierarchical model of intrinsic and extrinsic motivation. *Psychology of Sport and Exercise, 11*, 155–161.

Glenn, S. D., and Horn, T. S. (1993). Psychological and personal predictors of leadership behavior in female soccer athletes. *Journal of Applied Sport Psychology, 5*, 17–34.

Gould, D., and Voelker, D. (2010). Youth sport leadership development: Leveraging the sports captaincy experience. *Journal of Sport Psychology in Action, 1*, 1–13.

Gould, D., and Voelker, D. K. (2012). Enhancing youth leadership through sport and physical education. *Journal of Physical Education, Recreation and Dance, 83*(8), 38–41.

Gould, D., and Westfall, S. (2014). Promoting life skills in children and youth: Applications to sport contexts. In A. Rui Gomes, R. Resende, and A. Albuquerque (Eds.), *Positive Human Functioning from a Multidimensional Perspective. Vol. 2: Promoting Healthy Lifestyles* (pp. 53–77). New York: Nova.

Gould, D., Chung, Y., Smith, P., and White, J. (2006). Future directions in coaching life skills: Understanding high school coaches' views and needs. *Athletic Insights: The Online Journal of Sports Psychology, 18*, 28–38. Available from: www.athleticinsight.com/Vol18Iss3/CoachingLifeSkill.htm.

Gould, D., Voelker, D., and Blanton, J. (2012). Future developments in youth leadership research. In R. J. Schinke and S. J. Hanrahan (Eds.), *Sport for Development, Peace and Social Justice* (pp. 163–180). Morgantown, WV: Fitness Information Technology.

Gould, D., Voelker, D. K., and Griffes, K. (2013). How coaches mentor team captains. *The Sport Psychologist, 27*, 13–26.

Hammond-Diedrich, K. C. and Walsh, D. (2006). Empowering youth through a responsibility-based cross-age teacher program: An investigation into impact and possibilities. *Physical Educator, 63*, 134–142.

Hellison, D. (1995). *Teaching Responsibility Through Physical Activity*. Champaign, IL: Human Kinetics.

Holt, N. L., Black, D. E., Tamminen, K. A., Fox, K. R., and Mandigo, J. L. (2008). Levels of social complexity and dimensions of peer experiences in youth sport. *Journal of Sport and Exercise Psychology, 30*, 411–431.

Klonsky, B. G. (1991). Leaders' characteristics in same-sex sport groups: A study of interscholastic baseball and softball teams. *Perceptual and Motor Skills, 72*, 943–946.

Kuhn, P., and Weinberger, C. (2005). Leadership skills and wages. *Journal of Labor Economics, 23*, 395–436.

Larson, R. W. (2000). Toward a psychology of positive youth development. *American Psychologist, 55*, 170–183.

Libby, M., Sedonaen, M., and Bliss, S. (2006). The mystery of youth leadership development: The path of just communities. *New Directions for Youth Development, 109*, 13–25.

Loughead, T. M., Hardy, H., and Eys, M. A. (2006). The nature of leadership. *Journal of Sport Behavior, 29*, 142–158.

Martinek, T., and Hellison, D. (2009). *Youth Leadership in Sport and Physical Education*. New York, NY: Palgrave Macmillan.

Martinek, T., Schilling, T., and Hellison, D. (2006). The development of compassionate and caring leadership among adolescents. *Physical Education and Sport Pedagogy, 11*, 141–157.

Moran, M. M., and Weiss, M. R. (2006). Peer leadership in sport: Links with friendship, peer acceptance, psychological characteristics, and athletic ability. *Journal of Applied Sport Psychology, 18,* 97–113.

Northouse, P. G. (2010). *Leadership: Theory and Practice* (5th ed.). Thousand Oaks, CA: Sage.

Pease, D. G., and Zhang, J. J. (2002). Predictors of preadolescent athletic leadership behaviors as related to level of play. *International Sports Journal, 6,* 92–106.

Rowold, J. (2006). Transformational and transactional leadership in the martial arts. *Journal of Applied Sport Psychology, 18,* 312–325.

Schneider, B., Ehrhart, K. H., and Ehrhart, M. G. (2002). Understanding high school student leaders: II. Peer nominations of leaders and their correlates. *Leadership Quarterly, 13,* 275–299.

Schonfeld, A. (2008). Leadership development in athletes and coaches. In A. M. Lane (Ed.), *Sport and Exercise Psychology: Topics in Applied Psychology* (pp. 153–169). London, UK: Hodder Education Group.

Smith, R. E., Smoll, F. C., and Hunt, E. (1977). A system for the behavioral assessment of athletic coaches. *Research Quarterly, 48,* 401–407.

Smoll, F. L., and Smith, R. E. (1989). Leadership behaviors in sport: A theoretical model and research paradigm. *Journal of Applied Social Psychology, 19,* 1522–1551.

Smoll, F. L., and Smith, R. E. (2010). Conducting sport psychology training programs for coaches: Cognitive-behavioral principles and techniques. In J. M. Williams (Ed.), *Applied Sport Psychology: Personal Growth to Peak Performance* (6th ed., pp. 392–416). Mountain View, CA: Mayfield.

Todd, S. Y., and Kent, A. (2004). Perceptions of the role differentiation behaviors of ideal peer leaders: A study of adolescent athletes. *International Sports Journal, 8*(2), 105–118.

Van Linden, J. A., and Fertman, C. I. (1998). *Youth Leadership.* San Francisco, CA: Jossey-Bass.

Voelker, D. K., Gould, D., and Crawford, M. J. (2011). Understanding the experience of high school sport captains. *The Sport Psychologist, 25,* 47–66.

Waldron, J. J. (2012). A social norms approach to hazing prevention workshops. *Journal of Sport Psychology in Action, 3,* 12–20.

Ward, P. J., and Ellis, G. D. (2008). Characteristics of youth leadership influence adolescent peers to follow. *Journal of Park and Recreation Administration, 26,* 78–94.

Weinberg, R. S., and Gould, D. (2015). *Foundations of Sport and Exercise Psychology* (6th ed.). Champaign, IL: Human Kinetics.

Yukelson, D., Weinberg, R., Richardson, P., and Jackson, A. (1983). Interpersonal attraction and leadership within collegiate sport teams. *Journal of Sport Behavior, 6,* 28–36.

Zacharatos, A., Barling, J., and Kelloway, E. K. (2000). Development and effects of transformational leadership in adolescents. *Leadership Quarterly, 11,* 211–226.

13

POSITIVE YOUTH DEVELOPMENT PROGRAMMING WITH MARGINALIZED POPULATIONS

Tanya Forneris, Corliss Bean, and Tanya Halsall

Participation in sport and physical activity-based positive youth development (PYD) programs can foster a number of positive outcomes in youth (Fraser-Thomas et al., 2005; Gould and Carson, 2008; Weiss, 2008; Weiss and Wiese-Bjornstal, 2009). Such benefits, however, may be particularly important for youth from marginalized populations as they are often at greater risk of experiencing negative outcomes than other youth (Flynn, 2008; Pickett et al., 2002). The purpose of this chapter is to provide a brief overview of research and programming related to three different marginalized populations. The first population is female youth from families living on low incomes in Canada. The second population is Aboriginal youth in Canada.[1] The third population is youth from Low and Middle Income Countries (LMIC). In addition to the overview of research and programming with these three populations, we have also provided an in-depth case example of a life skills program in which we have been involved in developing, implementing, or evaluating with these three marginalized populations. The chapter concludes with an outline of future directions for sport and physical activity programs with marginalized youth.

Female youth from families living on low incomes

Gender and family affluence have been identified as two powerful determinants of youth development (World Health Organization, 2006). As such, it has been long recognized that female youth from families living on low incomes face several barriers to achieving optimal levels of development (Sabo and Veliz, 2008). For example, the Public Health Agency of Canada (PHAC, 2011) has recognized that female youth, compared to their male counterparts, score lower on all indicators of health and well-being including higher depressive symptoms, lower self-esteem, increased victimization due to bullying, and increased suicide attempts.

Furthermore, female youth living in poverty have a greater risk of dropping out of school, mental health problems, difficulties with the law, and engaging in risk-taking behavior (PHAC, 2011; Statistics Canada, 2001).

Over the past two decades, female-focused sport and physical activity-based PYD programs have grown significantly (Rauscher and Cooky, 2015), providing many female youth with opportunities to be more active and to develop life skills. Life skills have been defined as "skills that enable individuals to succeed in the different environments in which they live, such as school, home, and in their neighborhoods" (Danish et al., 2004, p. 40). Furthermore, research has shown that participation in such programs has the potential to develop and improve the interpersonal and intrapersonal skills of female youth such as leadership, confidence, self-esteem, self-worth, body image, and physical activity competence (DeBate et al., 2009; Duncan et al., 2015; Frelich et al., 2005; Waldron, 2007; Warner et al., 2009).

In a study conducted by Watson et al. (2000), female youth discussed the importance of having sport and physical activity programming that was fun, allowed them to be engaged with friends, and that took place in a non-competitive sporting environment. Consistent with these findings, Wright and colleagues (Wright et al., 2008; Wright et al., 2011) highlighted the importance of ensuring the program structure and activities are relevant to the youth, having a flexible leadership approach and using, whenever possible, a youth-driven approach that provides youth with voice and a sense of ownership. As a result, in recent years, researchers have recommended that sport and physical activity-based PYD programming incorporate intentional activities to develop life skills, enhance self-esteem, increase positive attitudes and motivation towards physical activity as well as provide a safe and supportive, task-oriented environment (Brown and Fry, 2014; DeBate et al., 2009; Futris et al., 2013; Rauscher et al., 2013). The following case example describes the Girls Just Wanna Have Fun (GJWHF) program, which integrated a number of these best practices including a youth-driven approach, intentional activities to teach life skills and foster positive peer relationships, as well as specific strategies to create a safe and supportive environment.

Case example: Girls Just Wanna Have Fun program

The GJWHF program was developed in response to an identified gap in programming for female youth at a local Boys and Girls Club (Bean et al., 2014). Annual reports from the local club indicated that only 19 percent of participants in sport and recreation programs were female. Once this gap was identified, pilot research was conducted with female youth from local clubhouses to aid in the development of a program that would incorporate recommendations from past research outlined above (Forneris et al., 2013a). Below is a detailed overview of the program as well as results highlighting the perceived impact of the program.

The GJWHF program was a physical activity-based life skills program with three main goals: (1) to provide female youth with opportunities to be physically active;

(2) to facilitate life skills development; and (3) to enable opportunities for youth voice. In order to achieve these three goals, the GJWHF program was predominantly based on Hellison's (2011) Teaching Personal and Social Responsibility (TPSR) model while also incorporating life skills activities from Danish's (2002) Sports United to Promote Education and Recreation (SUPER) program model (for more details see Bean et al., 2014).

The GJWHF program has been implemented for two years to date. In each year the program ran from September through to June with one program session per week. Each session was 60–75 minutes in length and involved five program leaders for ten to twelve youth participants who ranged from eleven to sixteen years of age. In addition, free transportation was provided for the youth to and from the program. To achieve the goals of the program a number of strategies were employed. First, the youth participated in a variety of physical activities throughout the program in two-week blocks (e.g. walking, swimming, basketball, volleyball, yoga, dance, kickboxing, lacrosse, cooperative games, and skating). Second, within each session the youth participated in activities that were specifically designed to teach life skills and each session focused on one life skill (e.g. communication, teamwork, responsibility, goal setting, seeking help, empowerment and confidence, leadership, appreciating differences). Third, youth were provided numerous opportunities to make choices about the program such as what physical activities they wanted to engage in, choice in life skill activities, and intentional leadership opportunities (e.g. to design and implement their own mini program to teach life skills to younger youth at the Boys and Girls Club). Fourth, the leaders focused on providing a supportive environment and fostering positive peer relationships by beginning and ending each session with the youth in small groups to discuss both current issues (successes and challenges) occurring in their lives and to reflect on what they were learning in the program.

To evaluate the strategies the leaders utilized and the impact of the program, a mixed-methods approach using semi-structured interviews, questionnaires, and leader logbooks was employed. The results indicated that participants perceived the GJWHF program as providing a trusting and caring environment and afforded positive and supportive all-female leaders. For example, the female youth reported that the girls' only environment was of great importance in fostering a physically and psychologically safe environment, which they explained helped them feel more at ease and free to be themselves. In addition, the integration of the intentional life skills activities was perceived as providing an opportunity to further connect with the leaders and their peers along with numerous developmental outcomes such as a positive future orientation, a sense of identity, physical skills, respect, confidence, emotional regulation, teamwork and leadership (Bean et al., 2014; Bean and Forneris, 2015; Bean et al., 2015). Furthermore, a two-year qualitative study revealed that the youth reported transferring a number of the skills learned in the program to other areas of their life, including at school, at home, and with their peers (Kendellen et al., 2014).

First Nation, Metis and Inuit youth in Canada

A recent report has described Canadian policy relating to the assimilation of FNMI peoples as cultural genocide, defined as "the destruction of those structures and practices that allow the group to continue as a group" (Truth and Reconciliation Commission of Canada [TRCC], 2015, p. 1). These policies include such practices as the seizure of land, the prohibition of traditional cultural practices and the division of families (TRCC, 2015; Wesley-Esquimaux and Smolewski, 2004). These influences have resulted in collective trauma (Crooks et al., 2010; Kral, 2012) and have created many health and social disparities between FNMI youth and their mainstream peers. These include increased rates of drug and alcohol use (National Aboriginal Health Organization, 2011), lower academic success (Aboriginal Affairs and Northern Development Canada, 2014) and increased rates of mental health issues and suicide (Chandler and Lalonde, 1998).

Leaders in the FNMI community have identified sport and physical activity as a potential opportunity to promote youth and community development (Forsyth and Wamsley, 2006). However, organizations must be cautious when considering the implementation of sports programs for FNMI youth development. In her examination of how the Indian Act shaped FNMI sport participation, Forsyth (2007) describes how Euro-Canadian sports (e.g. hockey, basketball) were legitimized as the most appropriate forms of sport for FNMI people. As such, Euro-Canadian sports were used as part of a larger strategy of assimilation. It is also important to understand FNMI youth perspectives regarding sport. McHugh et al. (2013) highlight FNMI youth experiences of sport through their participatory study using Photovoice. In this research, they explored the meanings of sport to urban FNMI youth. Their participants described sport as: (1) activities they grew up with; (2) fun; (3) a connection to nature and others; and (4) helping them believe in themselves.

Recently there has been an increased focus on evaluating sport and physical activity-based PYD programming for FNMI youth. For example, Active Circle is an initiative that was developed to promote the health and wellness of FNMI youth and communities through the development of sport and recreation programs (Active Circle, 2014). This initiative was launched in 2008 and is being implemented by Motivate Canada and the Aboriginal Sport Circle which supports Aboriginal youth and communities to become vibrant, active, and healthy individuals through sport and recreation. This project is currently being evaluated using participatory methods, including talking circles, Photovoice and Anishnaabe Symbol-Based Reflection.

Additionally, Galipeau and Giles (2014) recently evaluated Alberta's Future Leaders (AFL), a cross-cultural mentorship program that uses sport and recreation to develop leadership skills in FNMI youth. The initiative is run by the Alberta Sport, Recreation, Parks, and Wildlife Foundation and connects primarily non-FNMI mentors with a background in sport with FNMI mentees. Using a qualitative approach Galipeau and Giles found two major discourses that influenced the program's mentoring approach: "first, mentorship can help Aboriginal youth to avoid negative life trajectories and, second, youth leadership development is universal" (p. 149). However, it should be noted that a number of recommendations were made based on these findings to help minimize the perpetuation of power relations between the mentors and mentees. These recommendations included recruiting more FNMI youth workers and providing more cultural awareness education to staff. These recommendations are consistent with identified best practices for sport and physical activity-based programming for FNMI youth such as voluntary participation, a welcoming and culturally appropriate environment, partnership engagement, inclusion of FNMI role models, youth-driven program design, and the creation of youth leadership roles (Sutcliffe Group, 2007). Below is a description of the Nunavik Youth Hockey Development Program (NYHDP) which incorporated a number of these best practices including a voluntary participation structure, having local FNMI hockey coaches who act as role models, and the creation of leadership roles for the youth.

Case example: Nunavik Youth Hockey Development Program

The NYHDP was established in 2006 with the purpose of being both a crime prevention program and a vehicle to enhance the development of Inuit youth. More specifically, the NYHDP has a number of objectives, which include encouraging Inuit youth to be physically active, pursue education, and develop life skills that will help them succeed in the future (NYHDP, 2012). The program is offered to youth from ages five to seventeen in all fourteen villages within Nunavik at no cost and is comprised of two major components: the Community program and the Select program. The Community program takes place in all fourteen villages while the Select program is comprised of five competitive teams divided by age and gender that bring together youth from different villages to train and travel to one tournament in southern Canada each year. As part of the Select program, all youth are involved in a life skills component designed to enhance their individual and social development. Youth are chosen for the select team based on their participation in both the tryout camps and the life skills activities as the program emphasizes the importance of being well-rounded and not solely displaying good hockey skills. The life skills activities are intentionally structured and there is time set aside for reflection and debrief of the life skills activities. For example, for the life skill of "responsibility," an activity involved brainstorming situations in everyday life in which people are responsible and not responsible. From the examples brainstormed by the group, the youth were then asked to provide suggestions of solutions to the not-responsible behavior in order to help people to become more responsible.

Tied to both these NYHDP components is a third element, which is the certification of Local Hockey Trainers. Typically, these individuals are current or past participants of the NYHDP. Having Local Hockey Trainers not only provides an avenue where youth can give back to their village and act as leaders, but it also allows for the sustainability of the program. The Local Hockey Trainers act as coaches on the ice in their home village and are seen as role models for younger participants.

Recently, a comprehensive evaluation was conducted on the NYHDP (Bean, 2013). From the evaluation, it was observed that the program as a whole was perceived to have helped youth develop a positive sense of identity (Bean and Forneris, 2013). In addition, the youth who participated in the Select program believed they developed life skills such as teamwork, effort, persistence, and positive peer relationships. The youth also identified specific opportunities that the program provided to enable the transference of life skills they learned in the program to other areas of their life, including becoming a Local Hockey Trainer in their village, becoming a referee or time keeper, and participating in an active recess program at school to minimize bullying.

Youth from low and middle income countries

The number of sport-based PYD programs being implemented in LMICs has grown in recent years (Spaaij, 2009). This increase is due in part from the emphasis the United Nations has placed on sport for helping to reduce the inequalities experienced by LMICs through the achievement of the Millennium Development Goals. These goals include but are not limited to promoting health and education, and strengthening youth development (United Nations, 2006). There has also been an increase in the literature on programs implemented in LMICs, yet there remains a lack of literature on understanding what programs are most effective for whom and under what conditions (Coalter, 2007; Whitley et al., 2015b).

Although it is recognized that there are a variety of sport and physical activity-based programs being implemented globally, this section will focus on community-based programs that primarily focus on incorporating practices to foster local capacity building. The rationale for this focus is that if community-based programs are to be sustainable, and particularly those implemented in LMICs, it is critical to integrate capacity-building practices, such as training local leaders, that will empower the local community to take ownership of the program. For example, Wright and colleagues started a new initiative called the Belizean Youth Sport Coalition (BYSC), a project that focuses on promoting youth development through sport and physical activity through the development of a three-year training exchange program funded by the US Department of State (Wright, 2015). To date a number of exchanges have occurred including the training of 36 coaches and youth workers in Belize. From this training, eight coaches were selected to travel to the United States for advanced training in youth development and then these eight coaches were co-facilitators of training for 45 new coaches, youth workers, teachers, and community police in Belize. The next phase of the initiative is to further support the Belizean coach trainers and develop more training materials to build capacity towards full facilitation without the help of the US team to ensure program sustainability. In addition to capacity building, it has been recognized that the development of strong partnerships with local organizations as well as local involvement in the planning of the program are important for sustaining programming in LMICs (Whitley et al., 2015a). The program described below, Project Nepal, also focused on ensuring that these best practices were integrated into the design and implementation of the program.

Case example: Project Nepal

Project Nepal started out as a fourth-year student community project that has grown into a locally driven program. The program is a physical activity-based life skills program that was implemented in collaboration with a local Nepalese nongovernmental organization (NGO). The program was adapted from SUPER (Danish, 2002) and focused on five specific life skills (goal setting, communication, teamwork, confidence, and leadership; for more details see Forneris, 2013; Forneris et al., 2013b). A pilot version of the program was implemented in 2007 for students from four government (public) schools. The pilot program was set up so that students from grades six through eight would participate in one 45-minute program session every school day, for a period of three weeks. The program was implemented by teams of Canadian and Nepalese university students. Each school had a team of two Canadian students and one Nepalese student. The Canadian university students were studying kinesiology and, therefore, had a background in physical activity, while the Nepalese university students were volunteers with the local NGO and had already established relationships with the schools in which the program was being implemented.

Results from a mixed-methods evaluation of the pilot program indicated that the program was highly valued by the program leaders and school principals. In addition, the program was successful in helping the students learn about how to set goals for their future, how to work together, and develop confidence, particularly for female youth. As a result, in 2008, the program was implemented again but with an additional component of a life skills club. The purpose of the life skills club was to provide more intentional opportunities for the youth to take on leadership roles and to further enhance the development of life skills by having them plan and implement life skills activities for their younger peers at school. Each week the life skills club would meet to plan and/or implement a life skills activity for the duration of the school year. Although the students who comprised the life skills club were responsible for the planning and organizing of the life skills activities, there was a life skills club leader from the local NGO who oversaw the students' implementation of these activities.

Since the creation of the life skills clubs, the NGO has taken greater ownership of the program and this has resulted in program sustainability. Specifically, the NGO has developed its own Nepalese life skills manual for program implementation and has organized a number of life skills days and camps which involved inviting students from various schools across the school district to participate in different life skills activities. In addition, with the help of Dr. Doris

Watson from the University of Nevada Las Vegas, the NGO was able to organize a teacher training workshop based on the TPSR model which was implemented in the spring of 2011. The purpose of this workshop was to help local teachers acquire the skills to facilitate the development of their students both in and outside of the classroom. The workshop took place over the course of four days and was attended by sixteen teachers and thirteen of the youth workers from the local NGO. The teachers were partnered with the NGO youth workers who had all participated in life skills training in the past and therefore could help the teachers better understand the material and recognize how to integrate life skills activities into their lesson plans. To sustain the impact of this workshop, the NGO had its youth workers conduct school visits to help teachers integrate life skills using the TPSR model in the classroom. The NGO has also continued to expand the life skills programming to new schools throughout the country. In more recent months, Nepal has been working hard to rebuild after the earthquake that destroyed many homes and schools. During this time the NGO has used the life skills programming to bring together the youth and to help keep them engaged as many of the schools have postponed classes until the schools are rebuilt and it is safe to resume schooling.

Conclusion

Over the past twenty years there have been a number of advancements with regards to sport and physical activity-based PYD programming with marginalized populations. These advancements are due to the recognition that sport and physical activity can play an important role in fostering development, the increase in funding for PYD programming worldwide, and continued research on best practices for sport and physical activity-based PYD programming. In our experience with developing, implementing, and evaluating programs based on best practices identified to date, the key strategies that are consistent across these marginalized populations include providing a safe and fun environment for youth, intentional activities to develop life skills, and intentional opportunities to provide leadership roles that can lead to greater capacity building. Moving forward there is still a need for more rigorous evaluation research to understand the impact of sport and physical activity-based PYD programming and to better refine these best practices. First, there is a need for longitudinal research to examine the long-term impact of participation in such programs. Second, there is a need for research that examines life skills transfer to understand whether and how youth who participate in such programs transfer the skills to others areas of their lives. Third, there is a need for research that extends impact beyond the individual to understand whether there is a positive impact on the greater community, which would be particularly important with marginalized populations. It is also of critical importance to increase opportunities for knowledge translation into the community to help more programs incorporate a best practice approach. It is through this work that we help our youth thrive, as our youth are our future.

Acknowledgment

We would like to acknowledge the Social Sciences and Humanities Research Council of Canada for its funding to develop, implement, and evaluate the Girls Just Wanna Have Fun program.

Note

1 Aboriginal peoples in Canada are most often defined by the term First Nation, Metis and Inuit (FNMI) in recognition that there are three distinct Aboriginal groups who have distinct communities and cultures.

References

Aboriginal Affairs and Northern Development Canada. (2014). *2013–14 Departmental Performance Report*. Available from: https://www.aadnc-aandc.gc.ca/eng/1403268280586/1403268381797

Active Circle. (2014). *Active Circle Research Project*. Available from: http://www.activecircle.ca/en/research.html

Bean, C. N. (2013). *Program Evaluation: Nunavik Youth Hockey Development Program*. Report prepared for Quebec en Forme and Makivik Corporation.

Bean, C. N., and Forneris, T. (2013, October). *Engaging Inuit Youth in Hockey: A Pathway to Positive Youth Development*. Paper presented at Canadian Society for Psychomotor Learning and Sport Psychology Conference, Kelwona, BC.

Bean, C. N., and Forneris, T. (2015). Using time-series analysis to evaluate a female youth-driven physical activity-based life skills program based on the Teaching Personal and Social Responsibility model. *ÁGORA para la Educación Física y el Deporte, 17*, 94–114.

Bean, C. N., Forneris, T., and Halsall, T. (2014). Girls Just Wanna Have Fun: A process evaluation of a female youth-driven physical activity-based life skills program. *SpringerPlus, 3*, 401–415.

Bean, C., Forneris, T., and Fortier, M. (2015). Girls Just Wanna Have Fun: Understanding perceptions of effective strategies and outcomes in a female youth-driven physical activity-based life skills programme. *Journal of Sport for Development, 3*(4): 28–40.

Brown, T. A., and Fry, M. D. (2014). Evaluating the pilot of Strong Girls: A life skills/physical activity program for third and fourth grade girls. *Journal of Applied Sport Psychology, 26,* 52–65.

Chandler, M. J., and Lalonde, C. (1998). Cultural continuity as a hedge against suicide in Canada's First Nations. *Transcultural Psychiatry, 35,* 191–219.

Coalter, F. (2007). Sport clubs, social capital and social regeneration: Ill-defined interventions with hard to follow outcomes? *Sport in Society, 10,* 537–559.

Crooks, C. V., Chiodo, D., Thomas, D., Burns, S., and Camillo, C. (2010). *Engaging and Empowering Aboriginal Youth: A Toolkit for Service Providers* (2nd ed.). Bloomington, IN: Trafford.

Danish, S. J. (2002). *SUPER (Sports United to Promote Education and Recreation) Program: Leader Manual* (3rd ed.). Richmond, VA: Lifeskills Center, Virginia Commonwealth University.

Danish, S. J., Forneris, T., Hodge, K., and Heke, I. (2004). Enhancing youth development through sport. *World Leisure, 46*, 38–49.

DeBate, R. D., Gabriel, P. K., Zwald, M., Huberty, J., and Zhang, Y. (2009). Changes in psychosocial factors and physical activity frequency among third- to eighth-grade girls who participated in a developmentally focused youth sport program: A preliminary study. *Journal of School Health, 79*, 474–484.

Duncan, S. C., Strycker, L. A., and Chaumeton, N. R. (2015). Sports participation and positive correlates in African American, Latino, and White girls. *Developmental Science, 8*, 12–28.

Flynn, R. J. (2008). Communities that care: A comprehensive system for youth prevention and promotion, and Canadian applications to date. *Institute for Crime Prevention Review, 2*, 83–106.

Forneris, T. (2013). Project Nepal: The experience of implementing life skills programming in a developing country. In R. Schinke and R. Lidor (Eds.), *Case Studies in Sport Development: Contemporary Stories Promoting Health, Peace and Social Justice* (pp. 175–186). Morgantown, WV: Fitness Information Technology.

Forneris, T., Bean, C. N., Snowden, M., and Fortier, M. (2013a). Using youth-driven programs to encourage physical activity in adolescent girls: A preliminary study. *PHEnex Journal, 4*(3), 1–15.

Forneris, T., Whitley, M., and Barker, B. (2013b). The reality of implementing community-based sport and physical activity programs to enhance the development of underserved youth: Challenges and potential strategies. *Quest, 65*, 313–331.

Forsyth, J. (2007). The Indian Act and the (re)shaping of Canadian Aboriginal sport practices. *International Journal of Canadian Studies/Revue internationale d'études canadiennes,* (35), 95–111.

Forsyth, J., and Wamsley, K. B. (2006). 'Native to native ... we'll recapture our spirits': The world indigenous nations games and North American indigenous games as cultural resistance. *The International Journal of the History of Sport, 23*, 294–314.

Fraser-Thomas, J., Côté, J., and Deakin, J. (2005). Youth sport programs: An avenue to foster positive youth development. *Physical Education and Sport Pedagogy, 10*, 19–40.

Frelich, S. G., Patterson, D. L., and Romack, J. L. (2005). Enhancing self-concept through physical activity: The GoGirlGo! project in an economically disadvantaged minority female population. *Research Quarterly for Exercise and Sport, 76*, A99–A100.

Futris, T. G., Sutton, T. E., and Richardson, E. W. (2013). An evaluation of the relationship *Smarts Plus* program on adolescents in Georgia. *Journal of Human Sciences and Extension, 1*(2), 1–15.

Galipeau, M., and Giles, A. (2014). An examination of cross-cultural mentorship in Alberta's Future Leaders Program. In K. Young and C. Okada (Eds.), *Sport, Social Development and Peace* (Vol. 8, pp. 147–170). Bingley, UK: Emerald Group Publishing Limited.

Gould, D., and Carson, S. (2008). Life skills development through sport: Current status and future directions. *International Review of Sport and Exercise Psychology, 1*, 58–78.

Hellison, D. (2011). *Teaching Personal and Social Responsibility Through Physical Activity* (3rd ed). Champaign, IL: Human Kinetics.

Kendellen, K., Bean, C. N., and Forneris, T. (2014). Exploring life skill transfer in a physical activity-based life skills program: Planting the seeds for growth and success in female youth. *Journal of Sport and Exercise Psychology, 36*, S81.

Kral, M. J. (2012). Postcolonial suicide among Inuit in arctic Canada. *Culture, Medicine and Psychiatry, 36*, 306–325.

McHugh, T. L. F., Coppola, A. M., and Sinclair, S. (2013). An exploration of the meanings of sport to urban Aboriginal youth: A Photovoice approach. *Qualitative Research in Sport, Exercise and Health, 5,* 291–311.

National Aboriginal Health Organization. (2011). *Drug Abuse Major Concern among First Nations and Inuit.* Available from http://www.naho.ca/blog/2011/06/27/drug-abuse-major-concern-among-first-nations-and-inuit/

Nunavik Youth Hockey Development Program. (2012). *About the Nunavik Youth Hockey Development Program.* Available from http://www.nyhdp.ca/en/about

Pickett, W., Garner, M. J., Boyce, W. F., and King, M. A. (2002). Gradients in risk for youth injury associated with multiple-risk behaviours: A study of 11,329 Canadian adolescents. *Social Science and Medicine, 55,* 1055–1068.

Public Health Agency of Canada. (2011). *The Chief Public Health Officer's Report on the State of Public Health in Canada, 2011* (Chapter 3: The health and well-being of Canadian youth and young adults). Available from http://www.phac-aspc.gc.ca/cphorsphc-respcacsp/2011/cphorsphc-respcacsp-06-eng.php

Rauscher, L., and Cooky, C. (2015). Ready for anything the world gives her?: A critical look at sports-based positive youth development for girls. *Sex Roles* (in press), 1–11. http://link.springer.com/article/10.1007/s11199-014-0400-x

Rauscher, L., Kauer, K., and Wilson, B. D. M. (2013). The healthy body paradox: Organizational and interactional influences on preadolescent girls' body image in Los Angeles. *Gender and Society, 27,* 208–230.

Sabo, D., and Veliz, P. (2008). *Go Out and Play: Youth Sports in America.* East Meadow, NY: Women's Sports Foundation.

Spaaij, R. (2009). The social impact of sport: Diversities, complexities and contexts. *Sport in Society, 12,* 1109–1117.

Statistics Canada. (2001). *Children and Youth in Canada.* Available from http://publications.gc.ca/Collection/Statcan/85F0033M/85F0033MIE2001005.pdf

Sutcliffe Group. (2007). *Best Practices: Physical Activity Programs for Aboriginal Youth.* Available from www.nada.ca/wp-content/uploads/1070.pdf

Truth and Reconciliation Commission of Canada. (2015). *Honouring the Truth, Reconciling for the Future: Summary of the Final Report of the Truth and Reconciliation Commission of Canada.* Available from http://www.trc.ca/websites/trcinstitution/index.php?p=890

United Nations. (2006). *Report on the International Year of Sport and Physical Education: 2005.* Available from http://www.un.org/sport2005/a_year/IYSPE_Report_FINAL.pdf

Waldron, J. J. (2007). Influence of involvement in the girls on track program on self-perceptions of early adolescent girls. *Research Quarterly for Exercise and Sport, 78,* 520–531.

Warner, S., Dixon, M. A., and Schumann, C. (2009). Enhancing girls' physical activity and self-image: A case study of the GoGirlGo program. *Women in Sport and Physical Activity Journal, 18*(1), 28–41.

Watson, D. L., Poczwardowski, A., and Eisenman, P. (2000). After-school physical activity programs for adolescent girls. *Journal of Physical Education, Recreation and Dance, 71*(8), 17–21.

Weiss, M. R. (2008). 2007 CH McCloy Lecture: "Field of Dreams": Sport as a context for youth development. *Research Quarterly for Exercise and Sport, 79,* 434–449.

Weiss, M. R., and Wiese-Bjornstal, D. M. (2009). Promoting positive youth development through physical activity. *President's Council on Physical Fitness and Sports Research Digest, Series, 3*(10), 1–8.

Wesley-Esquimaux, C. C., and Smolewski, M. (2004). *Historic Trauma and Aboriginal Healing*. Ottawa, Ontario: The Aboriginal Healing Foundation Research Series. Available from www.ahf.ca/downloads/historic-trauma.pdf

Whitley, M. A., Forneris, T., and Barker, B. (2015a). The reality of sustaining community-based sport and physical activity programs to enhance the development of underserved youth: Challenges and potential strategies. *Quest, 67*(4), 409–423.

Whitley, M. A., Hayden, L. A., and Gould, D. (2015b). Growing up in the Kayamandi Township: II. Sport as a setting for the development and transfer of desirable competencies. *International Journal of Sport and Exercise Psychology*, 1–18.

World Health Organization. (2006). *Inequalities in Young People's Health: Health Behaviour in School-Aged Children, International Report from the 2006/2006 Survey*. Available from http://www.euro.who.int/__data/assets/pdf_file/0005/53852/E91416.pdf

Wright, P. M. (2015). Social change through sport: Rhetoric or reality? *Liikunta and Tiede, 50*, 38–41.

Wright, P. M., Stockton, M., and Hays, N. L. (2008). The personal-social responsibility model: Exploring a novel approach to promoting gender equity and increasing relevance for adolescent females in physical education. In J. Coulter (Ed.), *Progress in Exercise and Women's Health Research* (pp. 159–175). Hauppauage, NY: Nova Science Publishers, Inc.

Wright, E. M., Whitley, M. A., and Sabolboro, G. (2011). Conducting a TPSR program for an underserved girls' summer camp. *ÁGORA para la Educación Física y el Deporte, 14*, 5–24.

14

LEARNING RESPONSIBILITY THROUGH SPORT AND PHYSICAL ACTIVITY

Tom Martinek and Don Hellison

For years, sports have occupied a privileged place in our American culture. Their impact spans all ages, social classes, religions, races, and genders. Channeling children and youths' interest in sport can foster responsible behavior. Using the right strategy in sport programs can create experiences that are highly productive in both during school and after-school programs.

Responding to this challenge, responsibility-based programs have shown promise in addressing the developmental needs of children and youths (Halpern, 2003; Hamilton and Hamilton, 2004; Hirsch, 2005). The purpose of this chapter is to draw attention to a specific framework used to develop experiences that empower children to be personally and socially responsible. First, we offer a portrait of sport and physical activity programs that have focused on fostering personal and social responsibility. In-school, after-school, and community-based programs will be described. Special attention is given to programs guided by Don Hellison's Teaching Personal and Social Responsibility model (TPSR)—a nationally and internationally acclaimed model used in sport-based youth development programs (Hellison, 2011). While all programs function to promote the development of responsible behavior, each will have their own approach in program delivery. That is, many programs employ the TPSR framework from which activities are planned and taught in a way that creates opportunity for responsible decision-making and leadership. The specific qualities and missions of these programs will be given—all influenced by program goals related to the enhancement of personal and social responsibility. A common theme that runs through all of these programs is that given the right guidance all children are capable of becoming what Robert Coles calls "good people" (Cole, 2000).

We conclude with a description of the various ways in which these responsibility programs have been assessed. Both traditional approaches to evaluation as well as more unconventional assessment strategies will be explored. Each of these approaches will be connected to their potential contribution to the improvement of program effectiveness and delivery. We view evaluation in a way that promotes principles of positive youth programming, some guided prescriptions, some ways to problem solve, and a variety of ideas for sustaining quality programming. All of these, however, are idiosyncratic to the context in which the programs are delivered. So we will offer evaluation approaches as a broad array of ideas that hopefully serve those who teach responsibility-based programs in a variety of program settings.

Teaching responsibility through sport and physical activity

Within the past two decades, programmers and policy makers have begun to realize the contributory role that sport and physical activity can play in youth development programs. Several curricular models that rely on physical activity and sport to get children to acquire various skills were created. Each of these models provides certain developmental activities for youth that focus on fitness development, sport skill enhancement, or adoption of an active lifestyle. The shift to more responsibility-based applications of sport and physical activity especially became evident in the latter part of the twentieth century. With this movement, various approaches were developed by many scholars in physical education that exposed children to the concept of responsibility. There was John Cheffers (1987) who explored the effects of structural decision-making on the affective enhancement of inner-city children. Daryl Siedentop's Sport Education model (Siedentop, 1994) leaned on the notion that sport culture could be foundational in giving students opportunity to coach, keep statistics, officiate, and perform other duties. He also felt that authentic assessment could be maintained because records, leadership, and relevant sport involvement could be connected to the sport education experience. And there was Cathy Ennis's Sport for Peace model (Ennis et al., 1999) which resembled the Sport Education model but also emphasized conflict resolution.

More recently, others have also acknowledged the important role that sport and physical activity can play by linking programs to youth development goals and the teaching of responsibility. Al Petitpas's two national programs, First Tee and Play it Smart (Petitpas et al., 2008), Fraser-Thomas and her associates' applied sport model for positive youth development (Fraser-Thomas et al., 2005), and Sam Intrator and Don Siegel's (2014) mutlifaceted sport program called *Project Coach* have all brought forward the concept of empowerment and its role in enhancing responsible behavior through sport and physical activity. In many ways, they set the tone for inclusion of responsibility-based programming in various sport settings (Kirk et al., 2006).

Hellison's TPSR model

One other approach that has become the centerpiece for many sport- and physical-activity-based programs is Don Hellison's Teaching Personal and Social

Responsibility model (TPSR) (Hellison, 1978, 1985, 2003, 2011), a model that has withstood the test of time. Whereas in its early beginnings it was kept on the margins of the physical education profession, as problems with youth, especially those that were underserved, began to escalate, TPSR began to be adopted in a variety of settings (both in North America and in several other countries).

The TPSR model predates the youth development movement as its birth took place in the early 1970s of Hellison's career. His initial experience as a Marine platoon leader and working with low-income court-referred men gave him a sense of purpose in life. Later he took a teaching position in an alternative school where he was forced to search for some way to reach children who were unmotivated and hostile. Because there were no resources, he started to develop his own curriculum, which eventually became TPSR. The model included five levels which represented student goals. Level one is self-control and respect for the rights and feelings of others, level two relates to effort (trying your best), level three is self-direction, level four is caring and leading others, and the fifth level is taking it outside the gym—applying the levels in everyday life. The dimension of social responsibility is represented in levels one and four. The personal responsibility dimension includes levels two and three.

The TPSR model is undergirded by a set of core values which are closely aligned with several positive youth development principles created by Benson (1997), Lerner (2004), and the National Research Council and Institute of Medicine (2002). The essence of core values is "putting kids first." Core values need to be "a way of being" for program leaders. It needs to be who they are, the values that they live as they work with children, and the values they hope they will seriously consider as potential guidelines for their lives. TPSR strives to include all children depending on their interest. Not just play, not just competitive sports, it has many faces, or aspects, depending on the people involved. It allows children to be leaders and gives them other responsibilities that are not always associated with sport. Sometimes this is the first and only time that they are included and can contribute their talents.

The concepts of the TPSR model have been instilled in hundreds of youngsters through our own programs. Both of us have operated youth programs in conjunction with our university work. Our programs have provided great opportunities for undergraduate and graduate students to work with youth and in many instances develop ideas of creating future youth programs. The many programs that have been guided by the TPSR model have functioned in their own way. Resources, settings, funding, demographics, and space are some of the factors that have defined the character of these programs. After-school, in-school, and neighborhood programs typify the general settings of TPSR programs. Regardless of their uniqueness, they have all maintained the spirit of the TPSR model and its core values.

School-based programs

One of the settings that has employed TPSR programming has been the school. Many of these programs have been started in order to provide some scaffolding for certain students who struggle socially, emotionally, and academically. While academics continue to be a main priority in most schools, it is being recognized that social and emotional learning also plays a major role in children's lives. Thus, programs have recently begun to incorporate experiences that focus on relationship building and other interpersonal qualities (Weissberg and Cascarino, 2013).

Several of these programs have been supported through a partnership with a local university where its resources are interfaced with the school's program needs. For example, Tom's program, called the *Youth Leader Corps (YLC)*, is an after-school program at a local elementary school in North Carolina. Selected high school students are given opportunities to become leaders of their own sport program. Personal and social responsibility with a particular focus on caring and compassionate leadership are the cornerstones of the YLC program. The youth leaders are from an alternative high school (i.e. middle college) located on the University of North Carolina at Greensboro's campus.[1] The selection of the leaders is based on the recommendations of the teachers and school counselor. They create lessons that incorporate both sport skills and the responsibility goals, and teach them to elementary-age children at their school. The program runs once a week for the entire school year. The children are part of a special school program that focuses on keeping African American males engaged and successful in school. The Youth Leader Corps program has two main purposes. For the high school students, one of them is to develop key leadership attributes such as strategic thinking, problem solving, communication, emotional control, and conflict resolution (Wright, 2012; Wright et al., 2010). The second goal is to pass these attributes on to the elementary children through the TPSR experiences provided by the youth leaders.

Another example of a school-based program, one that is a part of a school–university partnership, is run by John McCarthy at Boston University. With his graduate students John provides a TPSR program, called *Get Ready*, for disengaged students at one of Boston's local high schools. The school is in a low-income neighborhood where students (and families) face the daily hardships associated with being poor. The program is run during the school day in conjunction with the regular school schedule. Similar to the Youth Leader Corps program, the program serves to assist the school in keeping students, especially those who struggle in the classroom, "on track." Having been a former coach John has honed his skills around the TPSR framework so that the experiences provided to the program participants insure exposure to responsibility-based learning.

At Northern Illinois University another university–school partnership has been developed by Paul Wright and Jenn Jacobs. Paul and Jenn agreed to start an after-school program for academically and social challenged students after being approached by a local elementary school principal. Special attention was given to elevating boys' engagement in after-school activities (e.g. clubs, sport, etc.). It also served to provide students psychological strength to cope with the challenges of schooling. The program is called *Project Leadership* and is guided by the TPSR model. The program runs twice a week at the school site. This program has become a "sports club" where students not only participate in physical activity but also engage in various community service projects (e.g. school wellness night, food drive, involvement in a community garden).

Dave Walsh at the San Francisco State University has implemented a *Kinesiology Career Club (KCC)*, where high school freshmen from an underserved area of the city are guided by Dave's undergraduate seniors who provide a special TPSR program that focuses on developing a career pathway in the field of kinesiology (Walsh, 2012). Based on the theory of "possible selves" (Oyserman and Markus, 1990; Oyserman et al., 2002), Dave has his students provide learning experiences that help high school students balance the perception of what they would like to become with what they are afraid of becoming. In other words, the intent is to heighten the students' motivation to pursue a career interest (i.e. in kinesiology) and to counter the thoughts of encountering future failure.

TPSR's international presence has also been felt in countries outside of the United States. One of these countries is New Zealand where the national curriculum strongly guides teaching and learning in high schools. The overall vision for the curriculum is to produce learners who are confident, connected, and actively involved as lifelong learners (Gordon, 2012, p. 26). Barrie Gordon, a professor at the University of Victoria at Wellington, made TPSR a presence and influence in New Zealand's physical education programs for years. Barrie's strong advocacy for the TPSR's inclusion in school physical education programs also trickled into universities' teacher education programs. Six New Zealand universities have their teacher education programs using TPSR as a primary pedagogical approach to teaching physical education.

A community-based program

Clearly the environment plays a significant role in how children form their values and dispositions toward working with others. The challenges that children face have always been instrumental is raising the risk level of children. It is fair to say that sometimes the challenges are so great to overcome that getting children to be responsible people is not tenable. One way to address this problem is to change the environmental conditions in which the children live (Bronfenbrenner and Morris, 2006; Martinek and Lee, 2012).

This is exactly what Amy and Rob Casteneda have done. This husband and wife team created a program called *Beyond the Ball*. The program serves Little Village, a low-income community located on the west side of Chicago. The program first started as a way to get neighborhood youth involved with something that was positive. Guided by the TPSR model, a transformative basketball program was started in a local elementary school. Besides giving the neighborhood children a chance to play in a safe environment, youth development principles were also employed in the program (i.e. conflict resolution, youth voice, service learning, community building, and leadership). Both Rob and Amy live in the community, and have made their program (and their home) an "open door" for the children in the neighborhood. Community evening events are also offered which bring families to mingle and socialize with one another. Racial and cultural lines are crossed and rival gangs participate together in a peaceful way. Thus, an important positive transition from negative to positive gang relations has been made.

Evaluation of responsibility-based programs

During the past two decades numerous studies have been conducted on TPSR programming. Most of this research has focused on testing, modifying, and affirming the effectiveness and fidelity of TPSR programs. The majority of these studies emerged from the work done by university professors and their graduate students where numerous research questions have been generated. Various research strategies have been used to address these questions. Some strategies have been traditional forms of inquiry and others have been less traditional (e.g. service-bonded inquiry) (Martinek et al., 2004). A study of studies by Hellison and Walsh (2002) provided a summary and analysis of 26 studies on TPSR programs and portrayed an array of research designs.

Because TPSR programs are often multifaceted, we often had to look beyond the traditional end products of program impact (e.g. better classroom behavior, improved academic performance). The question that has been frequently posed, however, is "What evidence really counts?" (Hellison, 2003). There will always be uncertainties about the impact of TPSR programs. But evaluating the outcomes of personal and social responsibility becomes a special challenge in the evaluation process. Testing the fidelity of any program requires much more. That is, the dynamic interplay among the values of the participants and program leaders, the goals of the program, and the external forces impacting delivery (e.g. schools and neighborhood) must become part of the research agenda. Quite often the approach to evaluation must be based on ideas, as opposed to just theory, to more effectively address the squirmy issues related to values acquisition and personal growth of program participants. Ultimate outcomes will always need to be acknowledged in the evaluation of TPSR programs. In fact, early TPSR studies have looked at program impact on grades and office referrals (Martinek et al., 1999), classroom behavior (Martinek et al., 2001), and attendance and performance ratings (Cutforth and Puckett, 1999). However, it is important not to ignore the mechanisms within the program that create such outcomes—thus avoiding the "black box" approach to evaluation. Knowing these factors would place program directors in a better position to make the necessary adjustments and changes to present program protocol.

Several studies have attempted to look at certain aspects of the program experience that impacted students' ability to transfer TPSR values. One of these studies by Okseon Lee (Lee and Martinek, 2013) focused on those experiences that impacted elementary-age participants' ability to apply TPSR values in their classrooms. Using interview and observational data the study showed that while TPSR values were evident in the behavior of the program participants, there was little application of them back at the school. Empowerment, opportunities to lead, and working with others created a program culture that supports the TPSR values. On the other hand, students reported that feelings of boredom, insecurity, and anger were prevalent features of the school. Thus, a "psycho-social border" (Phelan et al., 1998) was created between the program and school setting that challenged the students' ability to apply the TPSR values.

Transfer of TPSR values was also a focal point of a recent study by Melendez and Martinek (2015). This study looked at how past program involvement influenced the lives of former program participants (having participated in at least seven years). The study identified the extent to which specific TPSR values and life skills played a role in their lives. In addition, uncovering the specific types of program experiences and their impact on the lives of six former participants were explored. A multiple-case design was implemented to understand this phenomenon. Structured interviews were used in generating the following findings:

- Former participants considered that the two TPSR values (i.e. respect, helping others) were really important to their lives.
- They reported that they learned the TPSR value of helping others and leadership in their sport club experience.
- The TPSR value of helping others acquired in the program was most useful to the participants in their everyday lives.

In a more recent evaluation of the Youth Leader Corps program described above, Talbert (2015) looked at how exposure to leadership experiences based on TPSR values impacted the resiliency attributes of six high school students. Relationships with others, personal expectations, and pursuit of opportunities for personal growth were studied in relation to the students' participation in the program. A qualitative, multi-case study design was used to capture each individual's unique experiences within the program. Fourteen individual interviews were conducted with the leaders, their classroom teachers, parents/caregivers, and YLC staff.

Cross-case analysis showed two common themes emerging from the youth leaders' relationships with others: (a) connection and interaction with the children in the program; and (b) improved social competence. Two themes emerged for the second research question, impact on personal expectations: (a) improvements of self-worth; and (b) self-identify as a positive influence within a structured environment. The findings for the third research question, which pertained to pursuit of opportunities for personal growth, were limited and varied among each youth leader participant.

Semi-structured interviews, field notes, and participant journal entries provided the data source to examine the impact and processes of Dave Walsh's Kinesiology Career Club (Walsh et al., 2012). With a focus on widening the high school participants' view of a possible future in kinesiology, Walsh found that participants were able to connect the TPSR goals to their possible futures. They were also able to envision and explore a career in kinesiology, and link kinesiology to their own positive possible future. One of the important aspects of the study was the participants' exposure to the weekly guidance offered by the program staff (university students). A balance between hopes and fears was achieved by several of the participants. These findings also helped to inform the theory of possible selves (Oyserman et al., 2001).

Earlier we described Barrie Gordon's professional development work in the New Zealand pre- and in-service programs. In another program at the University of Sharbrooke, Canada, Sylvie Beaudoin studied how using TPSR strategies worked in an in-service program with two physical education teachers. The year-long study incorporated an action research approach with the teachers. The researcher examined which TPSR strategies were most effective in getting teachers to successfully deliver TPSR learning experiences in their classes. Semi-structured interviews, self reflections, and the researcher's blog were the data sources for the study. Results provided strong evidence that the use of four responsibility-based strategies were instrumental in supporting the implementation of TPSR experiences: (a) empowering teachers through self-supervision; (b) providing opportunities for success; (c) setting teacher expectations; and (d) nurturing a respectful relationship with the teachers (Beaudoin, 2012). Beaudoin's evaluation efforts extend the way we look at the utility of TPSR from studying program impact to examining the efficacy of professional development initiatives.

Conclusion

It is important to keep in mind that evaluation evidence can take one form or another. All of the studies that have been described (and there are plenty more) provide some glimpse of how TPSR has been useful in instilling some sense of responsibility in children. They also indicate an upswing in the work of professionals who are aligning sport experiences with youth development principles. We are also reminded that simple rhetoric in how to manage a child's behavior and build character through sport and physical activity are ineffective in abating the social problems and needs of children today (Hellison, 2003). Rather, helping children to grow personally and socially through the use of TPSR-guided experiences holds promise for addressing these challenges.

There are many times when the question of how early do you expose children to these experiences is asked. We believe it can happen at any age. In some of our programs we have seen children as young as five years old taking on the responsibility of sharing with others and engaging in helping types of behavior. An important point here is that, whatever the age may be, "seeds of responsibility" can be planted when programs are run with conviction and clear intent. Sometimes these seeds do not immediately germinate. That is, changes do not occur until years later (i.e. sleeper effects) thus making evaluation of program outcomes difficult.

An important take-away in all this is that TPSR is one of many approaches to help youngsters become personally and socially responsible. Many of these were not covered in this particular chapter. What we have done is offer a portrayal of

TPSR programming and research that stems from the work of those who see sport and physical activity as important allies in helping children become responsible people. Our own 40 plus years of working with children has taught us that using TPSR is more than just knowing what to do with it. Rather, it demands that both practitioners and researchers reflect on the question, "What's worth doing?!" The support that comes from social, economic, and political change will be important in creating programs that produce responsible individuals. Regardless if such changes come about, doing what's best for children must remain at the forefront in what we (and those cited in this chapter) do in our work with children—it is worth doing!

Note

1   The Youth Leader Corps (YLC) was originally an extension of an after-school elementary and middle school sport club based on the TPSR model (i.e. Project Effort). The YLC provided an opportunity for veteran sport club members to plan and run an after-school TPSR program for other children in the community. Recently, the Middle College has served as a new version of the original YLC model. For past references to the original concept of the Youth Leader Corps see Martinek and Schilling (2003); Hellison et al. (2008); Martinek and Hellison (2009); Melendez and Martinek (2015).

References

Beaudoin, S. (2012). Using responsibility-based strategies to empower in service physical education and health teachers to learn and implement TPSR. *Agora for Physical Education and Sport, 14,* 161–177.

Benson, P. (1997). *All Kids Are Our Kids: What Communities Must Do to Raise Caring and Responsible Children and Adolescents.* Minneapolis, MN: Search Institute.

Bronfenbrenner, U., and Morris, P. (2006). The bioecological model of human development. In I. W. Damon and R. M. Lerner (Eds.), *Handbook of Child Psychology: Volume 1: Theoretical Models of Human Development* (pp. 793–828). New York: John Wiley.

Cheffers, J. (1987). Tuesdays and Thursdays with Boston's inner-city youth. *Quest, 49,* 50–66.

Cole, R. (2000). *Lives of Moral Leadership.* New York: Random House.

Cutforth, N. and Puckett, K. (1999). An investigation into the organization, challenges, and impact of an urban apprentice teacher program. *Urban Review, 31,* 153–172.

Ennis, C. D., Solomon, M. A., Satina, B., Loftus, S. J., Mensch, J., and McCauley, M. T. (1999). Creating a sense of family in an urban school using the "sport for peace" curriculum. *Research Quarterly for Exercise and Sport, 70,* 273–285.

Fraser-Thomas, J., Côté, J., and Deakin, J. (2005). Youth sport programs: An avenue to foster positive youth development. *Physical Education and Sport Pedagogy, 10,* 19–40.

Gordon, B. (2012). Teaching personal and social responsibility through secondary school physical education: The New Zealand experience. *Agora for Physical Education and Sport, 14,* 25–37.

Halpern, R. (2003). *Making Play Work: The Promise of After-School Programs for Low Income Youth*. New York: Teachers College Press.

Hamiton, S. F., and Hamilton, M. A. (2004). *The Youth Development Handbook*. Thousand Oaks, CA: Sage.

Hellison, D. (1978). *Beyond Balls and Bats: Alienated Youth in the Gym*. Washington, DC: American Alliance for Health, Physical Education, Recreation, and Dance.

Hellison, D. (1985). *Goals and Strategies for Physical Education*. Champaign, IL: Human Kinetics.

Hellison, D. (2003). *Teaching Responsibility Through Physical Activity*. Champaign, IL: Human Kinetics.

Hellison, D. (2011). *Teaching Responsibility Through Physical Activity* (2nd ed.). Champaign, IL: Human Kinetics.

Hellison, D. and Walsh, D. (2002). Responsibility-based youth programs evaluation: Investigations of investigations. *Quest, 54*, 292–307.

Hellison, D., Martinek, T., and Walsh, D. (2008). Sport and responsible leadership among youth. In N. L. Holt (Ed.), *Positive Youth Development through Sport* (pp. 49–60). London: Routledge.

Hirsch, B. (2005). *A Place to Call Home: After School Programs for Urban Youth*. New York: Teachers College Press.

Intrator, S. M., and Siegel, D. (2014). *The Quest for Mastery – Positive Youth Development Through Out-Of-School Programs*. Cambridge, MA: Harvard University Press.

Kirk, D., MacDonald, D., and O'Sullivan, M. (2006). *The Handbook on Physical Education*. Thousand Oaks, CA: Sage.

Lee, O., and Martinek, T. (2013). Understanding the transfer of values-based youth sport program goals from a bioecological perspective. *Quest, 65*, 300–312.

Lerner, R. (2004). *Liberty: Thriving and Engagement among America's Youth*. Thousand Oaks, CA: Sage.

Martinek, T., and Schilling, T. (2003). Developing compassionate leadership in underserved youth. *Journal of Physical Education, Recreation, and Dance, 74*, 33–39.

Martinek, T., and Hellison, D. (2009). *Youth Leadership in Sport and Physical Education*. New York: Palgrave-Macmillan.

Martinek, T., and Lee, O. (2012). From community gyms to classrooms: A framework for values transfer in schools. *Journal of Physical Education, Recreation, and Dance, 83*, 33–38.

Martinek, T., McLaughlin, D., and Schilling, T. (1999). Project effort: Teaching responsibility beyond the gym. *Journal of Physical Education, Recreation, and Dance, 70*, 12–25.

Martinek, T., Schilling, T., and Johnson, D. (2001). Evaluation of a sport and mentoring program designed to foster personal and social responsibility in underserved youth. *The Urban Review, 33*, 29–45.

Martinek, T., Hellison, D., and Walsh D. (2004). Service-bonded inquiry revisited: A research model for the community engaged professor. *Quest, 56*, 397–412.

Melendez, A., and Martinek, T. (2015). Life after Project Effort: Applying values acquired in a responsibility-based physical activity program. *International Journal of Sport Science, 21*, 258–280.

National Research Council and Institute of Medicine (2002). *Community Programs to Promote Youth Development*. Washington, DC: National Academy Press.

Oyserman, D., and Markus, H. (1990). Possible selves and delinquency. *Journal of Personality and Social Psychology, 59*, 112–125.

Oyserman, D., Harrison, K., and Bybee, D. (2001). Can racial identity be promotive of academic efficacy in adolescence? *International Journal of Behavioral Development, 25,* 379–385.

Oyserman, D., Terry, K., and Bybee, D. (2002). A possible selves intervention to enhance school involvement. *Journal of Adolescence, 25,* 313–326.

Petitpas, A. A., Cornelius, A., and Van Raalte, J. (2008). It's all about relationships. In N. L. Holt (Ed.), *Positive Youth Development through Sport* (pp. 61–70). London: Routledge.

Phelan, P. K., Davidson, A. L., and Yu, H. C. (1998). *Adolescents' Worlds: Negotiating Family, Peers, and School.* New York: Teachers College Press.

Siedentop, D. (1994). *Sport Education: Quality Physical Education through Sport Experiences.* Champaign, IL: Human Kinetics.

Talbert, C. (2015). *Perceptions of a Youth Leadership Program's Impact On Resiliency.* Unpublished doctoral dissertation, University of North Carolina at Greensboro.

Walsh, D. S. (2012). A TPSR-based kinesiology career club for youth in underserved communities. *Agora for Physical Education and Sport, 14,* 55–77.

Walsh, D. S., Veri, M. J., and Scobie, D. (2012). Impact of the kinesiology career club: A TPSR-based possible futures program for youth in underserved communities. *Agora for Physical Education and Sport, 14,* 213–229.

Weissberg, R. P., and Cascarino, J. (2013). Academic learning + social-emotional learning = national priority. *Phi Delta Kappan, 95*(2), 8–13.

Wright, P. M. (2012). Offering a TPSR physical activity club to adolescent boys labeled 'at risk' in partnership with a community-based youth serving program. *Agora for Physical Education and Sport, 14,* 94–114.

Wright, P. M., Ding, S., and Pickering, M. (2010). Integrating a personal and social responsibility program into a lifetime wellness course for urban high school students: Assessing implementation and educational outcomes. *Sport, Education, and Society, 15,* 277–296.

PART 4

PYD, sport, and mental health

15

POSITIVE GROWTH IN SPORT

Katherine A. Tamminen and Kacey C. Neely

The study of positive growth emerged within the field of psychology amid a larger wave of research emphasizing positive functioning and human development. In the 1980s, scholars such as Ed Diener, Suzanne Kobasa, Martin Seligman, C. Richard Snyder, and Michael Rutter were advancing work in the areas of positive psychology, positive emotions, resilience, and hardiness. Their work was largely developed in response to calls for researchers to examine the full complexity of human experience, since much of the research in psychology and stress has focused on treating and preventing negative experiences (for reviews of the historical roots of positive psychology and posttraumatic growth, see Diener, 2009 and Tedeschi et al., 2009). At the same time, researchers examining stress among survivors of trauma and serious illnesses found that some individuals reported positive life changes in the aftermath of their experiences (e.g. Affleck et al., 1985; Affleck and Tennen, 1996). This work has led to a large body of research which aims to understand how traumatic events and life stressors can precipitate positive transformations in the way people view themselves.

In some ways, the development of positive growth as a domain of inquiry has mirrored the emergence of positive youth development (PYD) as a field of research in the early 1990s and 2000s. Both areas share philosophical similarities in terms of their emphasis on positive human functioning and development. Positive youth development researchers operate from a strength-based perspective that youth are resources to be developed rather than problems to be managed (Roth and Brooks-Gunn, 2003), and they have sought to understand the conditions and processes that contribute to optimal youth development. Similarly, researchers investigating positive growth operate from the perspective that negative events have the potential to precipitate positive transformations and changes in one's life, and they have sought to understand the conditions and processes that contribute to these positive changes following adversity or trauma.

Thus, positive growth and PYD share some conceptual foundations in terms of seeking to understand the positive aspects of human functioning. The purpose of this chapter is to review concepts related to positive growth, review recent research that has been conducted among athletes and in youth sport settings, provide suggestions for future research, and to consider some of the ethical implications for research on positive growth following adversity.

Theories and concepts of positive growth

As positive psychology has increased in popularity as a field of inquiry, multiple theoretical perspectives have been used to conceptualize and study positive growth. It is important to note that we use the term positive growth in this chapter as a broad term to refer to various related concepts including posttraumatic growth, adversarial growth, resilience, mental toughness, and hardiness; however, these concepts have specific definitions and conceptualizations. We review some of these concepts here, and we refer the reader to Calhoun and Tedeschi (2014) as well as Lopez and Snyder (2009) for comprehensive reviews of these and other concepts related to positive growth.

Posttraumatic growth

Posttraumatic growth (PTG) is one of the most commonly used terms when it comes to understanding the positive changes that people report following traumatic events, and it refers to "positive psychological change experienced as a result of the struggle with highly challenging life circumstances" (Tedeschi and Calhoun, 2004, p. 1). Tedeschi and Calhoun identified five domains of PTG: (a) having a greater appreciation of life and a changed sense of priorities in life; (b) closer relationships with others; (c) a greater sense of personal strength; (d) recognizing new possibilities for one's life; and (e) spiritual or religious growth. Tedeschi and Calhoun (2004; see also Calhoun and Tedeschi, 2014) proposed that growth is a process which involves the management of emotional distress, rumination or cognitive engagement with the stressful event, and self-disclosure (e.g. writing and talking about the experience), and that growth is also influenced by the individual's sociocultural context. One important element of this definition is the idea that adversity or trauma itself does not necessarily lead to PTG, but rather growth is thought to occur through the process of struggling with the traumatic event. Therefore, processes such as coping, benefit-finding, positive reinterpretation, and meaning-making are thought to be mechanisms through which positive psychological changes may occur. Another important element of this definition is that PTG is not considered to be a return to normal functioning after a disruptive life event; instead, PTG involves positive changes within an individual that moves them beyond their previous level of functioning (Clay et al., 2009; Tedeschi and Calhoun, 2004).

Adversarial growth

An alternative perspective for conceptualizing and studying positive growth was forwarded by Joseph and Linley (2005), whose organismic valuing theory of growth through adversity aimed to integrate various perspectives of psychological growth (see also Joseph et al., 2012). Within their theory, adversarial growth is viewed as a process of struggling with adversity that propels an individual to a higher level of functioning than that which existed prior to the event (Linley and Joseph, 2004). This theory suggests that individuals are actively motivated towards growth due to an innate 'completion tendency'—that is, individuals are constantly evaluating their experiences and are driven towards integrating these experiences into their sense of self. The process is considered to be ongoing until the individual has resolved discrepancies between their pre- and post-trauma assumptive worlds, and it is influenced by the individual's personality and their social context.

Resilience

Resilience is another concept that is sometimes used interchangeably with the terms positive or posttraumatic growth. Lepore and Revenson (2014) described resilience as "a propensity towards positive (or nonpathological) developmental outcomes under high-risk conditions" (p. 72), and it consists of recovery, resistance, and reconfiguration. Recovery refers to individuals' return to normal functioning after a stressful event, while resistance refers to individuals who maintain normal functioning during and after a stressful event. Reconfiguration is most similar to PTG, in that it refers to individuals whose cognitions, beliefs, and behaviours are re-shaped and changed through the process of dealing with stressful events. The main conceptual difference is that PTG concerns primarily the positive changes that individuals experience as a result of dealing with negative events, while reconfiguration can refer to both positive and negative outcomes and changes that a person might experience. For example, a talented young rugby player might experience a devastating, career-ending head injury and report that he gained greater appreciation for other aspects of his life after the injury. However, he may also avoid spending time with his former teammates to avoid bringing up feelings of regret that he can no longer play rugby. Thus, the athlete's reconfiguration following his injury includes both positive and negative changes in thoughts and behaviours.

Within the sport psychology literature, resilience has been defined as "the role of mental processes and behavior in promoting personal assets and protecting an individual from the potential negative effect of stressors" (Fletcher and Sarkar, 2013, p. 16). Resilience in sport typically emphasizes the maintenance of normal functioning or individuals' ability to return to normal functioning, rather than the promotion of positive growth following adversity. In the remainder of this chapter we review research on positive growth following adversity in sport, although we also refer the reader to Sarkar and Fletcher (2014) and Galli and Vealey (2008) for more information on resilience in sport.

Growth-precipitating events

Researchers have argued that highly traumatic events are necessary to shatter an individual's assumptions about the world in order to prompt psychological growth (Tedeschi and Calhoun, 2004), suggesting that PTG is reserved for individuals who have experienced major traumas such as life-threatening illness, war, natural disasters, plane crashes, and so on. However, recent research indicates that individuals report different types of growth following exposure to similar events, and the degree of growth is not consistently related to the degree of trauma (for a review, see Linley and Joseph, 2004). In fact, researchers have reported a curvilinear relationship between posttraumatic stress and PTG, such that PTG seems to be highest when individuals report moderate levels of posttraumatic stress (Levine et al., 2008). Calhoun and Tedeschi (2014) recently suggested that a determination of whether an event is considered "traumatic enough" can be made by considering the extent to which the event has disrupted the individual's assumptive world or their personal narrative. If the individual's view of oneself has been changed in such a way that they perceive themselves as fundamentally different "before" and "after" the event, then Calhoun and Tedeschi would argue that the event has likely initiated forms of cognitive engagement required to produce PTG (for a review of trauma in sport, see Day, 2012).

Additionally, scholars have argued that positive growth does not necessarily require seismic disruptions to one's personal narrative, and that individuals can find positive changes in their worldviews as they mature and change across the lifespan (Davis and Nolen-Hoeksema, 2009). People may find benefits which are "common but relatively transient and incidental by-products of experiencing adversity, including improved social relationships, minor or temporary adjustments to values and priorities, and the realization of new possibilities" (p. 642). Thus, some scholars suggest a valuable distinction can be made between the benefits that individuals develop through facing adversity in life, whereas PTG involves sustained changes to major commitments and life goals in response to dealing with major changes in one's identity or life narrative (Davis and Nolen-Hoeksema, 2009).

Positive growth research among athletes

A recent surge of research in sport psychology has explored the potential for positive growth and benefit-finding following adversity in sport, primarily among adult athletes. At the highest levels of competition, many Olympians believe the adversity they faced was crucial on their paths to winning gold medals. For example, Sarkar et al. (2014) examined the different types of adversity that Olympic champions (six males, four females; aged 33–70 years) experienced before eventually winning a gold medal. The most common types of adversity were non-selection for international competitions, significant sporting failures, and injury, while non-sporting adversity included political unrest and terrorism, and the death of a family member. Olympians often described these events as motivating factors to reach the highest levels in their sport, and adversity was viewed as a learning opportunity and increased their confidence to overcome future challenges and adversity.

Similar research by Howells and Fletcher (2015) explored adversity and growth-related experiences by analyzing the autobiographies of seven Olympic swimmers (four male; three female; ages 14–41 years). Swimmers' adversity included developmental stressors during childhood and adolescence, external stressors related to family and coaches, injury, disordered eating, and psychological adversity including body dissatisfaction, depression, and suicidal thoughts. The authors explained that the transition from adversity to growth started as swimmers tried to hide their adversity and maintain a state of normality. However, as normality became too challenging to sustain, athletes began to question their performance narratives and view sport from a different perspective. This questioning led to a search for meaning which appeared to be a critical aspect for facilitating growth, and it reflects the idea that positive growth occurs through a process of rumination and cognitive engagement with the meaning of adverse events (Tedeschi and Calhoun, 2004; Joseph and Linley, 2005). Athletes began to seek support from family and friends, highlighting the important role of social support in adversarial growth. The authors suggested that growth was evident through the athletes' superior performance following adversity, enhanced relationships, increased spirituality, and prosocial behaviours to support others.

Positive growth has also been investigated among high-performance varsity athletes. Galli and Reel (2012) interviewed eleven NCAA Division 1 athletes (eight females, three males; M age = 20.82 years) who scored a moderate to large degree of growth on the Post Traumatic Growth Inventory (PTGI; Tedeschi and Calhoun, 1996) to examine their perceptions of stress-related growth. Consistent with previous findings, adversity identified by the athletes included sport and non-sport related events (e.g. performance issues, injuries, academics, car accident, and depression), and athletes perceived growth in life philosophy, self-changes, and interpersonal changes. In another study of varsity athletes, Tamminen et al. (2013) interviewed five elite female athletes (aged 18–23 years) to explore perceptions of growth following adversity. Athletes described several different types of adverse events, including coach conflicts, injuries, eating disorders, and sexual abuse by a coach. Although the types of negative events were different for each athlete, common elements included feelings of isolation/withdrawal, emotional disruptions, and they questioned their identity and abilities as athletes, suggesting the adversities they faced had challenged their personal narratives. The athletes' perceived growth occurred as they found meaning in their experiences, particularly through gaining perspective of the role of sport in their lives. Through struggling with adversity, athletes realized their physical and mental strength, and developed a desire to help other athletes going through similar forms of adversity.

The aforementioned studies have explored athletes' experiences of positive growth following various types of adversity. However, some researchers have exclusively examined growth following injury. For example, Wadey et al. (2011)

examined athletes' perceptions of positive benefits gained following injury among ten competitive male athletes (*M* age = 21.7 years) involved in rugby, soccer, and basketball. Athletes described specific perceived benefits from three phases of injury recovery. During the onset of their injury, athletes reported an increase in their ability to express and regulate emotions and strengthened social networks. During the rehabilitation phase, athletes perceived that the inability to practice or play enabled them to develop a stronger relationship with their coach, increase their technical and tactical knowledge, and spend more time with family and friends, which strengthened other social relationships. In the return to sport phase, athletes reported becoming mentally tougher and developing more empathy for other injured athletes when they reflected back on the injury process. This research is valuable in proposing that different forms of growth may occur at different points in time for athletes struggling with adversity, and it supports the need for more longitudinal research examining positive growth in sport.

Stress-related growth following injury has also been examined in the adapted sport literature. Crawford et al. (2014) conducted interviews with twelve individuals with an acquired spinal cord injury (SCI) to examine how participation in ParaSport influenced the athletes' perceptions of growth. The athletes perceived social, emotional, and physical growth through their participation in ParaSport, and they described sport as being invaluable in the formation of new identities following SCI, including the re-establishment of an athletic identity. Other forms of growth included a new appreciation for life, strengthened relationships with family and friends, and a sense of community with ParaSport athletes to make new connections with other athletes. Participants believed they gained confidence, developed problem-solving skills as they learned to cope with new challenges and obstacles, and felt they became more caring individuals.

While the majority of sport research investigating positive growth has used primarily qualitative methodologies, one study used a quantitative approach to examine resilience, coping, and stress-related growth following injury among 206 athletes (148 males, 58 females; *M* age = 22.23 years; Salim et al., 2015). Results indicated that there was a significant positive relationship between hardiness and stress-related growth, suggesting that hardy individuals were more likely to report stress-related growth following injury. Results also indicated that certain emotion-focused coping strategies (i.e. positive reframing, emotional support) mediated the relationship between hardiness and stress-related growth. These findings suggest that athletes who are high in hardiness experience more positive growth following injury because they use more emotion-focused coping strategies as opposed to problem-focused coping strategies.

Sport as a context for positive growth: cyclones, earthquakes, and complex traumas

The research reviewed thus far has considered athletes' perceptions of positive growth in sport, primarily among varsity and elite-level athletes. However, some researchers have taken a different approach by examining sport as a context which may decrease posttraumatic distress and promote positive growth among children and adolescents in the aftermath of traumatic experiences that have occurred outside of sport. For example, McDermott and colleagues (2014) recently reported findings of a longitudinal study of posttraumatic distress among 371 children and adolescents in the aftermath of a cyclone in Australia. Findings showed that approximately 41 percent of primary school children and 19 percent of secondary school children reported moderate to severe PTSD at Time 1 (three months post-disaster). Follow-up measures at Time 2 (eighteen months post-disaster) indicated that 45 percent of primary school children and 25 percent of secondary school children continued to report a high degree of PTSD. Interestingly, social connectedness (e.g. measured as feelings of trust and belonging, having friends and participating in sports or clubs at school) was associated with PTSD symptomatology at T2. Among primary school students, low social connectedness at Time 1 was significantly associated with moderate to severe PTSD at Time 2, and secondary students who were high in social connectedness at Time 1 had significantly lower PTSD symptoms at Time 2. Although this study did not focus exclusively on sport as a context for positive growth, it does lend support to the idea that social connections are associated with better adjustment post-disaster, and the measurement of social connectedness explicitly referred to sport participation. Thus, sport may be one opportunity for promoting social interactions and social connectedness among youth.

Another study provided evidence that sport may be a tool for positive psychosocial development among traumatized youth in the aftermath of natural disaster. Kunz (2009) described the use of sport as an intervention to promote resilience among children following an earthquake in the city of Bam, Iran. Participants in the sport program included approximately 300 youth between six and eighteen years of age, who were among 75,000 families that had been relocated to refugee camps after the earthquake. Youth had opportunities to participate in daily recreational activities such as football, basketball, gymnastics, karate, and table tennis offered by coaches in protected warehouses and a sports stadium in a nearby village. Despite initial difficulties with hostile and aggressive or agitated behaviours, youth learned to support one another, they developed team spirit, and demonstrated respect for their coaches and peers over time. Kunz (2009) suggested that the success of the program in facilitating positive growth was due to the development of supportive relationships between coaches and the youth participants. Coaches were trusted adults whom the children could talk to about the earthquake and its aftermath, which likely facilitated cognitive processing of the earthquake to help youth overcome the traumatic experience.

Beyond the study of sport interventions in post-disaster settings, sport has also been examined as an intervention to promote positive psychological health among complexly traumatized adolescents. Complex trauma involves repeated exposure to traumas that occur in the context of a caregiving environment (e.g. abuse, neglect, exposure to domestic violence). D'Andrea et al. (2013) reported pilot data regarding a weekly sports-based intervention consisting of weekly games and skills development which emphasized four main therapeutic concepts: (a) "play to the whistle"—perseverance and putting aside one's frustration while pursuing goals; (b) "show up"—commitment to best performances and awareness of emotional reactions to distress; (c) "build your team"—leadership skills and responsibility; and (d) "fill the tank"—providing support for others and framing the game in terms of successes rather than failures. Adolescent girls who participated in the intervention reported decreases in internalizing and externalizing symptoms (e.g. lower anxiety/depression, withdrawal, somatic complaints, delinquency, and aggression), while participants who did not engage in the sport program exhibited an increase in internalizing and externalizing symptoms. Intervention participants also showed an increase in peer-to-peer helping behaviours and peer encouragement, suggesting their interpersonal skills improved as well as indices of mental health. D'Andrea et al. (2013) suggested that structured interventions which are designed to promote specific therapeutic goals have the potential to serve as promising adjunctive treatments for traumatized youth. However, further research is required to determine whether complexly traumatized adolescents also experience PTG as a result of participation in sport-based interventions.

Taken together, these studies align with the main tenets of PYD and they highlight the importance of youth sport as a context for promoting positive psychological growth for children and adolescents. Key features of sport settings which seem to promote positive growth following adversity include opportunities for youth to interact with peers, and the development of supportive relationships with adults and coaches. Lepore and Revenson (2014) noted that social environments that are safe and supportive and that have a high degree of social capital (e.g. social relationships, mutual trust, and community participation) can facilitate coping and reduce distress, thus contributing to resilience and growth. In addition to developing relationships with peers and adults, youth participating in sport programs have the opportunity to develop physical skills and a sense of accomplishment, confidence, and self-esteem, which are key factors for promoting PYD in sport (Fraser-Thomas et al., 2005; National Research Council and Institute of Medicine, 2002).

Summary and considerations for future research

It appears that athletes report various forms of adversity that vary in duration and intensity, however the types of growth and psychological changes that athletes report appeared to be similar across studies and they reflect the main domains of growth proposed by Tedeschi and Calhoun (2004). This body of work supports the theoretical contention that it is not the specific event or adversity per se that leads to positive psychological growth, but rather it is the cognitive processing, coping, and affective engagement that occurs in the aftermath of adversity that leads to perceived growth and positive change. Additionally, positive growth does not appear to be uniform across individuals; instead it seems that positive growth following adversity is likely to occur when the individual has opportunities for self-disclosure within supportive relationships in order to facilitate cognitive engagement, rumination, and affective processing in relation to the event. Moving forward, researchers have argued for the examination of the environmental contexts that are likely to promote positive psychological changes following adversity (Lepore and Revenson, 2014). We anticipate that greater attention to the role of coaches, peers, and sport psychologists will be valuable for advancing this area of research, as well as studies which examine the responses of others when athletes engage in self-disclosure about adversity in sport.

Most of the studies examining positive growth within sport contexts have sampled adult athletes, although many of the adverse experiences that athletes described had occurred when they were adolescents. This trend likely reflects the fact that positive growth research in sport is a relatively new area of inquiry, and there are also ethical and methodological challenges in studying traumatic experiences among youth. However, since young athletes do experience psychological distress following injury and other traumatic experiences in sport (e.g. Newcomer and Perna, 2003; Stirling and Kerr, 2007), and since they have the capacity to experience at least some forms of growth following adversity (Milam et al., 2004), it would be useful to examine how and in what contexts positive growth may occur for youth athletes.

There are several areas where youth sport PYD researchers may draw from concepts in the area of positive growth to advance research and theory. For example, drawing from Linley and Joseph's (2004) work on positive growth, we would suggest that individuals' innate "completion tendencies" and cognitive styles which promote the integration of experiences with one's sense of self (Horowitz, 1980) could be explored within theoretical models of PYD to examine how youth athletes' identity development, sense of self, and cognitive styles might be associated with developmental outcomes. Similarly, drawing from research examining positive growth following injury, findings would suggest that development and change is not a linear process, but that athletes might exhibit gains and setbacks in various developmental outcomes as a series of fits and starts across childhood and adolescence. Longitudinal research designs which are sensitive to the possibility for increases and decreases in developmental outcomes over a number of measurement periods are necessary to further explore this issue. Additionally, research on positive growth in sport may benefit from approaches used to study PYD in sport. Researchers have demonstrated that sport participation does not automatically confer developmental benefits to youth, but rather the potential for youth to experience positive outcomes depends on features of the sport environment and interactions between actors at multiple levels and in multiple contexts. Similarly, adversity does not automatically precipitate positive growth among athletes. Researchers are encouraged to consider the programmatic work that has been conducted in the area of PYD and take into account the features of the person as well as their social and structural environment that may contribute to experiences of growth following adversity.

While it is likely that many young athletes will perceive benefits through facing adversity in sport and some may even report forms of PTG in the aftermath of negative sport experiences, it is important to ask whether there is truly anything to be gained from adversity in sport. The more troublesome corollary to this question, and one which is arguably of greater concern when it comes to youth sport, is whether idealizing concepts such as adversarial growth and resilience in sport promotes and legitimizes negative sport experiences for youth. Some researchers have even argued that trauma should be a "development tool" which can be exploited to develop talent among high-performing athletes (Collins and MacNamara, 2012), however, we feel this position raises the possibility that coaches, parents, and other adults involved in youth sport may engage in questionable behaviours and justify their actions with the argument that adversity will promote growth and resilience among athletes (Stirling and Kerr, 2015). The question remains: What is at risk when we promote resilience and growth in sport, and is the potential for growth worth the distress associated with adversity? We also note the paradox that by studying the concepts of adversarial growth and resilience in youth sport, we may be implicitly contributing to the legitimization of these concepts which could perpetuate damaging conditions for youth athletes.

While issues surrounding the legitimization of adversity in sport are troubling, nothing will be gained by ignoring them. Conversely, we argue that researchers and practitioners *should* grapple with these issues in three main areas: (a) by exploring how the sport environment may be problematic in contributing to adversity among youth athletes in the first place; (b) by considering the ethical implications of promoting concepts such as resilience, mental toughness, and adversarial growth among young athletes; and (c) by examining how and under what conditions sport may be a context for promoting and supporting psychological growth among children and adolescents. If positive growth can and does occur in sport settings, then it is important that we thoughtfully and responsibly pursue these avenues of research in a manner which maximizes our knowledge of these processes without inadvertently promoting or perpetuating harmful sport practices.

References

Affleck, G., and Tennen, H. (1996). Construing benefits from adversity: Adaptational significance and dispositional underpinnings. *Journal of Personality, 64*, 899–922.

Affleck, G., Tennen, H., and Gershman, K. (1985). Cognitive adaptations to a high risk infant: The search for mastery, meaning and protection from future harm. *American Journal of Mental Deficiency, 89*, 653–656.

Calhoun, L. G., and Tedeschi, R. G. (2014). *Handbook of Posttraumatic Growth: Research and Practice*. New York: Psychology Press.

Clay, R., Knibbs, J., and Joseph, S. (2009). Measurement of posttraumatic growth in young people: A review. *Clinical Child Psychology and Psychiatry, 14*, 411–422.

Collins, D., and MacNamara, A. (2012). The rocky road to the top: Why talent needs trauma. *Sports Medicine, 42*, 907–914.

Crawford, J. J., Gayman, A. M., and Tracey, J. (2014). An examination of post-traumatic growth in Canadian and American ParaSport athletes with acquired spinal cord injury. *Psychology of Sport and Exercise, 15,* 399–406.

D'Andrea, W., Bergholz, L., Fortunato, A., and Spinazzola, J. (2013). Play to the whistle: A pilot investigation of a sports-based intervention for traumatized girls in residential treatment. *Journal of Family Violence, 28,* 739–749.

Davis, C. G., and Nolen-Hoeksema, S. (2009). Making sense of loss, perceiving benefits, and posttraumatic growth. In S. J. Lopez and C. R. Snyder (Eds.), *The Oxford Handbook of Positive Psychology* (2nd ed., pp. 641–650). Oxford: Oxford University Press.

Day, M. (2012). Coping with trauma in sport. In J. Thatcher, M. Jones, and D. Lavallee (Eds.), *Coping and Emotion in Sport* (2nd ed., pp. 62–78). London: Routledge.

Diener, E. (2009). Positive psychology: Past, present, and future. In S. J. Lopez and C. R. Snyder (Eds.), *The Oxford Handbook of Positive Psychology* (2nd ed., pp. 7–12). Oxford: Oxford University Press.

Fletcher, D., and Sarkar, M. (2013). Psychological resilience: A review and critique of definitions, concepts, and theory. *European Psychologist, 18,* 12–23.

Fraser-Thomas, J. L., Côté, J., and Deakin, J. (2005). Youth sport programs: An avenue to foster positive youth development. *Physical Education and Sport Pedagogy, 10,* 19–40.

Galli, N., and Reel, J. J. (2012). 'It was hard, but it was good': A qualitative exploration of stress-related growth in Division I intercollegiate athletes. *Qualitative Research in Sport, Exercise, and Health, 4,* 297–319.

Galli, N., and Vealey, R. S. (2008). "Bouncing back" from adversity: Athletes' experiences of resilience. *The Sport Psychologist, 22,* 316–335.

Horowitz, M. J. (1980). Psychological response to serious life events. In V. Hamilton and D. Warburton (Eds.), *Human Stress and Cognition* (pp. 235–266). New York: Wiley.

Howells, K., and Fletcher, D. (2015). Sink or swim: Adversity- and growth-related experiences in Olympic swimming champions. *Psychology of Sport and Exercise, 16,* 37–48.

Joseph, S., and Linley, P. A. (2005). Positive adjustment to threatening events: An organismic valuing theory of growth through adversity. *Review of General Psychology, 9,* 262–280.

Joseph, S., Murphy, D., and Regel, S. (2012). An affective-cognitive processing model of posttraumatic growth. *Clinical Psychology and Psychotherapy, 19,* 316–325.

Kunz, V. (2009). Sport as a post-disaster psychosocial intervention in Bam, Iran. *Sport in Society, 12,* 1147–1157.

Lepore, S. J., and Revenson, T. A. (2014). Resilience and posttraumatic growth: Recovery, resistance, and reconfiguration. In L. G. Calhoun and R. G. Tedeschi (Eds.), *Handbook of Posttraumatic Growth: Research and Practice.* New York: Psychology Press.

Levine, S. Z., Laufer, A., Hamama-Raz, Y., Stein, E., and Solomon, Z. (2008). Posttraumatic growth in adolescence: Examining its components and relationship with PTSD. *Journal of Traumatic Stress, 21,* 492–496.

Linley, P. A., and Joseph, S. (2004). Positive change following trauma and adversity: A review. *Journal of Traumatic Stress, 17,* 11–21.

Lopez, S. J., and Snyder, C. R. (2009). *The Oxford Handbook of Positive Psychology* (2nd ed.). Oxford: Oxford University Press.

McDermott, B., Cobham, V., Berry, H., and Kim, B. (2014). Correlates of persisting posttraumatic symptoms in children and adolescents 18 months after a cyclone disaster. *Australian and New Zealand Journal of Psychiatry, 48,* 80–86.

Milam, J. E., Ritt-Olson, A., and Unger, J. B. (2004). Posttraumatic growth among adolescents. *Journal of Adolescent Research, 19,* 192–204.

National Research Council and Institute of Medicine. (2002). *Community Programs to Promote Youth Development.* Washington: National Academy Press.

Newcomer, R. R., and Perna, F. M. (2003). Features of posttraumatic distress among adolescent athletes. *Journal of Athletic Training, 38,* 163–166.

Roth, J. L., and Brooks-Gunn, J. (2003). What exactly is a youth development program? Answers from research and practice. *Applied Developmental Science, 7,* 94–111.

Salim, J., Wadey, R., and Diss, C. (2015). Examining the relationship between hardiness and perceived stress-related growth in a sport injury context. *Psychology of Sport and Exercise, 19,* 10–17.

Sarkar, M., and Fletcher, D. (2014). Psychological resilience in sport performers: A review of stressors and protective factors. *Journal of Sports Sciences, 32,* 1419–1434.

Sarkar, M., Fletcher, D., and Brown, D. J. (2014). What doesn't kill me … : Adversity-related experiences are vital in the development of superior Olympic performance. *Journal of Science and Medicine in Sport, 18,* 475–479.

Stirling, A. E., and Kerr, G. (2007). Elite female swimmers' experiences of emotional abuse across time. *Journal of Emotional Abuse, 7,* 89–113.

Stirling, A. E., and Kerr, G. (2015). In the name of performance: Threats, belittlement, and degradation. In J. Baker, P. Safai, and J. Fraser-Thomas (Eds.), *Health and Elite Sport: Is High Performance Sport a Healthy Pursuit?* (pp. 83–98). New York: Routledge.

Tamminen, K. A., Holt, N. L., and Neely, K. C. (2013). Exploring adversity and the potential for growth among elite female athletes. *Psychology of Sport and Exercise, 14,* 28–36.

Tedeschi, R. G., and Calhoun, L. G. (1996). The posttraumatic growth inventory: Measuring the positive legacy of trauma. *Journal of Traumatic Stress, 9,* 455–471.

Tedeschi, R. G., and Calhoun, L. G. (2004). Posttraumatic growth: Conceptual foundations and empirical evidence. *Psychological Inquiry, 15,* 1–18.

Tedeschi, R. G., Park, C., and Calhoun, L. G. (2009). Posttraumatic growth: Conceptual issues. In R. G. Tedeschi, C. L. Park, and L. G. Calhoun (Eds.), *Posttraumatic Growth: Positive Changes in the Aftermath of Crisis* (pp. 1–22). Mahwah, NJ: Lawrence Erlbaum.

Wadey, R., Evans, L., Evans, K., and Mitchell, I. (2011). Perceived benefits following sport injury: A qualitative examination of their antecedents and underlying mechanisms. *Journal of Applied Sport Psychology, 23,* 142–158.

16

COACHING, POSITIVE YOUTH DEVELOPMENT, AND MENTAL HEALTH

Stewart A. Vella, Lauren A. Gardner, and Sarah K. Liddle

Half of all psychological disorders have their onset before the age of fourteen years (Kessler et al., 2005). Childhood psychological disorders persist through adolescence and are recognized as one of the most prominent contributors to the global burden of disease among young people (Costello et al., 2005). Furthermore, mental health problems during adolescence have a long-term impact because they reduce the likelihood of completing school, getting a job, and engaging as a productive member of society, and have significant costs to quality of life (Sawyer et al., 2000). A recent report from the European Union estimated that the direct cost of programs that aim to promote well-being and prevent the onset of mental health problems can be recouped within four years. In addition, the immeasurable benefits to quality of life are far longer-lasting (McDaid, 2011).

As a result, there is a recognized need for targeted early prevention and intervention (Kessler et al., 2005), with programs aimed at positive youth development (PYD) forming a key component of this need. The primary, but not exclusive, principle of the PYD approach has been to focus on the promotion of developmental assets and protective factors that work to facilitate resilience, positive social and emotional functioning, community engagement, and a high degree of agency among young people (Benson et al., 2006). This asset-based approach to development has been contrasted with a deficit-based or pathology-based approach where the definition of a healthy young person is of one that is simply disease or problem-free. Nonetheless, Benson and colleagues (2006) have suggested that harm-reduction strategies can supplement the asset-based approach in the promotion of optimal functioning. This may be especially so when harm-reduction strategies are used in a way that increase agency and facilitate developmental assets. For example, strategies that promote autonomous and informed help-seeking behaviors for mental health can simultaneously be used to minimize potential harm while promoting agency and building a set of skills or assets that can underpin resilience and optimal functioning in the future.

Organized leisure activities are seen as an important avenue for PYD programs, with sport being the most popular and time-consuming leisure activity for young people (Hansen and Larson, 2007). In countries such as Australia, the average time that young people spend in organized sports is over six hours each week (Vella et al., 2013a). Evidence suggests that participation in organized sports can be an effective "intervention" for PYD. For example, sports participation can enhance social and emotional functioning, enhance health-related quality of life, and protect against the development of mental illness during childhood and adolescence at a population level (Vella et al., 2014a, 2014b).

The design and implementation of organized sporting programs are important influences on developmental outcomes for young participants. While policy makers, sports organizations, parents, and coaches all have an important role to play in the promotion of positive outcomes (Fraser-Thomas et al., 2005), this chapter will focus on the role of the coach. Specifically, the purpose of this chapter is to provide an overview of a comprehensive set of strategies that may be used by coaches to promote PYD, including a range of promotion-based approaches and complementary harm-minimization strategies. We will first outline three evidence-based approaches to coaching youth sports and summarize current knowledge on the role of the coach–athlete relationship. We provide an overview of coach education as an "intervention" to promote PYD and outline emerging and complementary harm-minimization strategies for coaches.

Approaches to coaching and positive youth development

Coach behaviors have been linked with a diverse range of positive developmental outcomes for young people (Fraser-Thomas et al., 2005). Consequently, conceptualizations of coaching have stipulated athlete psychosocial growth and development as core elements of effective practice (Horn, 2008). Coaching effectiveness is defined as "the consistent application of integrated professional, interpersonal, and intrapersonal knowledge to improve athletes' competence, confidence, connection, and character" (Côté and Gilbert, 2009; p. 316). As such, sport psychology and coaching scholars have sought to provide evidence of the influence that certain coaching behaviors have on the developmental outcomes of young people who participate in sports. Notably, researchers have used several theories of coaching practice to study these issues, which are discussed below.

The Mastery Approach to Coaching (MAC) has perhaps the greatest body of evidence to support its influence on athlete development (Smoll and Smith, 2009). The basic aim of MAC is to help youth sport coaches facilitate a mastery climate. A mastery climate is characterized by a focus on learning and effort rather than winning. A coach-created mastery climate has been associated with young athletes' enjoyment of sport, the extent to which they like their coach, their intentions to play for their coach in the future, and greater life skill gains (Cumming et al., 2007; Gould et al., 2012).

Autonomy-supportive coaching is an application of self-determination theory (Deci and Ryan, 1985). An autonomy-supportive coach creates an environment that values self-initiation, provides choice, encourages independent problem-solving, and allows young athletes to participate in decision-making (Mageau and Vallerand, 2003). The level to which the environment is autonomy-supportive will in turn influence the satisfaction of three basic human needs of autonomy, competence, and relatedness (Deci and Ryan, 1985). When these three basic needs are met, young athletes are more likely to be motivated by intrinsic or autonomous factors, and in turn, experience more positive cognitive, affective, and behavioral outcomes (Mageau and Vallerand, 2003). These psychological processes have found support in the literature where youth sport coaches' autonomy-supportive behaviors have been shown to predict satisfaction of basic psychological needs, which in turn are associated with important developmental assets including self-esteem, prosocial behaviors, identity reflection, and initiative (Coatsworth and Conroy, 2009; Hodge and Lonsdale, 2011). Furthermore, increases in coaches' autonomy-supportive behaviors are associated with increases in basic psychological need satisfaction, which are in turn associated with increases in athlete well-being and decreases in burnout (Balaguer et al., 2012).

Transformational leaders stimulate their followers and inspire others to follow them in the absence of social exchanges such as rewards and punishments. By facilitating a shared vision they are able to motivate others and promote autonomous actions. There are four major components of transformational leadership: idealized influence; inspirational motivation; intellectual stimulation; and individual consideration (Bass and Riggio, 2006). Transformational leadership theory has been applied to coaching youth sports with the aim of helping coaches to facilitate positive developmental outcomes for young athletes (Vella et al., 2012, 2013b; also see Chapter 3). Among youth sport athletes the Transformational Leadership Approach to Coaching—an approach based in transformational leadership theory and applied to the youth sport context—has been associated with increased task cohesion, collective efficacy, perceived competence, enjoyment, and positive developmental experiences (Price and Weiss, 2013; Vella et al., 2013c).

Despite diverse theoretical foundations, all three approaches to coaching have been associated with positive developmental outcomes for young athletes. The strength of the evidence is limited given its cross-sectional nature, but offers some support for the theoretical propositions that underpin each approach. Nonetheless, strong theoretical foundations and an expanding evidence base allow coaching practitioners to select an approach to coaching that suits their needs. It may also be possible for coaches to pick and choose aspects of each approach that are consistent with their coaching philosophy and that are compatible with the context in which they operate. For a detailed exploration of these approaches to coaching and how they can be used to inform coaching practice aimed at PYD, see a summary provided by Vella and Perlman (2014).

The coach–athlete relationship

The coach–athlete relationship refers to the situation in which coaches' and athletes' cognitions, affect, and behaviors mutually and causally influence each other (Jowett and Ntoumanis, 2004). This dynamic relationship is particularly important in youth sports where coaches not only play an integral role in improving skill and performance, but also in facilitating optimal development (Fraser-Thomas et al., 2005; Vella et al., 2013c). For example, positive coach–athlete relationships have been associated with a range of developmental outcomes including improved personal and social skills, initiative, goal setting, greater motivation, persistence, critical thinking, leadership, and have been inversely associated with negative experiences (Gould et al., 2007; Smith and Smoll, 2002; Vella et al., 2013c). Given the value of the coach–athlete relationship in promoting PYD, it is important for researchers and coaches to understand how to enhance this relationship and the resultant developmental gains.

Theoretical approaches to understanding the coach–athlete relationship

One of the most prominent conceptualizations of the coach–athlete relationship is the 3+1Cs approach developed by Jowett and colleagues (Jowett, 2005). It is proposed that the quality of the coach–athlete relationship is shaped by four key constructs: closeness, commitment, complementarity, and co-orientation. Closeness refers to the affective element of the relationship through feelings of trust, liking, appreciation, and respect. Commitment is the cognitive component which refers to the intentions of athletes and coaches to maintain their relationship. Complementarity is the behavioral aspect, and it refers to the cooperative and reciprocal behaviors of coaches and athletes. Finally, co-orientation refers to the athletes' and coaches' interpersonal perceptions about one another and the common views they share. It is proposed that a high-quality, interdependent coach–athlete relationship is established when greater levels of these constructs are experienced.

More recently, Jowett and Poczwardowski (2007) collaborated to produce an integrated research model to guide future research. The model has three interrelated layers representing antecedents, components, and outcomes of good quality coach–athlete relationships. The antecedent variables in the first layer include individual difference characteristics (e.g. age, sex, and personality traits), the wider social-cultural-sport context (e.g. cultural norms, roles, and expectations) and relationship characteristics (e.g. relationship type and duration). The components of a good-quality coach–athlete relationship in the second layer include the feelings (e.g. closeness), thoughts (e.g. commitment), and behaviors (e.g. complementarity) of coaches and athletes. Finally, the outcomes outlined in the third layer include intrapersonal (e.g. motivation, self-satisfaction, and performance), interpersonal (e.g. a satisfying relationship or conflict), and group (e.g. team cohesion and social acceptance) outcomes. It is proposed that the second and third layers both affect and are affected by one another. Importantly, the layers are bound together by interpersonal communication which is at the heart of the coach–athlete relationship and has the ability to unite or tear apart the coach–athlete dyad (Jowett, 2005; Jowett and Poczwardowski, 2007).

Strategies to enhance the coach–athlete relationship and PYD

Previous research utilizing highly experienced and successful coaches found that performance and life skills were not coached separately, but rather through general coaching methods, with personal development viewed as being of the most significant importance (Camiré et al., 2011; Gould et al., 2007). Key coaching strategies and techniques to foster high-quality relationships and PYD may include:

- treating young athletes respectfully and maturely
- effective communication
- positive reinforcement and feedback
- developing trust
- demonstrating empathy
- team-building activities
- building on young athletes' previous experiences and assets
- being responsive and supportive
- short- and long-term goal setting
- providing a rationale for tasks and decisions
- encouraging young athletes to take initiative
- relating teachable moments to non-sports settings
- emphasizing discipline, a strong work ethic, and emotional control.

Conclusions and future recommendations regarding the coach–athlete relationship

The coach–athlete relationship is one of the most critical relationships in youth sport and it holds significant potential for facilitating optimal development among young people (Camiré et al., 2011; Fraser-Thomas et al., 2005). Despite this, the majority of youth sports coaches do not have the formal coaching education necessary to understand how to maintain, enhance, or repair this important relationship and foster developmental outcomes. The implementation of coach education and training programs that focus on building effective relationships is a necessary step to maximize the potential of coaches in facilitating PYD.

Coach education for PYD

It is clear that the role of the youth sport coach extends well beyond the development of technical and tactical skills. As such, coach education could be viewed as an important and potentially influential means of promoting effective PYD. Typically, large-scale coach education programs such as the American Sport Education Program (Martens, 2012) and the US National Federation of State High School Associations Fundamentals of Coaching (Barnson, 2011) have included topics relevant to PYD, including motivational climate, building confidence, and goal setting. Nonetheless, evaluations of large-scale coach education courses are absent. Despite this, several insights can be gleaned from coach education research that are helpful for coaches and coach educators who are looking to facilitate PYD.

Informal approaches to coach education such as mentoring from more experienced coaches can effectively create settings that harness PYD (MacDonald et al., 2010). Underpinning the effectiveness of informal coach education may be the opportunity to discuss and reflect upon one's coaching practice. Indeed, ongoing coach reflection is critical to coach development and may be particularly critical for learning how to coach for PYD (Vella and Gilbert, 2013). This should include both critical reflection and reflective practice (Gilbert and Trudel, 2013). Critical reflection is a deep self-analysis that is aimed at re-organizing one's philosophies and mental models of coaching. Indeed, reflecting on one's coaching philosophy has been suggested as a good place to start a reflective process when PYD is the aim (Holt, 2011). Reflective practice, on the other hand, involves explicit attempts to solve everyday coaching issues. Coach education programs that are designed to stimulate critical reflection may be the most beneficial for sustained behavioral change (Vella and Gilbert, 2013).

Practical tips to help coaches engage in reflective practice have been provided by Holt (2011). Simple questions such as: Can you clearly explain your coaching philosophy? What factors make it difficult for you to prioritize PYD? What specific activities do you give to your players to promote their development? Can you use sports to teach lessons that will be valuable in other areas of athletes' lives? Furthermore, some examples of questions that might be used to facilitate critical reflection might include: Why do I coach? Why do I coach the way I do? What does it feel like to be coached by me? How do I define success? (Ehrmann et al., 2011).

One problem that is often faced by coaches who undertake education programs with modules designed to facilitate reflection is their ability to adopt and sustain reflective practices (Paquette et al., 2014). It could be argued that until this problem is solved, coach education programs will likely be ineffective in promoting positive developmental outcomes for young athletes. Coaching for PYD will most likely require coaches who are comfortable and skilled at engaging in a deep level of critical reflection and reflective practice, and who are able to constantly change their coaching practice to meet the changing needs of their young athletes (Vella and Gilbert, 2013).

Coaches as community gatekeepers for mental health

While half of all psychological disorders have their onset before the age of fourteen years, most young people do not seek professional help (Rickwood et al., 2005).

When young people do reach out for help, they tend to seek out someone with whom they are familiar, and often young people need the encouragement of a trusted adult to seek professional help (Rickwood et al., 2005). A community gatekeeper is a person within the community who is most likely to have close or regular contact with young people and is in a position to help facilitate behaviors which can underpin continued health, and usually adopt harm-minimization strategies (Lipson, 2014). However, when used well, gatekeeping strategies can promote agency, autonomy, and informed efforts to deliberately seek out opportunities to develop skills that can underpin optimal functioning into the future. For example, investigations into the effectiveness of gatekeeper approaches to the prevention of mental health problems have documented positive outcomes for young people, particularly using school teachers as community gatekeepers (Wyman et al., 2008). Mazzer and Rickwood (2015) identified that coaches have the potential to be a useful source of support for young people's mental health, and that further training for coaches could boost their effectiveness. Coaches have regular contact with the members of their team, and are in a position to monitor behavior changes, identify concerns, and act to promote positive outcomes.

Gatekeeper training programs are often harm-minimization strategies that aim to increase knowledge about mental health issues, increase the ability of gatekeepers to recognize mental health problems and intervene appropriately, and increase help-seeking behaviors of young people (Lipson, 2014). There is still significant scope to tailor such programs to be compatible with the PYD approach by training gatekeepers to promote agency, autonomy, and targeted asset-building among young people. Further, while sport coaches have been identified as potential gatekeepers, more empirical research needs to be conducted to determine what content is most suited for coaches and the sports setting. To our knowledge, training of sports coaches as community gatekeepers has not yet been undertaken and evaluated. Future research might explore the effectiveness of a PYD approach to gatekeeper training, or explore its utility with sports coaches.

Mental health literacy for coaches

Another potential approach to enhance coaches' influence on PYD is increasing their mental health literacy. Mental health literacy consists of several distinct components, which may be typically considered as harm-minimization strategies. These include recognition of specific disorders or different types of psychological distress, knowledge and beliefs about causes, risk factors, self-help interventions and professional help available, attitudes facilitating recognition and help-seeking, and knowledge of how to seek mental health information (Kitchener and Jorm, 2008). Increasing mental health literacy can decrease the stigma of mental health, and improve the mental health of members within community groups such as sporting clubs (Wright et al., 2007). Nonetheless, mental health literacy training may also legitimately be used to educate coaches on those factors which underpin positive development and well-being.

One of the most influential methods of training mental health literacy is through the Mental Health First Aid program (MHFA; Kitchener and Jorm, 2008). Rural football coaches' knowledge of mental disorders, their capacity to recognize mental illness, and their confidence in helping someone with a mental health problem were all improved following MHFA training (Pierce et al., 2010). This suggests that encouraging coaches to participate in appropriate training could have important benefits for the mental health and well-being of young people. Future research should consider adapting the mental health literacy framework to be more compatible with a PYD approach. For example, coaches could be educated on the factors that underpin PYD, be trained to recognize the presence or absence of such factors, and help them build confidence to act.

Summary and conclusions

Coaches have an important and influential role in the promotion, prevention, and early intervention for mental health among young people. There are three notable evidence-based approaches to coaching which purport to help the coach facilitate PYD. Although the evidence base which underpins these approaches is less than convincing, they are nonetheless promising guidelines for coaches who want to incorporate PYD into their coaching practice. Similarly, evidence suggests that a good-quality coach–athlete relationship may facilitate PYD, and guidelines are also available to help coaches in this area of practice. To further consolidate benefits for athletes, coaches are encouraged to engage in reflective practice and critical reflection. Alternatively, gatekeeper and mental health literacy training for coaches can complement traditional approaches used to influence the mental health of young athletes if used to promote agency, autonomy, and to develop skills that can underpin future health. To move the field forward high-quality coach education programs need to be formulated, implemented, tested, and translated into policy and practice. Future research should focus on the formulation of coach education programs that are evidence- and theory-based, incorporate reflection as a core component, meet the needs of coaching practitioners, and that are scalable and sustainable. This might also include adapting the traditional harm-minimization strategies to include a PYD approach.

References

Balaguer, I., Gonzalez, L., Fabra, P., Castillo, I., Merce, J., and Duda, J. L. (2012). Coaches' interpersonal style, basic psychological needs and the well- and ill-being of young soccer players: A longitudinal analysis. *Journal of Sports Sciences, 30*, 1619–1629.

Barnson, S. C. (2011). *Supplement for Fundamentals of Coaching.* Indianapolis, IN: National Federation of State High School Associations.

Bass, B. M., and Riggio, R. E. (2006). *Transformational Leadership.* Mahwah, NJ: Lawrence Erlbaum Associates.

Benson, P. L., Scales, P. C., Hamilton, S. F., and Sesma Jr., A. (2006). Positive youth development: Theory, research and applications. In W. Damon and R. M. Lerner (Eds.), *Handbook of Child Psychology. Theoretical Models of Human Development* (6th ed., pp. 894–941). New York: Wiley and Sons.

Camiré, M., Forneris, T., Trudel, P., and Bernard, D. (2011). Strategies for helping coaches facilitate positive youth development through sport. *Journal of Sport Psychology in Action,* 2, 92–99.

Coatsworth, J. D., and Conroy, D. E. (2009). The effects of autonomy-supportive coaching, need satisfaction, and self-perceptions on initiative and identity on youth swimmers. *Developmental Psychology, 45,* 320–328.

Costello, E. J., Egger, H., and Angold, A. (2005). 1-year research update review: The epidemiology of child and adolescent psychiatric disorders: I. Methods and public health burden. *Journal of the American Academy of Child and Adolescent Psychiatry, 44,* 972–986.

Côté, J., and Gilbert, W. (2009). An integrative definition of coaching effectiveness and expertise. *International Journal of Sports Science and Coaching, 4,* 307–323.

Cumming, S. P., Smoll, F. L., Smith, R. E., and Grossbard, J. R. (2007). Is winning everything? The relative contributions of motivational climate and won-lost percentage in youth sports. *Journal of Applied Sport Psychology, 19,* 322–336.

Deci, E. L., and Ryan, R. M. (1985). *Intrinsic Motivation and Self-Determination in Human Behaviour.* New York: Plenum Press.

Ehrmann, J., Ehrmann, P., and Jordan, G. (2011). *InSideOut Coaching: How Sports Can Transform Lives.* New York: Simon and Schuster.

Fraser-Thomas, J. L., Côté, J., and Deakin, J. (2005). Youth sport programs: An avenue to foster positive youth development. *Physical Education and Sport Pedagogy, 10,* 19–40.

Gilbert, W., and Trudel, P. (2013). The role of deliberate practice in becoming an expert coach: Part 2 – Reflection. *Olympic Coach Magazine, 24,* 35–44.

Gould, D., Collins, K., Lauer, L., and Chung, Y. (2007). Coaching life skills through football: A study of award winning high school coaches. *Journal of Applied Sport Psychology, 19,* 16–37.

Gould, D., Flett, R., and Lauer, L. (2012). The relationship between psychosocial development and the sports climate experienced by underserved youth. *Psychology of Sport and Exercise, 13,* 80–87.

Hansen, D. M., and Larson, R. W. (2007). Amplifiers of developmental and negative experiences in organized activities: Dosage, motivation, lead-roles, and adult–youth ratios. *Journal of Applied Developmental Psychology, 28,* 360–374.

Hodge, K., and Lonsdale, C. (2011). Prosocial and antisocial behavior in sport: The role of coaching style, autonomous vs. controlled motivation, and moral disengagement. *Journal of Sport and Exercise Psychology, 33,* 527–547.

Holt, N. L. (2011). Sport and positive youth development. In I. Stafford (Ed.), *Coaching Children in Sport* (pp. 256–266). London: Routledge.

Horn, T. S. (2008). Coaching effectiveness in the sport domain. In T. S. Horn (Ed.), *Advances in Sport Psychology* (pp. 239–268). Champaign, IL: Human Kinetics.

Jowett, S. (2005). On enhancing and repairing the coach–athlete relationship. In S. Jowett and M. Jones (Eds.), *The Psychology of Coaching* (pp. 14–26). Leicester, UK: The British Psychological Society, Sport and Exercise Psychology Division.

Jowett, S., and Ntoumanis, N. (2004). The coach–athlete relationship questionnaire (CART-Q): Development and initial validation. *Scandinavian Journal of Medicine and Science in Sports, 14,* 245–257.

Jowett, S., and Poczwardowski, A. (2007). Understanding the coach–athlete relationship. In S. Jowett and D. Lavallee (Eds.), *Social Psychology in Sport* (pp. 3–14). Champaign, IL: Human Kinetics.

Kessler, R. C., Berglund, P., Demler, O., Jin, R., Merikangas, K. R., and Walters, E. E. (2005). Lifetime prevalence and age-of-onset distributions of DSM-IV disorders in the National Comorbidity Survey replication. *Archives of General Psychiatry, 62,* 593–602.

Kitchener, B. A., and Jorm, A. F. (2008). Mental Health First Aid: An international programme for early intervention. *Early Intervention in Psychiatry, 2,* 55–61.

Lipson, S. K. (2014). A comprehensive review of mental health gatekeeper-trainings for adolescents and young adults. *International Journal of Adolescent Medicine and Health, 26,* 309–320.

McDaid, D. (2011). *Making the Long-term Economic Case for Investing in Mental Health to Contribute to Sustainability.* European Union. Available at: http://ec.europa.eu/health/mental_health/docs/long_term_sustainability_en.pdf

MacDonald, D. J., Côté, J., and Deakin, J. (2010). The impact of informal coach training on the personal development of youth sport athletes. *International Journal of Sports Science and Coaching, 5,* 363–372.

Mageau, G. A., and Vallerand, R. J. (2003). The coach–athlete relationship: A motivational model. *Journal of Sports Sciences, 21,* 883–904.

Martens, R. (2012). *Successful Coaching* (4th ed.). Champaign, IL: Human Kinetics.

Mazzer, K. R., and Rickwood, D. J. (2015). Mental health in sport: Coaches' views of their role and efficacy in supporting young people's mental health. *International Journal of Health Promotion and Education, 53,* 102–113.

Paquette, K. J., Hussain, A., Trudel, P., and Camiré, M. (2014). A sport federation's attempt to restructure a coach education program using constructivist principles. *International Sport Coaching Journal, 1,* 75–85.

Pierce, D., Liaw, S. T., Dobell, J., and Anderson, R. J. (2010). Australian rural football club leaders as mental health advocates: An investigation of the impact of the Coach the Coach project. *International Journal of Mental Health Systems, 4,* 10.

Price, M. S., and Weiss, M. R. (2013). Relationships among coach leadership, peer leadership, and adolescent athletes' psychosocial and team outcomes: A test of transformational leadership theory. *Journal of Applied Sport Psychology, 25,* 265–279.

Rickwood, D. J., Deane, F. P., Wilson, C. J., and Ciarrochi, J. (2005). Young people's help-seeking for mental health problems. *Australian e-Journal for the Advancement of Mental Health, 4,* 218–251.

Sawyer, M. G., Arney, F. M., Baghurst, P. A., Clark, J. J., Graetz, B. W., Kosky, R. J., … Zubrick, S. R. (2000). The mental health of young people in Australia: Key findings from the child and adolescent component of the national survey of mental health and well-being. *Australian and New Zealand Journal of Psychiatry, 35,* 806–814.

Smith, R. E., and Smoll, F. L. (Eds.) (2002). *Way to Go Coach!* (2nd ed.). Portola Valley, CA: Warde.

Smoll, F. L., and Smith, R. E. (2009). *Mastery Approach to Coaching: A Leadership Guide for Youth Sports.* Seattle: Youth Enrichment in Sports.

Vella, S. A., and Gilbert, W. (2013). Coaching young athletes to positive development: Implication for coach training. In R. Gomes, R. Resende and A. Alburquerque (Eds.), *Adaptation, Performance, and Human Development.* New York: Nova Science.

Vella, S. A., and Perlman, D. J. (2014). Mastery, autonomy and transformational approaches to coaching: Common features and applications. *International Sport Coaching Journal, 1,* 173–179.

Vella, S. A., Oades, L. G., and Crowe, T. P. (2012). Validation of the Differentiated Transformational Leadership Inventory as a measure of coach leadership in youth soccer. *The Sport Psychologist, 26,* 203–224.

Vella, S. A., Cliff, D. P., Okely, A. D., Scully, M., and Morley, B. (2013a). Associations between organized sports participation and obesity-related health behaviors in Australian adolescents. *International Journal of Behavioral Nutrition and Physical Activity, 10,* 113.

Vella, S. A., Oades, L. G., and Crowe, T. P. (2013b). A pilot Transformational Leadership training program for sports coaches: Impact on the developmental experiences of adolescent athletes. *International Journal of Sports Science and Coaching, 8,* 513–530.

Vella, S. A., Oades, L. G., and Crowe, T. P. (2013c). The relationship between coach leadership, the coach–athlete relationship, team success, and the developmental experiences of young athletes. *Physical Education and Sport Pedagogy, 18,* 549–561.

Vella, S. A., Cliff, D. P., Magee, C. A., and Okely, A. D. (2014a). Associations between sports participation and psychological difficulties during childhood: A two-year follow up. *Journal of Science and Medicine in Sport, 18,* 304–309.

Vella, S. A., Cliff, D. P., Magee, C. A., and Okely, A. D. (2014b). Sports participation and parent-reported health-related quality of life in children: Longitudinal associations. *Journal of Pediatrics, 164,* 1469–1474.

Wright, A., Jorm, A. F., Harris, M. G., and McGorry, P. D. (2007). What's in a name? Is accurate recognition and labelling of mental disorders by young people associated with better help-seeking and treatment preferences? *Social Psychiatry and Psychiatric Epidemiology, 42,* 244–250.

Wyman, P. A., Brown, C. H., Inman, J., Cross, W., Schmeelk-Cone, K., Guo, J., and Pena, J. B. (2008). Randomized trial of a gatekeeper program for suicide prevention: 1-year impact on secondary school staff. *Journal of Consulting and Clinical Psychology, 76,* 104.

17

PROMOTING MENTAL HEALTH IN YOUTH SPORT

David Carless and Kitrina Douglas

In this chapter we consider the effects of involvement in sport on the mental health of young people. We offer our own perspective on this topic with the intention of stimulating dialogue and creative responses to the question of how to promote young people's mental health in and through sport. To do so, we: (a) outline recent literature concerning mental health among young people; (b) reflect on our own experiences in sport as young people using dialogical (Frank, 2010) and duoethnography (Sawyer and Norris, 2015) approaches; and (c) draw on our ongoing narrative research into the experiences of elite and professional sportspeople (e.g. Douglas and Carless, 2015).

Although the participants in our studies have mostly been adults, our life story methodology has allowed us to generate retrospective insights into individuals' prior experiences of sport as young people. These experiences cover a wide range of team and individual sports, as well as a range of different contexts including school sport, leisure time and family sport, and athlete development initiatives. The essence of our argument is that sport has both positive and negative effects on young people's mental health, the direction of the effect depending more on the *cultural environment* in which participation occurs than the objective details of the activity (such as the nature, type or intensity of the activity). Given the importance of cultural environment on mental health outcomes (see Carless and Douglas, 2010, 2012), we focus our attention here on the cultural narratives that circulate and are enacted within sporting subcultures.

Children and young people's mental health

A recently published policy document, *Future in Mind* (Department of Health, 2015), summarizes facts and figures concerning mental health among British children and young people. It is reported that one in ten children aged between five and sixteen years has a mental health problem (Green et al., 2005), with the most common mental health issues being conduct disorders (5.8 per cent), anxiety (3.3 per cent), severe ADHD (1.5 per cent), and depression (0.9 per cent). Additionally, it is estimated that 10–13 per cent of fifteen- to sixteen-year-olds have self-harmed (Hawton et al., 2002). While mental health problems appear less common among children than adults, the report notes that the life chances of young people who are affected are 'significantly reduced in terms of their physical health, their educational and work prospects, their chances of committing a crime and even the length of their life' (Department of Health, 2015, p. 21). Mental health when young, then, has long-term implications for development, well-being and life prospects.

The *Future in Mind* document states that 'treating different, specific health issues separately will not tackle the overall wellbeing of this generation of children and young people' (p. 21). Instead, it is argued, young people's 'mental and physical health are intertwined, and at the heart of health and wellbeing are their relationships with others' (p. 21). These statements are important as they indicate the need for a holistic approach to health and well-being that takes seriously the social, cultural and relational environments in which young people live. These contexts – which include home, family, school and leisure environments – can have profound impacts on mental health. Bullying, for example, is reported by 34–46 per cent of school children in England and linked to elevated rates of anxiety, depression and self-harm in adulthood (Copeland et al., 2013). Here, a social, cultural and relational experience can be seen to directly impact mental health – young people who are exposed to frequent, persistent bullying have higher rates of psychiatric disorder (Copeland et al., 2013).

This holistic perspective works from the understanding that there is more to mental health than the presence or absence of disorder. We are drawn to the broad and humanistic definition of mental health as 'the emotional and spiritual resilience which enables us to enjoy life and to survive pain, disappointment and sadness. It is a positive sense of well-being and an underlying belief in our own and others' dignity and worth' (Department of Health, 2003, p. 8). In the United States, mental health has been similarly broadly defined as 'a state of successful performance of mental function, resulting in productive activities, fulfilling relationships with other people, and the ability to adapt to change and to cope with adversity' (United States Department of Health and Human Services, 1999, p. 4). It is from this integrated social, cultural and relational position that the effects of sport on the mental health of young people need to be considered.

Looking back to move forward, part one

> *David:* Looking back, my personal experience of mental health as a young person in sport was quite contradictory. On the one hand, sport was beneficial for me as a boy and young man. Wearing the goalkeeping kit in hockey at 11 and 12 made me feel special, like I was valued, that I had some

worth. Later, around 14, I started training, in inverted commas, for hockey and rugby. I'd go for runs along the canal, take Buster our dog with me, and time myself doing perhaps a 20-minute run. About that time, I also started training on the school's multi-gym. I remember the rugby coach helping me with my pass from the base of the scrum. I got one-to-one attention, I felt special. Those relationships with the PE and sport teachers were important to me – it was a more informal, friendly, equal relationship than I experienced with other teachers. Then there were matches on Saturdays, going somewhere on a day trip or even a little tour. I think these positive mental health effects helped me get along on a day-to-day basis. But there were also some real negatives. I can see now how sport was also harmful to my mental health and development. The clearest example was being held very tightly to an exclusively heterosexual story and identity. In a sport like rugby, a degree of physical closeness and intimacy, through changing and showering together, is common. I vividly remember feeling attracted to some teammates. But it felt, to me anyway, impossible to act on that attraction. Something in the culture seemed to prohibit same-sex sexual relationships. As a young person, I never met anybody in sport who identified as anything other than heterosexual. I never heard one single boy or man voice his attraction to other males. It was as if everybody was straight. I felt completely alone. Now, with hindsight, I understand that sport culture knocked me back, constantly, into a heterosexual identity. The singular (heterosexual) story that dominated sport culture made it difficult or impossible to share and develop alternative stories (gay or bisexual). The dominance of this story – which did not fit my experience – shaped my actions, constrained my identity and, I think, adversely affected my mental health.

Why do stories matter for mental health?

There are good reasons to believe that mental health is related to narrative processes such as people's ability and opportunity to create and share stories of their lives that fit their experience. According to McAdams (1993), developing one's life story contributes to mental health through bringing a sense of meaning and purpose to life which helps avoid malaise and stagnation. A person's life story is not, however, developed in isolation, but instead depends upon the broader narratives that circulate within her or his cultural environment (McLeod, 1997). These narratives are not always immediately obvious. Narrative theorists hold that who we *are* (our identity) and what we *do* (our behaviours) is shaped not only by the stories we tell but also by the cultural narratives in which we are immersed (see Bruner, 1986; Crossley, 2000; McAdams, 1993; McLeod, 1997). It is on this basis that Frank (2010) suggests that 'stories and narratives are resources for people, and they conduct people, as a conductor conducts an orchestra; they set a tempo, indicate emphases, and instigate performance options' (pp. 14–15). The availability of particular narratives encourages and legitimizes particular identities and behaviours.

An absence of narrative resources within a particular cultural context will limit identity and behaviour options.

Sustaining a story calls for behaviours that fit that story. Because one's story draws on one or more cultural narratives, a cultural narrative 'calls' the teller to act in ways that fit its plot (see Frank, 1995; Lindemann, 2014). When our experience does not fit an available cultural narrative, a degree of psychological tension is likely to result. Good mental health, as McLeod (1997) suggests, requires us to achieve a satisfactory fit between what we desire and do (as agentic beings), what we say we do (through personal stories) and what our subculture calls us to do (through cultural narratives). These theoretical insights make some sense of the experiences David recounts above where his experience (of same-sex attraction) was at odds with the dominant cultural narrative in sport (of heterosexuality). As recent autoethnographic studies (Carless, 2010, 2012a) show, the lack of narrative resources that fit a person's embodied experience can constrain identity development and prohibit relational interconnection. This can lead to isolation and alienation. David's account above offers a snapshot of the consequences of these processes (see Carless, 2010, 2012a, 2012b, 2013 for fleshed-out accounts). But it is not only in terms of sexuality that dominant cultural narratives can create psychological tensions and difficulties for young people in sport.

Looking back to move forward, part two

> *Kitrina:* As a child, I didn't like it when people said they'd beaten me. It made me feel, within, I couldn't say exactly what it was, but it wasn't good. I can remember going for a run with my cousin and at the end she'd run ahead, because she was quicker than me, and I didn't like that.
>
> *David:* Almost like she was tricking you?
>
> *Kitrina:* No, I wouldn't say that, just the fact that she was quicker supposedly meant she was better.
>
> *David:* So because she *could* out-sprint you, she would. Rather than finish the race together?
>
> *Kitrina:* Yes. I knew there was something I didn't like in that process – something that was tearing apart rather than being together.
>
> *David:* Separation. Or separat*ing*.
>
> *Kitrina:* Yes, but it was a feeling rather than anything that was spoken.

A dominant narrative in sport

The above account portrays a young person – Kitrina – experiencing a degree of tension through running up against an enactment of what we've called the dominant narrative in sport: *the performance narrative* (Douglas and Carless, 2006, 2009, 2015). This narrative plot is essentially about winning, beating others, about being the best, the fastest, or the strongest. It articulates a desire to achieve a type of esteem and glory that go with being 'a winner' – even if only through 'friendly' rivalry with a family member. Over time, the quest to win means performance-related concerns come to infuse all areas of life, such that 'sport is life and life is sport'. It is a story of single-minded dedication to sport performance that requires all other areas of life and self to be relegated. Within and beyond sport culture it is widely assumed that living according to these values is the *only* way to be successful in sport. It is for this reason that we consider the performance narrative to be *dominant* – because it is the most commonly circulated and endorsed type of story in sport.

In our research with elite and professional athletes, we have documented how young people are sometimes socialized into living their lives according to the terms of the performance narrative (e.g. Carless and Douglas, 2013a). Ryan (a rower) and Luke (a runner) describe times when, as youngsters, they had been pressured to change how they lived to better fit the values of the performance narrative. For example, both described limiting or ending relationships which were seen by others to 'get in the way' of their sport performance. We have witnessed similar accounts across different sports, including golf, hockey and rugby union (see Carless and Douglas, 2009, 2013b). All these individuals recounted how the words and actions of powerful or influential *others* within sport culture (e.g. coaches, managers, other athletes, parents, performance directors) coerced them into a particular way of talking about and living their lives in the (mistaken) belief that this was necessary in order to achieve success.

The consequences of this coercion, however, are not benign. Through our longitudinal research with golfers (e.g. Carless and Douglas, 2009; Douglas and Carless, 2006, 2009), we have seen how performance stories tend to be associated with negative mental health consequences. We have documented how for performance storytellers: (a) self-worth is fragile and psychological well-being fluctuates, through being contingent on performance outcomes; (b) single-minded dedication to performance can foreclose identity and life horizons through relegating or suppressing other areas of life; and (c) withdrawal, retirement or career-ending injury are regarded fearfully as times of potentially insurmountable loss. When sport is organized, promoted or experienced in line with the plot of the performance narrative, we suggest that it's potential to lead to adverse mental health outcomes is increased.

Looking back to move forward, part three

> *David*: In recent years I've talked with a number of drama therapists, actors and contemporary dancers about what an individual might gain through having the opportunity to 'play' different roles through the performing arts. For example, in both drama and dance, an individual is asked to perform a *variety* of roles and act or dance *different* parts. Through their bodies, actors and dancers learn different movement patterns, take chances, and are encouraged to explore and experiment. In terms of sexuality and gender, for example, by playing a woman, acting a 'camp' role or an openly gay part, a

young man might be challenged to broaden a singular conception of gender or sexual identity. Becoming different parts on the stage might allow the performer to 'try on' different personas, opening up story and identity options, and movement patterns in a way that I would see as being good for mental health. In team sport, it's the opposite. As a young person, I was socialized into playing the quite narrow part of 'athlete' – a heterosexual role that is also about being competitive, tough, performance-focused and 'masculine' in an exclusive and hegemonic way. This includes the way I walk, hold my body, throw a ball or take a hit. In contrast, my dance and drama colleagues and friends are used to playing a whole array of parts. They didn't even have to decide whether they were *playing* a part or *becoming* a part. 'Oh this part feels like it fits!' Whereas in theatre they got to explore different parts without pressure or expectation, in sport I felt expected to conform to a particular part. I never got to try different parts on because *this* is the part of 'athlete' – as scripted by the performance narrative. There were loads of parts it might have been good to try – romantic, same-sex relationship parts perhaps? But those parts seemed incompatible with being a sportsman.

Negotiating life in sport

Through our research with professional golfers, we have shown that success at the highest level in sport *is* possible without following the script of the performance narrative (Douglas and Carless, 2006, 2009, 2015; Carless and Douglas, 2009; Douglas, 2009). Subsequently, we have shown this to also be the case in other sports (Carless and Douglas, 2013a, 2013b). Across this research, numerous athletes story and live their lives in line with alternative scripts, such as the *discovery narrative* (a story of a life of exploration and discovery over and above performance outcomes) and *relational narrative* (a story of complex interdependent connection between two or more people in which performance is a by-product).

Although mental health issues may still arise for tellers of discovery and relational life stories, they do not appear to be as severe as they can be for those who adhere to a performance life story. These individuals do not seem to experience fragile self-worth, foreclosed identity, or debilitating fear/loss concerning career cessation. If psychological difficulties do arise, they tend to be the result of being pressured by others to conform to the performance script. At these times, discovery and relationally oriented individuals need to find a way to *resist* these often powerful cultural pressures – they must, quite literally, resist 'the part of athlete' as scripted by the performance narrative (Carless and Douglas, 2013b; Douglas, 2014). To do so, they require alternative narrative resources (such as discovery or relational stories) to support and sustain their personal stories.

Because powerful or influential others within sport culture frequently assume success is only achievable through adhering to the performance story, some sportspeople change their story (what they say) and behaviour (what they do) to align with the performance narrative. By doing so, their long-term mental well-being and development is jeopardized. Others, particularly those in the early stages of their careers in sport, feel compelled to *play* 'the part of athlete', much like an actor playing a predetermined role. Rather than living or resisting the part of athlete, these individuals consciously present themselves or perform in line with the script of the performance narrative. When they perceive it necessary to do so (e.g. when selection, sponsorship or support are at stake), they modify their story and behaviour by telling and enacting performance stories. Outside sport, however, they maintain a multidimensional life story and enact a wider set of behaviours based on alternative narrative types (see Carless and Douglas, 2013b).

While we believe that playing the part of athlete is better for long-term mental health than living the part, there are three reasons why it may still be problematic. First, recounting performance tales over time potentially erodes the behaviours that stem from the existence of alternative stories. These behaviours cannot be sustained because they are at odds with the recounted performance stories. Second, self-policing behaviour to ensure performance actions are publicly visible reduces the available space and time for non-performance-oriented behaviours. As a result, the alternative life story derived from those actions may perish. Third, if a person continually presents an illusory self, how can others ever really get to know her or him? Adverse relational consequences may follow for those who repeatedly play the part of athlete.

Looking back to move forward, part four

> *Kitrina:* At weekends we did family things and there wasn't any pressure to play in school teams. My parents weren't running us around to different sport things. We just went to my Dad's football games and I played with my cousins – we'd be running around in the fields and making up games. He'd meet up with his mates beforehand, all my uncles, decide whose cars we were going in to the match – there was a lot of fun and laughter. Then we'd all arrive somewhere, our dads would disappear into the changing rooms and we'd just be let loose – so a lot of trust and freedom. Also, from when I was 11, although we had tennis lessons and badminton lessons, we also had music lessons and drama lessons. Because my sister was really into drama, I got really into drama too. My mother would take me to drama festivals in Bath and Bristol where I'd perform and then we'd have a great day out – we'd go for cake and wander around Bath. So there wasn't one area I felt I was excelling in and had to do well in to gain acceptance. There were several areas and I seemed to be doing alright wherever I was. Looking back, I can't find any signs of there being pressure for me to do well in anything, no expectation that I had to be brilliant or go on and get a career or go to university.
>
> *David:* Did that change when you started playing golf at 17?
>
> *Kitrina:* Well it was left very much for me to do it. After a lesson at the driving range, my Dad said, 'Do you fancy playing golf for a year?' I said

yes. We sat down and he said, 'This is what we'll do then. You'll have £1000 a year and it's up to you to manage it. It's up to you to decide what you want to do.' So I was the boss. There was, again, no pressure to do any particular thing, he wasn't chipping in (forgive the pun) saying, 'Oh that's not a good choice,' or checking up I was practising and so on. I didn't have anyone telling me what to do. I had to go and find out what to do and then get on with it.

David: So it wasn't like some master plan was set up: 'This is what you will do over the year…' 'You must be at these training weekends…' 'You must move to this centre…'

Kitrina: No, not at all. I was empowered. I felt autonomous. I felt it was my decision. I was scared a little by this initially, but I was in an environment where I was also held, and made to feel that whatever the outcome (that is, even if I didn't become a tour player) it wouldn't be a failure, it was all a good experience, which seems to be important.

David: You were held? Can you say a bit more about that?

Kitrina: There wasn't anything in my upbringing that would lead me to fear where I was at any moment. Like, going off road, and not having a map – I was exploring the terrain, and there were no wrong routes, so I never felt lost. Some turns mean I take a bit longer, but that was OK. I felt that I could always get help, that I wasn't being evaluated by whatever the outcome was. Only positives could come from it, whatever the outcome. That said, I don't want to give the impression there were never days when I didn't find playing golf really difficult, or boring, or unfair, and so on.

David: What I hear when you say that is a sense of, 'You're OK as you are'. You didn't have to become something else to be OK. For me, thinking about young people's mental health in sport, there's a need for *us* – family, teachers, coaches, whoever – to be able to communicate to young people that, 'You're OK, you are enough as you are. You don't have to achieve this or go in this direction to be OK. Yet, at the same time, there is the possibility that you *could* be something else – and that would be OK too. You *can* change – you don't *have* to stay the same to be OK.'

Kitrina: Hilde Lindemann (2014) talks about that, how parents have a really tricky job of holding on to certain aspects of a child's identity while letting go of other things that no longer define the person.

David: So there's an onus on those of us who work with young people to become like that. The performance narrative isn't 'natural' – youngsters have to be channeled or coerced into that story. It happens in complex interpersonal ways that aren't immediately visible but can be seen if you look hard enough. The power that enacts this coercion is about, 'You will be OK … provided you are *this*. You need to become *this* to be successful, to be OK.' So there's an implicit sense that you have to become something that you are not and *then* you'll be alright. But in reality, you actually never get there. You might get it for a moment – 'I've done it, I'm OK,

I'm loved' – but it's fleeting. Whereas young people need exposure to different possibilities within a safe space of being held. So: 'What you are is alright, you don't have to change at all. But here's a menu of possibilities if you do get hungry.' As adults working with young people in sport, perhaps the question we need to consider is: 'Are *our* stories and actions coercing somebody towards a singular way of being, or are we supporting the way that person *is* while allowing the *possibility* of change and development?'

Conclusion

Through our shared research journey, we have come to the view that to promote long-term mental health, those of us who work in sport need to create opportunities for young people to be able to explore themselves, to find a self that feels like it fits, and negotiate a way of living that might involve diverse roles and identities. We maintain this perspective in the face of some others who seem to believe that to be well, and to do well in sport, you must become *this* – you must live according to the terms of the performance narrative. While some do achieve sporting success this way, this story and way of being does not bode well for lifelong development and mental health. In contrast, people who maintain multidimensional life stories (e.g. discovery and relational narratives) appear more likely to experience positive identity development and mental health.

An issue we have frequently heard raised by concerned parents is the narrow and restrictive player pathways instigated in youth sport – at the elite level but increasingly in school and leisure settings too. Although player pathways may have been created as a guide, many now mirror the performance narrative in that one particular route is promoted or enforced. Some parents feel pressured to conform to this, even when they have concerns about it. Given the considerable problems of the singular approach encapsulated in performance stories, there is a strong case for widening and expanding player pathways.

We suggest practitioners who wish to promote long-term mental health for young people in sport might consider four approaches:

1. *Reflect on your own stories and actions* – the words and actions of coaches, teachers and parents are often highly influential for young people. To what extent do you uncritically reproduce the dominant performance narrative in what you say and do?
2. *Make alternative stories available* – other types of story do occasionally surface in the media. We offer numerous alternative stories in our recent book (Douglas and Carless, 2015). Can you bring some of these stories to the attention of the young people you work with?
3. *Value diversity and difference* – for alternative stories and ways of being to gain purchase, they need to be valued and taken seriously. To what extent do you demonstrate this valuing of diversity in your day-to-day practice?

4. *Include other experiences as a resource for story diversification* – personal stories are developed on the back of lived experience. A good way, therefore, to encourage alternative and multidimensional *stories* (and identities) is to include alternative and multidimensional *activities* to support story development.

References

Bruner J. S. (1986). *Actual Minds, Possible Worlds*. Cambridge, MA: Harvard University Press.

Carless, D. (2010). Who the hell was *that*? Stories, bodies and actions in the world. *Qualitative Research in Psychology, 7*, 332–344.

Carless, D. (2012a). Negotiating sexuality and masculinity in school sport: An autoethnography. *Sport, Education and Society, 17*, 607–625.

Carless, D. (2012b). Young men, sport and sexuality: A poetic exploration. In F. Dowling, H. Fitzgerald, and A. Flintoff (Eds.), *Equity and Difference in Physical Education, Youth Sport and Health: A Narrative Approach* (pp. 67–71). London: Routledge.

Carless, D. (2013). Cultural constraints: Experiencing same-sex attraction in sport and dance. In N. Short, L. Turner and A. Grant (Eds.), *Contemporary British Autoethnography: A Handbook for Postgraduate Qualitative Researchers* (pp. 49–61). Rotterdam: Sense Publishers.

Carless, D., and Douglas, K. (2009). 'We haven't got a seat on the bus for you' or 'All the seats are mine': Narratives and career transition in professional golf. *Qualitative Research in Sport and Exercise, 1*, 51–66.

Carless, D., and Douglas, K. (2010). *Sport and Physical Activity for Mental Health*. Oxford: Wiley-Blackwell.

Carless, D., and Douglas, K. (2012). The ethos of physical activity delivery in mental health: A narrative study of service user experiences. *Issues in Mental Health Nursing, 33*, 165–171.

Carless, D., and Douglas, K. (2013a). 'In the boat' but 'selling myself short': Stories, narratives, and identity development in elite sport. *The Sport Psychologist, 27*, 27–39.

Carless, D., and Douglas, K. (2013b). Living, resisting, and playing the part of athlete: Narrative tensions in elite sport. *Psychology of Sport and Exercise, 14*, 701–708.

Copeland, W. E., Wolke, D., Angold, A., and Costello, E. J. (2013). Adult psychiatric outcomes of bullying and being bullied by peers in childhood and adolescence. *JAMA Psychiatry, 70*, 419–426.

Crossley, M. (2000). *Introducing Narrative Psychology: Self, Trauma and the Construction of Meaning*. Milton Keynes: Open University Press.

Department of Health. (2003). *Promoting Mental Health: Strategy and Action Plan 2003–2008*. Belfast: Department of Health, Social Services and Public Safety. Crown Copyright.

Department of Health. (2015). *Future in Mind: Promoting, Protecting and Improving Our Children and Young People's Mental Health and Wellbeing*. Available from https://www.gov.uk/government/uploads/system/uploads/attachment_data/file/414024/Childrens_Mental_Health.pdf

Douglas, K. (2009). Storying my self: Negotiating a relational identity in professional sport. *Qualitative Research in Sport and Exercise, 1*, 176–190.

Douglas, K. (2014). Challenging interpretive privilege in elite and professional sport: One [athlete's] story, revised, reshaped, reclaimed. *Qualitative Research in Sport, Exercise and Health, 6,* 220–243.

Douglas, K., and Carless, D. (2006). Performance, discovery, and relational narratives among women professional tournament golfers. *Women in Sport and Physical Activity Journal, 15*(2), 14–27.

Douglas, K., and Carless, D. (2009). Abandoning the performance narrative: Two women's stories of transition from professional golf. *Journal of Applied Sport Psychology, 2,* 213–230.

Douglas, K., and Carless, D. (2015). *Life Story Research in Sport: Understanding the Experiences of Elite and Professional Athletes Through Narrative.* Abingdon, UK: Routledge.

Frank, A. W. (1995). *The Wounded Storyteller.* Chicago, IL: University of Chicago Press.

Frank, A. W. (2010). *Letting Stories Breathe: A Socio-Narratology.* Chicago, IL: University of Chicago Press.

Green, H., McGinnity, A., Meltzer, H., Ford, T., and Goodman, R. (2005). *Mental Health of Children and Young People in Great Britain, 2004.* A survey carried out by the Office for National Statistics on behalf of the Department of Health and the Scottish Executive. Basingstoke, UK: Palgrave Macmillan.

Hawton, K., Rodham, K., Evans, E., and Weatherall, R. (2002). Deliberate self harm in adolescents: Self report survey in schools in England. *British Medical Journal, 325,* 1207–1211.

Lindemann, H. (2014). *Holding and Letting Go: The Social Practice of Personal Identities.* New York, NY: Oxford University Press.

McAdams, D. (1993). *The Stories We Live By.* New York: The Guilford Press.

McLeod, J. (1997). *Narrative and Psychotherapy.* London: Sage.

Sawyer, R., and Norris, J. (2015). Duoethnography: A retrospective 10 years after. *International Review of Qualitative Research, 8,* 1–4.

United States Department of Health and Human Services. (1999). *Mental Health: A Report of the Surgeon General.* Rockville, MD: U.S. DHHS.

Conclusion

18

FUTURE DIRECTIONS FOR POSITIVE YOUTH DEVELOPMENT THROUGH SPORT

Nicholas L. Holt, Colin J. Deal, and Christine L. Smyth

The purpose of this chapter is to highlight future directions for positive youth development (PYD) through sport. In doing so we reflect on some important methodological and conceptual issues the contributors to this book identified. We then pay particular attention to definitional issues and the contention that PYD research is old wine in new bottles. At the end of the chapter we present a model of PYD through sport that may be useful for guiding future research and practice.

Methodological issues

Understanding processes

Several authors highlighted the need to generate better understandings of the processes through which PYD outcomes may be acquired via participation in sport (e.g. Chapter 4 by Hodge and colleagues, Chapter 10 by Camiré and Kendellen, Chapter 11 by Turnnidge and colleagues, and Chapter 14 by Martinek and Hellison). Essentially these arguments are consistent with the suggestion put forward in Larson's (2000) important article, in which he highlighted the need to unpack the "black box" of how participation in youth programs leads to various positive developmental outcomes. Process is notoriously difficult to study but it clearly remains a pressing issue for the advancement of PYD through sport. Specifically, continued research is needed to establish what features of sport programs work, under what circumstances, for whom, and the mechanisms that produce or limit the attainment of positive developmental outcomes (Coalter, 2010; Holt et al., 2013b; Levermore, 2008).

Conducting rigorous evaluations of interventions

There is a gap between research and practice, which may (in part) be due to the shortage of high-quality evaluation research in PYD through sport. Contributors (e.g. Chapter 1 by Weiss, Chapter 9 by Harwood and Johnston, and Chapter 10 by Camiré and Kendellen) noted the need to bridge the research-to-practice gap through rigorous intervention research to facilitate the development of theory- and evidence-based best practices. Without such research we are unable to determine if existing programs are effective or how they may be improved (see Chapter 2 by Coakley and Chapter 4 by Hodge and colleagues). Martinek and Hellison (Chapter 14) commented on the difficulty of conducting program evaluations. Moving forward, PYD through sport researchers need to do a better job of designing and conducting more rigorous intervention and evaluation research, which may ultimately contribute to narrowing the gap between research and practice.

Conducting longitudinal research

A limitation of existing research on PYD through sport is the lack of longitudinal studies. As Coakley (Chapter 2) explained, it is naïve to suggest that positive development has occurred in connection with sport-based programs unless longitudinal research tells us otherwise. Richard Lerner and colleagues have conducted the most comprehensive longitudinal study of PYD to date (e.g. Lerner et al., 2009). Although Lerner and colleagues included sport participation as a variable in their work, this is not a direct study of the long-term effects of participating in sport. Longitudinal research will also enable researchers to examine the long-term implications of PYD interventions. Whereas long-term change is difficult to assess, Vest Ettekal and colleagues (Chapter 6) provided some important advice for measuring and analyzing change. We have absolutely no doubt that whoever is able to publish a comprehensive longitudinal study of PYD through sport will make a seminal contribution to the field.

Advancing quantitative measurement

Another significant limitation faced by researchers of PYD through sport has been the general lack of appropriate quantitative measures for various PYD-related constructs (see Chapter 4 by Hodge and colleagues, Chapter 7 by MacDonald and McIssac). If we continue to assert that sport is a unique context (e.g. Côté et al., 2009), then we must use measures specifically designed for sport. In Chapter 7, MacDonald and McIssac called for researchers to continue to develop novel ways of assessing PYD. We must, however, remain cognizant of the fact that the creation of sport-specific measures of PYD will preclude studies comparing PYD through sport with PYD through other types of adult-organized activities.

Using theory in more sophisticated ways

Several contributors to this book highlighted theoretical issues that require further attention in the study of PYD through sport. For instance, Hodge and colleagues (Chapter 4) discussed that research in the area of life skills has been largely atheoretical. Nowhere is this more obvious than in the evaluation of existing programs. More use of theory may also help to address Camiré and Kendellen's suggestion (Chapter 10) that there is a need for more evidence-informed practical strategies to help program leaders and coaches promote PYD. Combined, these suggestions echo Gould and Carson's (2008) observation that the lack of theory in PYD through sport research "practically constrains the field, as practitioners do not have an overarching framework to guide their interventions" (p. 65).

Conceptual issues

Defining PYD through sport

MacDonald and McIsaac (Chapter 7) argued there is a need for a clear definition of PYD through sport. Whether a definition of PYD through sport as a singular construct is needed is a matter for continued scholarly debate. Given the freedom afforded to me (Nick) by virtue of being the editor of this book, I think this is a good place to offer my own view on how to define PYD. This is not a definition of PYD as a singular construct. Rather, it is a definition of what PYD through sport research involves – the definition of the area of inquiry that involves multiple constructs (highlighted in italics below). I submit that:

> PYD through *sport* is intended to facilitate youth development via *experiences* and *processes* that enable participants in *adult-supervised programs* to gain *transferable personal and social life skills*, along with *physical competencies*. These skill and competency outcomes will enable participants in youth sport programs to *thrive* and *contribute to their communities*, both now and in the future.

Allow me to explain some of the decisions I made in writing this definition, which is entirely based on my own understanding of the literature rather than on some kind of expert consensus (though that does seem like a good idea for a paper). I used the word *sport* to refer to sport in all its forms, from recreational leagues to summer camps to after-school programs to elite youth sport. I clearly focused on *adult-supervised programs*. I think development can occur through unsupervised active free play (see Lee et al., 2015), but the essence of PYD is that it involves adults (e.g. coaches, parents) and organized programs.

I delineated between *experiences* and *processes*, and view personal and social life skills and physical competencies as *outcomes*, based on the suggestions put forward by MacDonald and McIsaac (Chapter 7). I brought in the concept of *transferable life skills* because those personal and social skills and physical competencies learned in sport must transfer to other areas of children's and adolescents' lives for PYD to have occurred. *Personal and social life skills* refer to psychosocial characteristics rather than isolated behaviors (see Hodge and colleagues in Chapter 4). I ensured that *physical competencies* are included in this definition because PYD through sport involves a physical element that is not necessarily found in non-sport settings. I emphasized that the point of PYD is to provide opportunities to *thrive*, both now and in the future, because ultimately youth who experience PYD through sport will do well in adulthood. Finally, I included *contribution to community* because PYD should not be confined to the development of the individual. I hope this definition is useful and look forward to critical scholarly debate about its merits and weaknesses. Furthermore, I think each of the terms highlighted above in italics reflect specific constructs that must be operationally defined if they are used in a particular research study.

Is PYD a new area of inquiry in youth sport?

Weiss (Chapter 1) argued that PYD is old wine in new bottles, by which she meant that there is a legacy of a century of youth sport research (the old wine) that has not been fully recognized by contemporary PYD research (the new bottles). We wholeheartedly agree with her that there is a great deal of research in sport psychology which predates the introduction of PYD nomenclature. We also endorse the argument Weiss put forward that some of the early PYD research conducted by developmental psychologists did not extensively draw on youth sport psychology research. That said, we are pleased to note that this trend appears to be changing. For example, in Chapter 3 Agans and colleagues (from Richard Lerner's lab) did in fact draw on some important research from the youth sport psychology literature, including Roberts (2012), Shields et al. (2007), Weiss and Wiese-Bjornstal (2009) and others.

However, we want to take a closer look at the contention that PYD itself is old wine in new bottles. We think that contemporary PYD research is a *different* way of looking at developmental aspects of participation in youth sport that represents a marked contrast to much of the early work in sport psychology. That is, PYD research reflects a move away from the social psychology theories in the areas of moral development, social relationships, self-perceptions, motivation, observational learning, and achievement orientations that dominated the early sport psychology research (see Weiss, Chapter 1).

Certainly researchers using PYD perspectives "stand on the shoulders" of the giants who created and paved the way for serious academic study of youth sport. Yet, as several contributors to this chapter noted, PYD is underpinned by Bronfenbrenner's ecological theory (e.g. Bronfenbrenner, 2005) and—in Richard Lerner's work—the relational developmental systems (RDS) metatheoretical perspective (e.g. Lerner et al., 2015). Such ecological perspectives rarely featured in early youth sport psychology research. Indeed, in their review of sport and exercise psychology research, Spence and Lee (2003) noted that while intra-individual factors had been thoroughly explored, less attention had been paid to extra-individual (i.e. social ecological) factors. Within the realm of physical activity (the focus of their review), Spence and Lee noted that models that focus on intra-individual factors can, at best, explain 20–40 percent of variance in physical activity. Broader ecological models include both intra- and extra-individual factors and portray behavior as a complex interplay between people and their social ecological settings. Following this same logic, PYD is the result of mutually influential relations among individuals and their contexts (Lerner et al., 2015).

Youth sport is just one aspect of a complex system that is interconnected or fused with other aspects of the system. In other words, youth sport is a microsystem (García Bengoechea, 2002) and part of other, more distal, ecological systems. We think some of the early work in sport psychology Weiss discussed was primarily focused on proximal processes in the microsystem of youth sport without paying a great deal of attention to other (more distal) ecological systems that influence development. These systems extend beyond the role of parents, peers, and coaches in sport to also consider other social networks and community influences.

Rather than old wine in new bottles, a more precise criticism of the PYD literature, highlighted by several contributors to this book (e.g. in Chapter 3 by Agans and colleagues and in Chapter 5 by Strachan and colleagues), is that researchers have tended to study sport as an isolated system rather than an integrated part of a wider system of related social ecological factors. Simply using PYD concepts but only focusing on the microsystem leaves researchers open to the criticism that PYD research is old wine in new bottles. If youth sport settings are microsystems, influenced by more distal systems (e.g. community, policy, culture), it is necessary to consider multiple ecological factors that influence, and are influenced by, behaviors in the microsystem of youth sport.

Obviously it is incredibly challenging to include multiple ecological levels in a single study. Indeed, we have published studies looking at aspects of PYD that did not adequately account for more distal ecological systems, focusing narrowly on the microsystem of youth sport (e.g. Holt et al., 2009; Holt et al., 2008). However, in other studies we were able to draw on broader social influences, such as connections with community stakeholders in the delivery of a sport-based after-school program (Holt et al., 2013a) and broader structural issues that constrained the benefits young men from an inner city gained through their involvement in a sport program (Holt et al., 2013b). Hence, PYD provides opportunities to move beyond focusing on psychosocial development within a microsystem. By paying more attention to the other systematic influences on the microsystem of youth sport, as well as considering how involvement in sport programs may help youth contribute to communities and thrive in adulthood, researchers will be able to challenge the assertion that PYD is old wine in new bottles.

Linking theory and practice: toward a model of positive youth development through sport

Over the past year my (Nick's) team in the Child and Adolescent Sport and Activity lab at the University of Alberta has been working with other PYD researchers (Martin Camiré, Jean Côté, Jessica Fraser-Thomas, Dany MacDonald, Leisha Strachan, and Katherine Tamminen) on a grant funded by the Social Sciences and Humanities Research Council of Canada. Our work through this grant addresses two pressing issues that currently constrain the continued advancement of PYD research in sport. First, it addresses the suggestion there is a lack of sufficient theory to drive practice (Gould and Carson, 2008; Hodge et al., 2012). Second, it addresses the research-to-practice gap in terms of "operationalizing" how to deliver PYD in sport settings (cf. Vella et al., 2013).

A crucial step in bridging the research-to-practice gap is to synthesize knowledge (Graham and Tetroe, 2009). We are in the final throes of completing a large qualitative meta-study of PYD through sport research (Holt et al., 2016). This involved reviewing and synthesizing over 60 qualitative studies in order to produce a model of PYD through sport grounded in the literature (Figure 18.1). In addition to being supported by the results of our meta-study, the main components of this model are grounded in other relevant literature (much of which has been reviewed by contributors to this book). Here, we present the first iteration of the model for readers to digest. In creating this model we have adopted a parsimonious approach and specifically focused on identifying testable relationships with a practical focus. Due to its practical focus, the central components of this model focus on the microsystem of youth sport, explaining ways in which the provision of sport

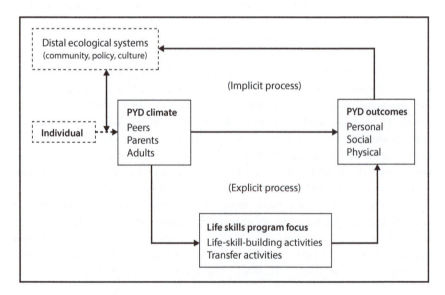

FIGURE 18.1   A model of positive youth development through sport

programs can support PYD. However, it also includes more distal ecological systems that may produce or constrain the potential benefits that may be gained through participation in sport.

Indeed, the entire model is framed within the context of distal ecological systems. This is because the broader theoretical literature clearly and consistently highlights that social-ecological systems influence, and are influenced by, behavior (Lerner et al., 2012). Sport programs are a microsystem (García Bengoechea, 2002) and interactions in this microsystem can be influenced by features of the broader macrosystem within which sport programs (and those who participate in sport programs) are located. Hence, the entire model is framed within the context of *distal ecological systems*. It is also important to consider the characteristics of individuals who enter sport programs. Not only may socio-demographic factors (e.g. gender, ethnicity, and socioeconomic status) be important, individual difference variables (e.g. traits and dispositions) may have an influence on the ways in which individuals acquire PYD outcomes through their involvement in sport.

The model then focuses on the microsystem of youth sport to provide a very practical focus that may help guide the delivery of youth sport programs in the future. It begins with the PYD climate created by peers, parents, and other adults. With regard to *peers*, strong peer relationships among youth, including feelings of belonging to a wider community, have been associated with PYD (e.g. Fraser-Thomas and Côté, 2009), and the provision of opportunities for peer leadership is important (see Chapter 12 by Gould). In terms of interactions with *parents*, autonomy-supportive or authoritative approaches have been associated with positive outcomes for young athletes (see Holt and Knight, 2014 for a review). With regard to other *adults* (namely coaches), mastery-oriented approaches to coaching have been associated with positive outcomes (Smith and Smoll, 2007), and there is some emerging evidence that transformational leadership approaches to coaching may also be useful for promoting PYD (e.g. see Chapter 11 by Turnnidge and colleagues). Of course, the very notion of a PYD climate reflects the extensive work on motivational climate that has been conducted in youth sport (see Harwood et al., 2015, for a review).

Core concepts in terms of life skills programs are based on a range of studies. *Life-skill-building activities* include establishing high expectations and accountability for behavior (e.g. Flett et al., 2013; Harwood, 2008; Holt et al., 2012) and role modeling desired behaviors (e.g. Camiré et al., 2012; Trottier and Robitaille, 2014; Turnnidge et al., 2012). *Transfer activities* reported in the literature primarily involved coaches reinforcing the importance of transfer and having discussions with their athletes (e.g. Chinkov and Holt, 2015; Goudas and Giannoudis, 2010; Wright and Burton, 2008). Finally, *personal, social, and physical outcomes* are benefits associated with youth sport programs (see Holt and Neely, 2011 for a review).

We propose that it is possible for PYD outcomes to be gained through *implicit learning* in sport programs if a suitable PYD climate is in place (the arrow between PYD climate and PYD outcomes). We also propose a mechanism for *explicit learning* of PYD outcomes. That is, PYD outcomes can be achieved if, within the context of a PYD climate, there is a life skills program focus (i.e. life-skills-building activities and transfer activities). This is represented by the arrows linking PYD climate to life skills program focus to PYD outcomes in Figure 18.1 (also see Turnnidge et al., 2014 for further discussion of implicit and explicit transfer mechanisms). By gaining PYD outcomes youth will be able to thrive and contribute to their communities (the arrow linking PYD outcomes back to distal ecological systems).

This model of PYD through sport provides testable relationships which may guide future research. Five hypotheses are proposed:

1. Distal ecological systems and individual factors influence PYD through sport.
2. A PYD climate (based on relationships between athletes and peers, parents, and other adults) can produce PYD outcomes (i.e. through implicit processes).
3. PYD outcomes can be attained if a life skills program focus (involving life-skills-building activities and transfer activities) is in place (i.e. through explicit processes) and in the presence of a PYD climate.
4. The combined effects of a PYD climate *and* a life skills focus will produce more PYD outcomes than a PYD climate alone.
5. Gaining PYD outcomes in and through sport will facilitate transfer and enable youth to thrive and contribute to their communities.

This model may, in addition to providing a guide for practice, help drive future research. For instance, research could examine the extent to which programs with features of a PYD climate produce PYD outcomes. The model also provides a framework for assessing the effects of sport programs with PYD skill-building activities versus other types of programs that do not have an explicit PYD focus. Finally, it provides a guide for longitudinal research to assess the long-term implications of thriving and sport participation in terms of contribution to community.

Conclusion

This book represents the most comprehensive collection of research and scholarship in the area of PYD through sport ever compiled. It demonstrates there has been some remarkable progress in the field since the publication of the first edition (Holt, 2008). Yet, some of the issues discussed in the future directions chapter of the first edition (Holt and Jones, 2008) remain as key areas discussed in the current chapter (e.g. the need to evaluate interventions, to improve measurement approaches, and to conduct longitudinal research). Another issue is that researchers have still yet to clearly "establish if different sporting contexts are associated with different types of developmental outcomes" (Holt and Jones, 2008, p. 127), which brings us back to the issue of further unpacking the black box of youth sport participation. Perhaps the model of PYD through sport may be useful for unpacking the black box, but we encourage researchers to embrace theoretical diversity. If a third edition of this book is ever published, we expect it to be replete with accounts of intervention and longitudinal studies conducted from a range of theoretical perspectives.

Furthermore, we remain somewhat frustrated that PYD remains largely absent from coach education programs (Vella et al., 2013) and the youth sport system more generally. Recently I (Nick) had a conversation with a policy analyst from Sport Canada (the federal government agency responsible for sport), during which she noted that despite the large number of PYD researchers in Canada, PYD remains largely absent from the Canadian sport system. I had an incredulous response to this comment (something along the lines of "that's your job isn't it?"). But, upon reflection, this led me to an important realization. It is no longer sufficient for researchers to simply publish studies in good journals and then hope the research gets picked up and applied by sport administrators and practitioners.

We, the researchers, must drive the push to knowledge translation by working with stakeholders from the outset of our research. This will help ensure that research is relevant to stakeholders' needs. Such "integrated knowledge translation" approaches have been shown to improve the relevance and use of research evidence by knowledge users in practice, program, and policy contexts (e.g. Innvaer et al., 2002). The model of PYD through sport presented here is an attempt to synthesize knowledge and provide suggestions to help bridge the research-to-practice gap and we anticipate it will be refined and adapted based on future work with stakeholders. In this vein, researchers must also be prepared to create "knowledge products" (beyond academic papers and conference presentations) that stakeholders can easily use. Perhaps then we will be able to realize a future in which practices to promote PYD are a routine feature of the youth sport programs delivered to millions of children and adolescents around the world every day. What a bright future that would be.

Acknowledgment

The production of this chapter was supported, in part, by a Partnership Development Grant from the Social Sciences and Humanities Research Council of Canada (grant # 890-2014-0022) held by Nicholas L. Holt (as principal investigator).

References

Bronfenbrenner, U. (Ed.). (2005). *Making Human Beings Human: Bioecological Perspectives on Human Development*. Thousand Oaks, CA: Sage.

Brown, T., and Fry, M. D. (2011). Strong girls: A physical-activity/life-skills intervention for girls transitioning to junior high. *Journal of Sport Psychology in Action, 2,* 57–69.

Camiré, M., Trudel, P., and Forneris, T. (2012). Coaching and transferring life skills: Philosophies and strategies used by model high school coaches. *The Sport Psychologist, 26,* 243–260.

Chinkov, A., and Holt, N. (2015). Implicit transfer of life skills through participation in Brazilian jiu-jitsu. *Journal of Applied Sport Psychology*. Advance online publication doi:10. 1080/10413200.2015.1086447

Coalter, F. (2010). The politics of sport-for-development: Limited focus programmes and broad gauge problems? *International Review for the Sociology of Sport, 45*, 295–314.

Côté, J., Lidor, R., and Hackfort, D. (2009). ISSP position stand: To sample or to specialize? Seven postulates about youth sport activities that lead to continued participation and elite performance. *International Journal of Sport and Exercise Psychology, 7*, 7–17.

Flett, M. R., Gould, D., Griffes, K. R., and Lauer, L. (2013). Tough love for underserved youth: A comparison of more and less effective coaching. *The Sport Psychologist, 27*, 325–337.

Fraser-Thomas, J., and Côté, J. (2009). Understanding adolescents' positive and negative developmental experiences in sport. *The Sport Psychologist, 23*, 3–23.

García Bengoechea, E. (2002). Integrating knowledge and expanding horizons in developmental sport psychology: A bioecological perspective. *Quest, 54*, 1–20.

Goudas, M., and Giannoudis, G. (2010). A qualitative evaluation of a life-skills program in a physical education context. *Hellenic Journal of Psychology, 7*, 315–334.

Gould, D., and Carson, S. (2008). Life skills development through sport: Current status and future directions. *International Review of Sport and Exercise Psychology, 1*, 58–78.

Graham, I. D., and Tetroe, J. (2009). Planned action theories. In S. Straus, J. Tetroe, and I. D. Graham (Eds.), *Knowledge Translation in Health Care: Moving from Evidence to Practice* (pp. 185–195). Oxford, UK: Blackwell.

Harwood, C. (2008). Developmental consulting in professional football academy: The 5Cs coaching efficacy program. *The Sport Psychologist, 22*, 109–133.

Harwood, C., Keegan, R. J., Smith, J. M. J., and Raine, A. S. (2015). A systematic review of the intrapersonal correlates of motivational climate perceptions in sport and physical activity. *Psychology of Sport and Exercise, 18*, 9–15.

Hodge, K., Danish, S., and Martin, J. (2012). Developing a conceptual framework for life skills interventions. *The Counseling Psychologist, 41*, 1125–1152.

Holt, N. L. (Ed.) (2008). *Positive Youth Development through Sport*. London: Routledge.

Holt, N. L., and Jones, M. I. (2008). Future directions for positive youth development and sport. In N. L. Holt (Ed.), *Positive Youth Development through Sport* (pp. 122–132). London: Routledge.

Holt, N. L., and Neely, K. C. (2011). Positive youth development through sport: A review. *Revista de Iberoamericana de Psicología del Ejercicio y el Deporte (English version), 6*, 299–316.

Holt, N. L., and Knight, C. J. (2014). *Parenting in Youth Sport: From Research to Practice*. London: Routledge.

Holt, N. L., Tink, L. N., Mandigo, J. L. and Fox, K. R. (2008). Do youth learn life skills through their involvement in high school sport? *Canadian Journal of Education, 31*, 281–304.

Holt, N. L., Tamminen, K. A., Tink, L. N., and Black, D. E. (2009). An interpretive analysis of life skills associated with sport participation. *Qualitative Research in Sport and Exercise, 1*, 160–175.

Holt, N. L., Sehn, Z. L., Spence, J. C., Newton, A. S., and Ball, G. D. C. (2012). Physical education and sport programs at an inner city school: Exploring possibilities for positive youth development. *Physical Education and Sport Pedagogy, 17*, 97–113.

Holt, N. L., McHugh, T. L. F., Tink, L. N., Kingsley, B. C., Coppola, A. M., Neely, K. C., and McDonald, R. (2013a). Developing sport-based after-school programmes using a participatory action research approach. *Qualitative Research in Sport, Exercise, and Health,* 5, 332–355.

Holt, N. L., Scherer, J., and Koch, J. (2013b). An ethnographic study of issues surrounding the provision of sport opportunities to young men from a western Canadian inner-city. *Psychology of Sport and Exercise, 14,* 538–548.

Holt, N. L., Neely, K. C., Slater, L. G., Camiré, M., Côté, J., Fraser-Thomas, J., MacDonald, D., Strachan, L., and Tamminen, K. A. (2016). *A Model of Positive Youth Development Through Sport Based on Results From a Qualitative Meta-Study.* Unpublished manuscript. University of Alberta, Edmonton, Alberta, Canada.

Innvaer, S., Vist, G., Trommald, M., and Oxman, A. (2002). Health policy-makers' perceptions of their use of evidence: A systematic review. *Journal of Health Services Research Policy, 7,* 239–244.

Larson, R. W. (2000). Toward a psychology of positive youth development. *American Psychologist, 55,* 170–183.

Lee, H., Tamminen, K. A., Clark, A. M., Slater, L., Spence, J. C., and Holt, N. L. (2015). A meta-study of qualitative research examining determinants of children's independent active free play. *International Journal of Behavioral Nutrition and Physical Activity, 12,* 5.

Lerner, R. M., von Eye, A., Lerner, J. V., and Lewin-Bizan, S. (2009). Exploring the foundations and functions of adolescent thriving within the 4-H study of positive youth development: A view of the issues. *Journal of Applied Developmental Psychology, 30,* 567–570.

Lerner, R. M., Bowers, E. P., Geldhof, G. J., Gestsdóttir, S., and DeSouza, L. (2012). Promoting positive youth development in the face of contextual changes and challenges: The roles of individual strengths and ecological assets. *New Directions for Youth Development, 135,* 119–128.

Lerner, R. M., Lerner, J. V., Bowers, E. P., and Geldhof, G. J. (2015). Positive youth development and relational-developmental-systems. In W. F. Overton and P. C. Molenaar (Eds.), *Handbook of Child Psychology and Developmental Science. Vol. 1: Theory and Method* (7th ed., pp. 607–651). Hoboken, NJ: Wiley.

Levermore, R. (2008). Sport: A new engine of development? *Progress in Development Studies, 8,* 183–190.

Roberts, G. C. (2012). Motivation in sport and exercise from an achievement goal theory perspective: After 30 years, where are we? In G. C. Roberts and D. C. Treasure (Eds.), *Advances in Motivation in Sport and Exercise* (pp. 5–58). Champaign, IL: Human Kinetics.

Shields, D. L., LaVoi, N. M., Bredemeier, B. L., and Power, F. C. (2007). Predictors of poor sportspersonship in youth sports: Personal attitudes and social influences. *Journal of Sport and Exercise Psychology, 29,* 747–762.

Smith, R. E., and Smoll, F. L. (2007). Social-cognitive approach to coaching behaviors. In S. Jowett and D. Lavallee (Eds.), *Social Psychology in Sport* (pp. 75–89). Champaign, IL: Human Kinetics.

Spence, J. C., and Lee, R. E. (2003). Toward a comprehensive model of physical activity. *Psychology of Sport and Exercise, 4,* 7–24.

Trottier, C., and Robitaille, S. (2014). Fostering life skills development in high school and community sport: A comparative analysis of the coach's role. *The Sport Psychologist, 28,* 10–21.

Turnnidge, J., Vierimaa, M., and Côté, J. (2012). An in-depth investigation of a model sport program for athletes with a physical disability. *Psychology, 3,* 1131–1141.

Turnnidge, J., Côté, J., and Hancock, D. J. (2014). Positive youth development from sport to life: Explicit or implicit transfer? *Quest, 66,* 203–217.

Vella, S. A., Oades, L. G., and Crowe, T. P. (2013). The relationship between coach leadership, the coach–athletes relationship, team success, and the positive developmental experiences of adolescent soccer players. *Physical Education and Sport Pedagogy, 18,* 549–561.

Weiss, M., and Wiese-Bjornstal, D. (2009). Promoting positive youth development through physical activity. *President's Council on Physical Fitness and Sports Research Digest, 10*(3), 1–8.

Wright, P. M., and Burton, S. (2008). Implementation and outcomes of a responsibility-based physical activity program integrated into an intact high school physical education class. *Journal of Teaching in Physical Education, 27,* 138–154.

INDEX